HN59.2 .F38 1993
Fast, Howard,
War and peace
3 4369 00076662 3

D0212674

War AND Peace

OBSERVATIONS ON OUR TIMES

Other Books by Howard Fast

BEING RED
THE CONFESSION OF JOE CULLEN
THE PLEDGE
THE DINNER PARTY
CITIZEN TOM PAINE (A Play)
THE IMMIGRANT'S DAUGHTER
THE OUTSIDER
MAX
TIME AND THE RIDDLE: THIRTY-ONE ZEN STORIES
THE LEGACY
THE ESTABLISHMENT
THE MAGIC DOOR
SECOND GENERATION
THE IMMIGRANTS
THE ART OF ZEN MEDITATION
A TOUCH OF INFINITY
THE HESSIAN
THE CROSSING
THE GENERAL ZAPPED AN ANGEL
THE JEWS: STORY OF A PEOPLE
THE HUNTER AND THE TRAP
TORQUEMADA
THE HILL
TWO VALLEYS
AGRIPPA'S DAUGHTER
POWER
THE EDGE OF TOMORROW
APRIL MORNING
THE GOLDEN RIVER
THE WINSTON AFFAIR
MOSES, PRINCE OF EGYPT
SYLVIA
THE LAST SUPPER
SILAS TIMBERMAN
THE PASSION OF SACCO AND VANZETTI
SPARTACUS
THE PROUD AND THE FREE
DEPARTURE
MY GLORIOUS BROTHERS
CLARKTON
THE AMERICAN
FREEDOM ROAD
CITIZEN TOM PAINE
THE UNVANQUISHED
THE LAST FRONTIER
CONCEIVED IN LIBERTY
PLACE IN THE CITY
THE CHILDREN
STRANGE YESTERDAY

War AND Peace

OBSERVATIONS ON OUR TIMES

HOWARD FAST

M.E. Sharpe
Armonk, New York
London, England

Available in the United Kingdom and Europe from M.E. Sharpe, Publishers, 3 Henrietta Street, London WC2E 8LU.

Library of Congress Cataloging-in-Publication Data

Fast, Howard, 1914–
War and peace: observations on our times /
by Howard Fast.
p. cm.
ISBN 1-56324-207-9
1. United States—Social conditions— 2. United States—
Politics and government—1989– 3. Pacifism.
I. Title.
HN59.2.F38 1992
306′.0973—dc20
92-26859
CIP

Printed in the United States of America

The paper used in this publication meets the minimum requirements of American National Standard for Information Sciences—Permanence of Paper for Printed Library Materials, ANSI Z39.48-1984.

MV 10 9 8 7 6 5 4 3 2 1

To the memory of Barney and Ida Fast

Contents

Preface

In 1987, *The New York Observer,* a weekly newspaper published by Arthur Carter and edited by John Sicher, appeared in New York City. I read it occasionally, became increasingly charmed by its open approach and rejection of dogma, and finally decided that I would like to write for it. In December of 1988, I met with John Sicher, and he welcomed me onto his staff. The agreement was that I would write about any matter that interested me, and that what I wrote would be printed as I wrote it. Thus began a cordial and rather unusual relationship between writer and editor that continued for the following three years, until the end of Mr. Sicher's term as editor. During that time no column of mine was ever rejected, nor was there any instance of opposition to my way of thinking.

It was for me a remarkable opportunity to spell out some of the beliefs that were the result of a long and active life, a literary life that was also a political life, of saying what had all too long been left unsaid.

Almost half a century ago, nurtured by a poverty-stricken youth and an abiding belief in socialism as the road out of man's agony, I joined the Communist Party of the United States. Twelve years later, I saw the dreams men dreamed of the brotherhood of man dissolve in the narration of cruelty and horror that Nikita S. Khrushchev delivered to the 20th Congress of the Communist Party of the Soviet Union. As with millions of others who shared my belief in socialism and in the Soviet Union as the beginning of a socialist world, I had to come to terms with my life and my thinking. I had to learn to look at the world in a new way, and above all, I had to learn to look at all things newly, without any of the conviction of the past.

I was born in 1914, close to eighty years ago, and the background to my lifetime includes a series of horrors inflicted by human beings upon other human beings unmatched in all the history of the world. If we add to the 25 million dead of World War I, 50 million accounted dead of World War II and all the uncounted thousands of war dead in the years since, we arrive at a total of more than 100 million human beings—such a slaughter as to numb the mind and make a true effort at empathy almost impossible. This is why I call this collection of essays by the title of *War and Peace;* but the murder of people by the recognized mayhem which we call war is only a part of the horror of the twentieth century. The collateral killing and suffering by starvation, murder of civilians as distinguished from the organized murder of soldiers, and death by disease make this century one that will be recalled with disgust and disbelief by future generations—that is, assuming that we leave a viable planet to those future generations.

Historians have come by generations of glib stupidity to regard war as a measure of history, and rare is the historian who places a moral measure upon his or her narrative; and by this I do not mean the assertion or argument or gathering of proof as to right or wrong of armed struggle; I mean a deeper and different inquiry into the practice of inflicting death upon another person, whatsoever the reason. It is not the gains or losses or reasons for war that elude those who write on the subject; it is the nature of the practice.

Religion adds two facets to this strange and terrible art: the first is the promise, in both Islam and Christianity, that the dead rise up from the field of battle and take their place in that "paradise" that rewards believers with immortality; and the second is the institutionalized belief that God slavers with satisfaction at bloodshed in whatsoever they, the combatants, consider His holy cause, as witnessed in "The Battle Hymn of the Republic": "Mine eyes have seen the glory of the coming of the Lord! He is trampling out the vintage where the grapes of wrath are stored! He has loosed the fateful lightning of His terrible swift sword—" and so forth and so on, ad nauseam. It is worth noting that the above hymn was the musical and liturgical accompaniment to Sherman's march to the sea in the American Civil War, a march so barbarous and savage and destructive to General Sherman's Southern countrymen that it remained unmatched for sheer horror until Adolf Hitler's invasion of the Soviet Union.

People will reject this and argue for the metaphorical significance of melody as simply an emotional factor, but this same emotional factor is a built-in factor of warfare. The obscene "Horst Wessel" hymn of the Nazi movement in Germany was based on a beautiful and stirring melody, and it might be useful to remember that the original words of "The Battle Hymn of the Republic" were:

> We'll hang Jeff Davis to a sour apple tree,
> Down goes McGinty to the bottom of the sea . . .

Julia Ward Howe heard Union soldiers singing the above words as they marched through Washington, and thought it a shame that this fine old melody should be so denigrated. Whereupon, she wrote her own contribution to the pious murder that was embarked upon, not to overturn slavery but to halt Southern expansion westward.

But can you do that? Can you indict this gifted and gentle woman for her emotional and justifiable bias against human slavery? Wasn't her cause just? Isn't the cause of freedom always just?

So the arguments go and so they have always gone, but such arguments are always based upon the absolute verity of war as a part of human existence. The mechanism is built into our thinking as human beings. Realizing at the dawn of history that no social group can survive unstructured and unlimited murder, we separated the act of murder into two sections, and this separation has survived through the centuries. Put baldly, the separation which allows what we call civilization to exist functions thus: the man in civilian clothes and life is denied the right to kill; the man in uniform is given that right. And this is so deeply ingrained as part of our thinking, indeed of our very existence, that to challenge it appears utterly absurd.

Certainly this curious elevation of the irrational must occur to any thoughtful person who watches the progression of any notorious murder trial. Lawyers, frequently well paid and famous, are hired to defend the accused. The state puts forth its own attorneys for the prosecution. Evidence is meticulously gathered and presented through the examination and cross-examination of many witnesses. Sometimes, a whole staff of lawyers searches through decades of legal opinion to support its case. Such trials can drag on for weeks and even for months. And then, when the jury finally delivers its verdict, the defendant—in the United States—has recourse to a lengthy and complex process of appeal. At the very same time, a soldier in an airplane can drop a bomb that kills half a dozen people or half a hundred people, men, women, children, old people, infants, people unknown to said airman, people who have done no harm to said airman; and for this bit of slaughter the killer is not arrested, undergoes no trial, and may indeed be given a medal for valor.

But of course! What the devil is Fast up to, spelling out these simplistic notions? War is war! Peace is peace!

But it is not simplistic, and the contradiction I pose above is central to the tragedy of human existence. I deal with it again and again in the essays that make up this book; for out of this contradiction flow most of the problems of our time. The three-year period covered by these essays includes the final year of Ronald Reagan's presidency and the first two years of George Bush's presidency, and since well over a hundred essays are included here, all of them will by no means deal directly with the contradiction I propose above. Yet almost all of them reflect part of the enormous net of cause and effect flung out by the dedication to war as a way of life; and if I tend to use humor and total irreverence more than a serious social essayist might, it is because I have always felt that humor can be more convincing than anger. In any case, the line between humor and tragedy is very thin. The enormous tragedy of Mr. Bush's war against Panama is heightened rather than lessened by the grim joke of his presenting as a cause and justification for that war the fact that an American woman was insulted by a Panamanian soldier.

The eight years of Ronald Reagan and the two following years of George Bush transformed America into a very different kind of society from what it had been. In those twelve years, the United States became in effect a gigantic arsenal, a country so dedicated to the production of guns in every form and the machinery of war in every form and state known to science, that it is in effect a murder weapon beyond either the dreams or the nightmares of the past. All of this was backed by the government's argument that unless we armed ourselves to this ultimate degree, we would be destroyed by the Soviet Union; and in order to achieve this grotesque goal, our people were mortgaged to the tune of better than a trillion dollars, while our cities and our national infrastructure crumbled and our quality of life deteriorated.

The military threat posed by the Soviet Union, real or imagined, disappeared with the disintegration of the Soviet Union, but the vast military apparatus lay upon the country like a great spider. Ever since the conclusion of World War II, in 1945, every government of this country had conditioned its moves and motivations according to the

"Soviet threat." The ideology of America became the ideology of a war machine; the future was a future of war; the hope no more than a hope of some of us surviving destruction; and the vast profits of the war industries became the dominant force in government.

The result of the creation of this enormous war machine was an unending river of weapons. Once armed, the United States could no longer justify the river of weapons, and even the creation of new advanced planes and tanks and submarines and missiles could not satisfy the greed and the profits of the weapons makers, the colossal armaments industry. The result of this was that we became arms merchants to the world, followed competitively by the Soviet Union, the British, the French, the Swiss, and whatever other industrial nations could enter the arms market. Throughout the world, we replaced muzzle-loading muskets with hand-held machine guns, rockets, and high-powered planes.

The destabilizing effect of this transition of an industrial power from civilian production to war production was felt in every corner of the earth; in Afghanistan, for example, tribal wars once fought with flintlocks and limited casualties were now undertaken with the most modern weapons and unlimited casualties. In Vietnam, millions died and a fertile land was criminally wasted. Regional wars, fought with the most modern weapons, became the order of the day, and in place after place, the terrible specter of additional atomic bombs arose. Ronald Reagan undertook a science-fiction project of creating a protective net across the United States that would ward off any atom bombs, while we could bomb our "enemies" at will; and his successor, George Bush, undertook two wars, one against Panama and the second against Iraq, without any real cause or reason except an arrogant domination of this hemisphere and an even more arrogant determination to control the oil of the Middle East.

I pose the above, not as an all too brief recollection of history, but as a background for the essays which follow. I did not begin my life as a pacifist. My pacifism was the result of many years of living and seeing and reflecting. I saw enormous acts of legalized murder being shrugged off again and again by those who make and control public opinion. The great Holocaust of World War II, the calculated murder of millions, is dropped out of memory as casually as a train wreck or ship sinking, and so it is with an ever increasing list of atrocities. It is only a few years since gangs inspired by the Indonesian government, in a single night of bloodthirsty madness, put over a million people of the political opposition to death—yet in all our dealings with Indonesia, not a congressman or a senator pauses to remember this awful thing.

I could go on and on, moving from these gargantuan horrors to the mother in Brooklyn, New York, who receives a phone call from the high school her fourteen year old son attends, informing her that in the corridors of the school, her son has been shot to death. The violence that has permeated our country is not innate in our people; human beings do not have violent genes; but an ideology of violence has been created that permeates every corner of our society—and, indeed, of world society.

I write as an outsider. I do not believe that there is any valid reason for taking a human life, and in the essays that follow I underscore this belief. Most, but not all, of these essays deal with violence and matters of war and peace—yet there is hardly a one of them that does not reflect the insanity of our times. We have eschewed common sense, reason, and simple logic. By all objective definition, we have become a society of the insane, and like criminals in revolt, we are destroying our habitat, the planet earth.

A Note on the Essays

Beginning this task was an interesting problem for me. John Sicher had said, "Write what you please." There was a world stood upon its head! Does anyone write what he wishes, what he thinks, what he never says aloud, what the boss might be enraged over, what his readers might turn away from in anger or fear? And since anything that rates a headline in the American press or a sound byte on the tube is written on and squeezed dry by a thousand reporters and commentators and anchormen, is there any way to say what none of them had said?

Strangely enough, the answer is yes. There is a way of looking at events that is eschewed by almost every commentator. The subject I chose to begin my time on *The New York Observer* was a segment of the ongoing "war against the women." There's a phrase that I came to use again and again, as I more and more clearly came to understand the nature of this war that man has waged against women since history began. It is a story of three women and a federal prosecutor, a small, heartbreaking moment in the endless struggle.

Chapter 1

The War Against Women

A Telling Indictment

Hortense Gabel, a distinguished New York judge, was arrested and tried along with Bess Myerson, both accused of exchanging favors. Judge Gabel had reduced the alimony payments of a close friend of Myerson's, and Miss Myerson had given employment to Judge Gabel's daughter, who testified against her mother in the trial.

There is a very old story about a young man who loved an evil woman. He gave her all that he owned, but it was not enough, and when he pleaded for her favor she said to him: "Bring me the living heart of your mother, torn from her breast, and that will prove that you love me."

With that, he raced home, took a knife, slashed open his mother's breast, tore out her living heart and then, holding it, ran with his gift to the evil woman—but as he ran, he tripped and fell and his mother's heart, still clutched in his hand, whispered to him: "Did you hurt yourself, my child?"

How often I thought of this ancient tale as I watched Hortense Gabel having her heart torn to shreds by her poor sick child, and how often I wondered whether there was a more telling indictment of our society than this dreadful trial. Mrs. Gabel is 76. She is a wise and gentle woman who has given years of her life to public service, first as a housing official and then as a judge. There has never been a word of corruption spoken against her, yet together with Bess Myerson, for reasons that made no sense whatsoever, she endured a public crucifixion of the soul for weeks on end. I don't know Bess Myerson, I have never met her, but through the media I witnessed her personal agony, arrested and denounced as a shoplifter, mocked, harassed, stripped naked, alone, friendless, deserted by the people who had used her and her beauty—in particular, Mayor Koch, who had once so proudly displayed her as his dinner companion. [Ed Koch was mayor of New York from 1977 to 1989.]

And U.S. Attorney Rudolph Giuliani—does he know what he has done? Did he know what he was doing? Is there anywhere in his makeup a shred of compassion? Has no one ever whispered to him that this metropolitan area is saturated with crime, that our jails are bursting, that District Attorney Robert Morgenthau's 400-plus district attorneys are plea-bargaining eight hours a day because there is no time or room in the courts? Has no one informed him that brutal and violent men are being returned to the streets in short time because there are no judges to try their cases? All of my life in and around New York, I have heard of political deals made, one hand washing the other, favors owed and favors given—and no one being indicted or going to the slammer for such small gifts. But apparently Mr. Giuliani had heard nothing of these goings on until his eyes were opened by the suggestion that Justice Gabel might have done a favor for Bess Myerson; and then, happily, he devoted hundreds of thousands of dollars of taxpayers' money and weeks of courtroom space to those two terrifying enemies of society, Hortense Gabel and Bess Myerson.

Here and there, we have been hearing that Mr. Giuliani hankers to be mayor of New York City, an interesting anticipation of future shock after Mr. Koch. I remember watching Mr. Koch and Ms. Myerson during the campaign of 1977. Here was this tall, graceful woman, walking with her hand upon Mr. Koch's arm, smiling and dissipating any notion that the future Mayor might be less than lovable. After all, this was the same gifted woman whom Mayor John Lindsay had appointed Commissioner of Consumer Affairs in the 1960s; and then, in 1983, Mr. Koch made her his Cultural Affairs Commissioner. And all through those years, again and again, Ed Koch and Bess Myerson were seen together at dinners and charity functions.

And of course when Ms. Myerson was put on trial, not for stealing money but for giving employment to an unhappy woman who needed work and approval so desperately, Mayor Koch rallied to her defense, telling the press what a fine woman this was, testifying to her integrity, skill and character, denouncing Mr. Giuliani's indictment, standing in defense of a woman he had once at least pretended to love and value—standing up as a gentleman and shouting for all the world to hear: "This is wrong!"

Or did he?

Understandably, he was much too preoccupied trying to work out a way for homeless people to pay for a night's lodging in a city shelter. And even after a jury of 12 good men and women had found Hortense Gabel and Bess Myerson not guilty of the crimes they were accused of, Mr. Koch had only a whisper of a sort of congratulations for Bess Myerson.

As for Mr. Giuliani, he had only a few words to the effect that this was the jury's opinion and that it hadn't changed his mind at all.

January 9, 1989

The Crazy Notion of Women's Equality

For some months now, I have had on my desk the August 1989 issue of *Fortune* magazine—not to treasure its financial advice, but because its lead article begged me to say something in response. Yet what that response should be puzzled me. Then, in the process of thinking through my own position on the question of choice in the current abortion struggle, I came up with some answers.

First the article: It is titled "The CEO's Second Wife," written by one Julie Connelly, and in a perfectly straightforward manner it presents a history of very wealthy men who run large corporations, and who, having come to power, find that their first wives are inadequate to their needs, neither young enough nor sufficiently beautiful, and thereupon dump said first wives and marry proper mates for tycoons. Ms. Connelly sees no need to argue her case; she simply presents it as a fact of today's world:

"Enter the second wife, a decade or two younger than her husband, sometimes several inches taller, beautiful, and very often accomplished. The second wife certifies her husband's status and, if possible given the material she has to work with, dispels the notion that men peak sexually at age 18."

A few pages later, Ms. Connelly further clarifies the situation: "The big loser is usually the first wife. Her fate is sealed in these four words: She Didn't Keep Up. The mistake the first wife too often makes is allowing her children to become the focus of her life instead of her husband."

And in case you still don't get the message: "In some cases the man with the old, nice matronly first wife is looked down upon. Why can't he do better for himself?"

Indeed, why can't he? The deal's the thing, and without getting moralistic about this tribute by *Fortune* magazine to the facts of life in today's America, one is forced to ask about the reverse: the right of women to do the same thing. Oh, it has happened, and many a wealthy woman has purchased herself a proper pair of gonads, but the circumstances are quite different: The gigolo sells his product. Being a "man," he is not a part of a large commodity market; the woman is—although in many cases she will respond with anger to the notion that women are considered "things." But the fact is that they have been considered *things* through all the several thousand years of civilization, and today there is no country on the face of the earth where the woman is not degraded, punished, bought and sold, and in some places put to death at the will or the whim of her husband—a condition prevalent even today in certain parts of Brazil.

So the gilding and juicing of the practice by *Fortune* magazine does not really separate the American situation from places in what we call "the third world," and, thereby, I return to the question of choice. The neatest and most successful trick of the anti-abortion forces has been to force the media to report the struggle in terms of a woman aborting a pregnancy, thereby narrowing and clouding the issue.

The fact of the matter is that when women demand the right of choice, they are not only asking for the right of a woman to say whether or not she will carry to term; they are asking for the right of a woman to exercise the privilege of equality. All women are oppressed, and it is a total and ghastly shame of the human race that there is no exception to this anywhere on earth. The oppression of women is so old, so absolutely matter of fact that it is simply accepted, and who in the media or in books or anywhere has dared to state:

"It is the absolute right of women, here in the United States, constituting 50 percent of the population, to hold 50 percent of the seats in Congress and in every legislative body in the land"?

Crazy notion, isn't it? And wasn't I writing something about some silly piece in *Fortune* magazine and how did I get to *choice* and to this crazy notion of women holding half the elective posts in America, and why don't I stick to the plain fact of the matter, which is that most women are content with things the way they are? And as for saying that women are treated as commodities, not people, I'll get my head handed to me for that, because every decent woman in America will stand up and tell me how wrong I am.

Or am I?

On the other hand, the fact that women constitute half the population of this country and of the earth makes for a potential more powerful and upsetting than any atomic weapon; and someday women will become aware of that simple fact. And when I contemplate the possibility of that besotted lot called Congress becoming half female, I am not at all disturbed. Not one small bit.

December 11, 1989

A Term of Contempt

Even after 14 women were brutally murdered in Canada by a lunatic carrying a semi-automatic assault rifle, there was no outcry in either Congress or the White House against either the ownership or the manufacture of such rifles in the United States. The fact that this horror occurred in Canada should add to no one's sense of ease or security, for thousands of these guns are in the hands of American civilians.

In a civilized society, there is no conceivable use or reason for such weapons. I have little admiration for hunters, but the hunter who goes after game with a rapid-fire infantry weapon deserves only contempt and should be locked up by local law. It may well be that I refer too often to the elocutionary orgasm that convulsed Congress in the matter of flag-burning, but I find a pressing need to compare this strange explosion of Congressional indignation with its silence in the face of every imaginable horror—and of course, in this instance, the mindless murder of 14 innocent women.

Again, let the fact that it happened in Canada bemuse no one; in a larger sense, it happened here, for the thing that is called "the American way of life" washes over the borders, especially to the north. What happened in this case cannot be dismissed as the insane act of one individual, and if we think of it in this manner, we will bog down in a concept of a society increasingly condemned to madness. Hypocrisy, racism, greed and the worship of power are something else; though they lead to madness, unlike clinical insanity, they are social and not genetic manifestations.

The 14 women were murdered for only one reason, because they were women. They were not singled out, they were not specified, they were simply women and they were put to death by a man who hated women.

And this hatred—so visibly monstrous on this specific occasion—is a socially nurtured miasma, acceptable in our society and in practically every other society, a pattern for mirth, for comedy and, above all, for contempt. It is in the nature of war—and I ask you to see war as the sickness of nations—that before one can kill another human being without reason or need, one must strip the enemy of humanity and reduce them to the status of animals; for everyone knows that to kill an animal is permissible and even admirable in all moralities and religions.

Yes, it was something more than a random act of murder that killed the 14 women; it was an incident in man's war against women—and while that statement calls for some thinking, it is by no means a figment of the imagination. The women were killed because of their sex, and while most men look upon the act with horror and are unable to think of it as an incident in the ghastly war that men have waged against women through the ages, we must be reminded that in every crazed serial murder, the victims were women. Jack the Ripper was not simply a demented killer; he is a symbol that has occurred and reoccurred through the ages, and which goes on today with the obsessive murder of women. Every police station in every city in America knows his pattern and has had to deal with it.

And of course, this thinking leads to the matter of *choice*. It would have to, for the great deceit of our time is to set the matter of *choice* in religious or ethical terms. In reality, it is nothing of the sort; it is something else entirely, the denial to the largest oppressed group on this planet—namely women—of their freedom. And this must be spelled out again and again and again. The issue is not abortion; the issue is *choice*.

The major difference here is that religion has gotten into the act. Not that religion is fighting against women's freedom for the first time; in almost every step of women's struggle for emancipation, fundamentalist religion stood in opposition.

The word "squaw," from the American Indian *ethkwewa* (Algonquin) was picked up by the early settlers as a term of contempt. The word means woman, and the woman among the tribal American Indians was never held in contempt. Fully the equal of the male, she decided questions of war and peace, chose the war chiefs, sat in the councils and, in time of famine, determined who should live and who should die. There is a very large and fully documented record of colonial women, kidnapped by Indians, who when rescued refused to give up the tribal life and fought tooth and nail to remain with the Indians.

It was left to civilization to teach the Indians such refinements of civilization as alcoholism, despair, and the degradation of women.

January 8, 1990

Rape

Some thoughts about women and rape:

There has never been a proven case of a tribal American Indian—that is, one living in a functioning tribe—committing rape. On the other hand, of the few hundred cases we have of white women captured by Indians, at least 75 percent when liberated fought like tigers not to be taken back to their white husbands. History has fudged this—as our written and taught history fudges most things—but it tells us something about the treatment of women. Among the American Indians, women were equal. Among the Iroquois, the *mothers* ruled the tribes.

Rape is not an act of response to a sexual need; it is an act of pure hostility and utter contempt for the victim, performed by the most degraded elements of a society so corrupt that it has reduced women to dehumanized *things,* bereft of any right to be seen as persons. Do I put it too strongly? Let's look at the semantics of this condition. As Americans, we have a greater tendency to think and allow our thinking to be controlled in terms of trigger-words than the people of any other society. Let's look at some trigger-words:

For men, in common conversational usage, only two words—guy or hunk. Both are terms of respect.

For women, in common conversational usage—gal, broad, bimbo, moll, tomato, dish, pig, doll, piece of ass, piece of tail, bitch, whore, hooker and certain others that the editor would not print. Except for the first, all of these are words of contempt and degradation. Don't laugh it off. Don't say, So what? As you speak, you think. As a society speaks, so does it think and act, and in our society mentation has been replaced by the cliché and the trigger-word.

In Victorian England, a very class-conscious society, the degradation of women took special forms. The right of an upper-class master to exact sexual services from his servants was tacitly accepted; when the reverse was novelized, as in *Lady Chatterly's Lover,* the critics went out of their minds. But even in England, so brazen a reduction of women to chattel status as the laws advocated by the right-to-lifers was never entertained. The notion of telling women that certain functions of their bodies could take place only as the state wills is so barbaric that the very thought of democracy wilts in its presence, and a human being subject to such thinking hasn't even a pretense of human rights.

Such thinking about the status of women in America begins to make a framework of fact that cannot be negated by the argument that we have women in Congress, in the Administration and in the highest echelons of business and the arts; this only goes to speak for the intelligence and courage and determination of a great many women—

not to either the intelligence or decency of the society they struggle against, or, better said, the men in that society.

Let's look at another aspect of this framework we have created around women. In any home that has cable television, a child of 6 or 8 or 10 or 15, a male, a female, any child who can punch a button can tune in the public-access channel and watch nude women masturbating, parading naked, drooling out every forbidden sex word and giving you a telephone number you can call to get your fill of verbal pornography, women used and displayed in a manner so tasteless and revolting that it would have horrified this country a few decades ago. Now it's par for the course, a business that rakes in millions of dollars a day by taking the best thing in human existence, love and sex, and turning it into a nightmare.

The women are presented not as people but as things, a little more titillating than department store dummies since they are functioning with a heartbeat, but entitled to no more respect.

Shall we talk about rape? Every day in these United States there are thousands of cases of rape—in Harlem, for example, as many as 20 in one week, none of them very newsworthy since they don't have the circumstances that surrounded the poor woman in the park. We have more rape cases, even proportionally, than any country on earth, and the knuckleheads in the media drool into their microphones mumbling Why? Why? Why?

Why indeed? On television, did you ever see a man and a woman, a boy and a girl, kiss each other gently, lovingly? In the demented world of television, a world of hate, violence, murder and assorted lunacy, a kiss is exhibited as an attempt to crawl into the other's mouth—never as an act of gentle love—and sex, most often, as a sort of modified rape. We have robbed the women of the right to be seen as human beings; the kids who grow up with six hours or more of television each day see what the tube gives them. Is it any wonder that they accept a rite of passage that is sold to them day in and day out?

June 5, 1992

Chapter 2

The War Against the Public

A Question of Economics

Enter now, Mr. D'emas (pronounced De EM is, "e" as in "empty"). Ever since the Dialogues of Plato, *the* naive *has been a convenient literary device for dialectical inquiry. To be in this position, as I was, where I could give vent to my opinions of organized society and not resort to a naive would have been unthinkable; whereupon you will meet D'emas again and again in the course of these essays.*

D'emas *is the Yiddish word for "truth," and since the naive is practically a fixture in Yiddish writing, it seemed proper to thus name my savage.*

But of course the naive is a "savage" only in the sense that he lacks the sophistication that has directed and manipulated the thinking of the so-called civilized to a point where the connection between mentation and the objective reality is either vague or entirely lacking. The naive is not stupid; indeed, his intelligence is if anything superior to the sophisticate's, but it is balanced with humility and self-deprecation. D'emas is apologetic, unassuming because he is faced with the "power and the glory" of civilization. When he sets foot into a world of social insanity, he is not critical but uneasy, with a sense of being very much out of place. He would be a part of this wonderful world, if only he could understand it.

It's not simply that my friend D'emas is a savage, having come from a place most unlike New York City, where they have neither television nor film. It's his stubborn refusal or inability to understand civilization. Returning from a walk on Madison Avenue, he was terribly upset about the homeless people he saw along the way.

"In this awful cold weather," he said, shaking his head, "New York is a frightful place."

"Now don't lay it all on New York," I told him. "There are more than two million homeless people nationwide and, believe it or not, there are cities with more of them than New York. Everyone dumps on New York."

"Oh, no," D'emas said. "New York is a fine place and I would never dump on it, but I was walking up Madison Avenue and I saw this lovely silk shirt with pink stripes and I priced it—and you know, it was $400."

"Well, Madison Avenue is expensive, but what has that got to do with homeless people?"

"It just seems that if you people can pay $400 for a shirt, you're very rich."

"Quite so," I informed him proudly. "We are the richest nation on the face of the earth. We are richer than Germany, France and England combined."

"Oh? Then they must have more than two million homeless people."

"Absolutely not. One thing has nothing to do with the other."

D'emas always gets upset when he feels he is offending me. "I'm trying so hard to think civilized, the way they do in a free society, but in my land, one can live pretty decently on $400 a year," he said.

"Because you are primitives."

"I suppose so. But when one of us is homeless, we all get together and build him a home."

"Exactly—which proves my point. It's one thing to be a savage and think like a savage, but we can't just get together and build a home for a homeless person. The free world doesn't work that way. I mean, nothing is free, and if we started giving away homes to homeless people, our whole structure would collapse."

"But," D'emas argued, "you do provide free homes—and very nice ones. Mr. Bush has a fine home, and he doesn't pay rent, and neither does Mr. Koch with his fine mansion [Gracie Mansion, residence of New York mayors] on the river, and there are thousands of governors and mayors and presidents of universities and ministers and priests and rabbis, not to mention army officers and soldiers, and none of them pay rent, and there must be all told maybe 15 or 20 million of them . . . ."

"D'emas, stop!" I shouted. "Even a savage has no right to be so confused. You are mixing apples and oranges, and that is simply not done in our society."

"You mean what I said is not true?"

"I mean you are mixing apples and oranges. Do you know what it would cost to build homes for our two million homeless?"

"I really have no idea."

"Let me tell you, then, and listen very seriously, my young friend. You must understand civilization if you are to exist at all in this world. The price of building two million homes equals 10 percent of the annual budget of the Pentagon. Not only that, but the amount of labor needed to build two million additional homes would practically wipe out unemployment and might even create a labor shortage—which would drive wages up and could be potentially disastrous. Meanwhile, the Pentagon might have to forego building three additional atomic submarines, any one of which could totally depopulate Europe in about 10 minutes. Do you understand what I'm saying?"

After a long moment, D'emas shook his head. "I'm afraid not," he said.

"I am trying to make clear to you that the problem of two million homeless people lying around on the streets and freezing to death in cold weather is not a question of compassion but one of economics."

"Yes," D'emas said. "I'm grateful that we don't practice voodoo economics on our island."

"Voodoo economics?"

"Yes, when your Mr. Reagan put together his budget and his tax laws that resulted in this, your Mr. Bush called it voodoo economics. Or am I mistaken?"

I had to admit that he was not mistaken.

March 13, 1989

Voodoo Economics

There are four schools of economics in these United States.

The first is called BOOM, and, much-simplified but not distorted, its practitioners hold that we will build a pathway to Eden, during which the market will rise forever and the road to happiness will be solidly based on hamburgers and fried chicken and cola drinks.

The second school is called BUST, and its practitioners hold that we are doomed because hamburgers and fried chicken and cola drinks are not enough, and a great depression awaits us.

The third school of economics is called MUDDLE, and it is based on the belief that somehow we will muddle along.

The fourth school of economics is called VOODOO, and, since it is the economic theory that has directed the economy of the nation during the past nine years, it is worth examining. There has been a great mystery about Voodoo economics, and many scholarly and erudite tomes have been published, as well as countless articles, all directed toward the patriotic goal of utter confusion. The great strength of Voodoo economics resides in the fact that its operation is so simple that a child could understand it, but that simplicity is operational, and since nothing simple or easily understandable emerges from the clown-show we call the Congress of the United States, Voodoo economics must be clothed with awesome budgets and endless discussion. Let's strip it down a bit.

Begin with yourself as an example. If you could borrow money at any rate of interest, and then borrow more as you needed it, and more and more and more, and no matter how great the interest became, borrow to pay the interest, and borrow more to live on, and so on through all your years on earth, you would be engaging in Voodoo economics. Well, before you start licking your lips, let's translate that into the practice of the gentlemen in Washington.

The Federal Government borrows money through the sale of notes, bills and bonds. These are all the same, in that they represent a promise by the Feds to redeem the loans at a given date for dollars. At the date of this writing, the gross amount of that unpaid loan amounts to just about three-and-one-half trillion dollars. Since a trillion dollars is not easily visualized, let me write the sum out: $3,500,000,000,000.

Who lends us that money? The Arabs, with dollars we pay for their oil; the Japanese, with dollars we pay for their products; the Germans, the French, the English and, of course, our own rich, who patriotically put up billions.

And do you know what we pay for this largess? Well, a rich American who buys a million dollars worth of Government bonds collects $85,000 a year from his grateful Government. You want to know what the others collect? You can get out your slide rule, or you can take my word for it: $300,000,000,000, give or take a few million.

This, by the way, is a bit more than half of all the Federal income tax collected in 1989. And where do we get the money to pay that gigantic carrying charge? Simple. We borrow more money.

Onward and upward: By the year of 2000, the carrying charge alone will be more than two-thirds of a trillion dollars. But who cares? Let tomorrow take care of tomorrow.

And what do we do with the billions and trillions that we borrow? We make prosperity. We pour money into the Pentagon, and this great idiot arms machine creates thousands of jobs for men and women to make tools of death, which, happily, are not used, as well as shoes and blankets and shirts and towels and everything else a bloated Army and Navy require. We scatter a little into the entitlements, we lend money to the petty dictators and murderers who run our client states, we pay off the bums and crooks who are grabbing up the savings-and-loans that went broke, we overpay thousands of Government workers—and the net result is prosperity.

And, just as a footnote to the above, we use some of the money to pay the legal bills of former Attorney General Edwin Meese III, compensation for what his lawyers cost him when he was indicted for funny business in the Wedtech affair. Said sum being $460,509.

So here you have a short and simple explanation of what Voodoo economics consists of and how it functions. Since the indebtedness is in dollars, and we print the dollars as well as the notes we use to endorse our borrowing, people will tell you we are in no danger. But that line of defense is an outrageous lie. No matter how many dollars and bonds we print, the loans and the interest come out of the skill and sweat of the citizens of this country—and we are witnessing the creation of a future of grotesque inflation and great misery.

Only a fool can believe that we borrow this money without collateral. The collateral is the hopes and lives of our children and our grandchildren.

July 30–August 6, 1990

Think Before You Cross the Picket Line

Few things that I have seen in recent months disturbed me as much as the crowds of people, men and women, young and old, rushing to cross the Eastern Airlines picket line to buy the cheap $12 handout of Frank Lorenzo. We've forgotten what crossing a picket line means—that stepping across it to avoid some petty inconvenience wipes out not only the hopes and dreams of people like ourselves, but only too often the food on the tables of the men and women who walk the picket line, not to mention whole families destroyed.

When that blissful and mindless destroyer, Ronald Reagan, broke the strike of the air controllers, he drove a stake deep into the heart of the American trade union movement; and at that moment there should have been a roar of citizen outrage that would have bounced him out of the White House; but there was no roar of outrage, and the cowardly boobs we elect to Congress did not even whisper a dissent.

So I am asking you to think once again about the meaning of trade unionism, and to set aside the notion that the trade union benefits only those who belong to it:

We have eight- and six-hour work days because the trade union movement fought for them.

We have pension plans because the trade union movement originated the plan and fought for it.

The whole idea of medical insurance and protection of the workers in the shop comes from the trade union movement.

You travel in safety in plane, train, bus and ship because the trade union movement originated and fought for these safety measures.

There would not be decent low-income housing if the trade union movement had not originated the idea and fought for it.

There would be no child labor laws if the trade union movement had not fought for and won these laws.

There would be no protection for workers in coal, steel and cotton if the trade unions had not fought for protective legislation.

And the women's movement for the vote, for equal pay for equal work would not be what it is today if not for the backing of the trade union movement.

There is no ghost of Christmas past and Christmas future, as Charles Dickens learned from the angry cries of British workers who read his *Christmas Carol.* Scrooge was and is Scrooge, and if Bob Cratchet wanted a decent wage and a future for Tiny Tim, he'd damn well have to join a union.

God help us, how easily we forget! Between 1820 and 1850, a whole generation of New England workers, descendants of the men who fought in the American Revolution, was wiped out of existence in the cotton mills of Maine, Massachusetts and Connecticut. Children were put into the mills at age 8, just as they were put into the mines, before they even reached puberty, and they lived in the mills and the mines and they died before they ever reached maturity, their passage into teen age marked by the blood they coughed up out of their lungs. The trade unions—not the government—put an end to that.

And when freedom-loving New Englanders brought over the Irish immigrants, to replace the dead Yankees in the mills and to build the new railroads, there was an Irish song to spell it out: "You work all day for sugar in your tay, down upon the railroad."

And we, the people of this country, stand by quietly and meekly as a

Frank Lorenzo says, "To hell with it! I do as I please!" And then he offers us a $12 junket to Washington and we scramble through the picket lines like trained rabbits, clapping our hands for the bargain we got.

We build monuments to celebrate war, but where are the monuments for the thousands of men and women who died to create our trade unions? If the unions are smashed, then, believe me, we will all suffer and this country will never again be what it is. I don't speak as some theoretical intellectual. For 15 years I covered trade unions, and for 32 years I have been a dues-paying member of one of the finest craft trade unions in America, The Writers' Guild of America. This union not only gives us a living wage, but it pays our medical and dental bills, it provides pensions, and it cares for widows and orphans. We have just come through a long, bitter strike, and we won because we stood firm and because decent people did not cross our picket lines.

So before you cross another picket line, add up what we in the trade union movement have given you, and think about it.

April 10, 1989

The Plight of America's Cities

The thing is that they don't know New York, they don't like New York, they don't understand New York and, when you come right down to it, they are afraid of New York. But then it may be that they don't know any other city in America any better than they know New York. I imagine that if you could penetrate their minds—considering that they have any in a human sense—you would find a map of America spotted with every golf course and every golf club in the land, green patches, like oases in the desert, surrounded by prim suburban houses, fading off into a blurred no-man's-land with dark blotches called cities.

I speak, of course, of that curious conglomeration of people who run the country from a most curious place called the District of Columbia, better known as Washington. Let's think about Washington for a moment: It cannot properly be called a city—any more than any other company town could claim the right to be called a city, and it is a company town. But even as a company town, it lacks the central factor that maintains a company town—that is, production. Washington reaps, but it does not sow. With very few exceptions the entire place eats at the trough of tax dollars. The main citizens nose deep in the trough, and the less favored take the gleanings, and from there on down everyone takes a piece of it—even to the drug trade that saturates the District of Columbia. For when you come right down to it, our tax dollars pay for every sniff of cocaine, every pebble of crack consumed in the District.

All this is not to put down our nation's capital, but to try, if very imperfectly, to comprehend why this huge, astronomically expensive institution that we have created on the banks of the Potomac is utterly indifferent to the plight of America's cities, the crumbling of our infrastructure, and of course the deep crisis of that queen of all cities, New York. This question is pertinent not only to our present metropolitan woes, but to every person and place and problem in America.

Nor can this question be considered narrowly. One cannot even think about the billions of dollars we have given to the gang of cutthroats who run El Salvador and whose latest obscenity is the murder of the six Jesuit priests, without contemplating that the same amount of money would have built housing for every homeless person in New York, or repaired every bridge in the city, or built Westway three times over, or fulfilled all the needs of our local AIDS program.

But if one carries on with this line of thought—if one realizes that the billions given to the Pentagon to waste, the billions to the Afghan barbarians to murder each other, the billions to the Contras to murder the women and children of Nicaragua and, not to go unmentioned, the raise in pay that Congress sneaked through, one must come to the conclusion that the crisis of our cities is not the result of any lack of funds but rather a lack of understanding on the part of our national Government as to what cities are.

I began this piece with some comments about the District of Columbia. It differs from all other capitals of great nations in that it is neither the heart of our country nor the expression of our country. The Statue of Liberty stands in New York Harbor because New York is the vanguard beacon of liberty to all of mankind. It has the same verve, zest and explosive creativity that are a part of Paris, of London, of Rome, of Prague—yes, and even of Moscow. All of these cities are first an expression of people and nation and art—and only second a place of government. Washington is simply a place of government—if indeed one can call the witlessness that happens there a process of government.

The result, God help us, is that the country Washington purports to govern is slowly disintegrating. If we were blessed with a sane government, capable of a minimal practice of common sense, the future would be a beacon of hope instead of a gloomy promise of disaster. If they could stop fighting about abortion and seeing Communist ghosts in the poverty-stricken starvation areas of the third world, and if they could stop pouring trillions of our dollars into the insatiable maw of that group of uniformed nuts called the Pentagon, then they might turn their attention to saving the cities—for the cities are still the source of invention, art and civilization. I should think they would sit up and take notice of what is happening in Hungary, Poland, Germany and Czechoslovakia, where millions of people have taken to the streets to shout they have had enough.

The mini-minds of the media have not yet grasped that what we witness in Europe is not exactly a local condition. There are millions here at home, and one day they might open their eyes and gather together with the realization that they too have been snookered.

December 18, 1989

Guardians of the Free World

There is a country called Afghanistan, and its legal, elected government was supported by the Soviet Union; whereupon we armed and fed a collection of benighted and savage tribes and set them about the overthrow of the legal government. We labeled them "freedom fighters," although their treatment of women was the worst on the planet, and their notion of freedom was the right to kill, rape and burn.

But no matter. The covey of mindless boobs we call our Congress set about feeding them money like it was going out of style, almost $4 billion to date, and right now, in the midst of this current budget crisis, our President George Bush and his Chief of Staff, the curious John Sununu, who peers out from behind the Bush at photo opportunities, are working the Congress to turn over $300 million more to the freedom-loving Afghans, who have been using our money to grow more poppies and send a stream of heroin into the United States. The guns we turned over to them are no longer used to fight the legal government, but to fight each other for a larger share in the heroin trade.

Net cost: $4,300,000,000.00.

Origins of the funds: the American taxpayer, who hasn't even a notion of what they do with his or her buck.

Among those taxpayers, a dear old lady friend who will not leave her small apartment in New York City. Her friend and companion was mugged and beaten so badly that she will never walk again.

"But," this friend of ours said, "what can we do? We need more police, but where will the money come from to pay for them?"

She pays her taxes like a good citizen, and not in a hundred years would it occur to her that some of the money she pays in taxes to the Federal Government went to these same Afghan dope runners, and some of it goes to the murder squads we finance in El Salvador, who have already murdered some 70,000 women, men, children, Catholic priests and nuns, and some of it went to a private army called the Contras, which we maintained in Nicaragua in an attempt to overthrow the legal government, and which repaid our misbegotten kindness by running thousands of pounds of cocaine into our country, and some of it went to poison our land forever with atomic waste—and so forth and so on for perhaps a thousand pages in a saga of past and continuing infamy.

How could she entertain such a notion? She would say to me, "How can that be? And why? Why should we bankrupt and destroy ourselves?"

And then, what could I answer her? That a man will starve his children to feed a habit? And how would one name the habit of a club of fools called the Congress who work and dream only of re-election?

In Los Angeles, they did a series of autopsies on teen-age youngsters who live in the bowl rather than on the heights—incidentally the bowl is where most Los Angelenos live—kids killed in accidents and gang wars, and they found that the lungs of each and every one of these youngsters were already partially destroyed from the polluted air that Los Angelenos breathe. Yet we are now engaged in putting together the basis for a great war with only one real object—control of the largest petroleum deposits on earth, so that we may continue to poison our atmosphere and to destroy the lungs and the life expectancy of our citizens. And as I have said before in this column, the money spent on a single day of this war enterprise could pay for all the cops Mayor Dinkins needs.

We live in the choicest piece of real estate on the planet earth. We have a climate as varied and salubrious as any place on earth. We can grow enough food to feed half the world, and we have a tradition of work and invention unequaled elsewhere. We are so positioned as to be invasion-proof, with borders to the north and south that need not be defended. We lead the world in creativity. Our film and theater and literature are honored the world over, and the wise men who wrote our Constitution created a blueprint for a democratic government that would survive long past their time.

And with all of this, we have corrupted the Constitution and the Government, giving all the reins of power to the rich and the mindless. Our great industrial machine has surrendered the making of the tools and products of peace to the Japanese and the Germans and the Koreans, while here at home it devotes itself to a demented production of the tools of death. Half the wealth and energy of our country goes to making the engines of death, and we turn somersaults to find enemies on which to use these murderous products. We have poisoned our earth and air to a point where the very future of the planet is in jeopardy.

But the Afghan drug lords honor us, for we support the free world.

October 22, 1990

So Ends 1990

Forty percent of our population is functionally illiterate. Last year, 2 million American children left school without learning to read or write; 90 percent of the students in a typical inner-city high school could not name the first or the second President of the United States. Half of all black and Hispanic children under the age of six come from homes where the income is below the poverty level, and over 40 million Americans, in terms of income, health care, education and nutrition constitute a third world country.

We are a nation already in debt by an amount in excess of $3 trillion, and servicing our debt costs about $300 billion a year; and on top of this we are undertaking a demented adventure in Saudi Arabia that will cost us in excess of $100 billion while our President, George Bush, goes begging among the oil sheiks for a few dollars to cool the heat at home.

Until 1970, the United States had a balance-of-trade surplus. Now we have a trade deficit in the billions, and it grows larger every week. A doddering actor whom we elevated to the Presidency managed, in eight years, to reduce this country to a financial horror-dump. Among his many legacies, there is a trillion-dollar savings-and-loan bill, which the taxpayers must pay. Another of his legacies is a trillion-dollar pile of military junk, a good bit of it destined to rot and rust in the Arabian desert, a loss sweated out of the hides of the taxpayers.

The year 1990 was the last year of the junk-bond con, a final blow to the surrender of American industrialists to the Japanese and the Koreans and the Germans. But out of this wreckage of the greatest industrial machine the world had ever seen, there did emerge something positive—namely a million-and-a-half millionaires and a company of CEOs who, on an average, earned 90 times as much as the workers in their industries. Many a British 18th-century squire on his landed estate did not have as high a multiple over the peasants who worked his fields as the CEO over the average worker.

What other good news in the realm of industry to grace the year? Well, there was a time when a high school graduate could find work as a machinist, a factory worker, a mechanic or any one of a hundred other industrial jobs. But we have surrendered so much of our heavy industry to the Japanese and the Koreans and the Germans that today, for the most part, the high school graduate can look forward to nothing more than pushing hamburgers or pumping gas or some similar service job, a scene that not only does away with the solid working-class household and family that has been the blood and bones of this country, but which feeds thousands of youngsters into the world of crime.

Yet here is one field in which we lead the entire world—we have become the crime and murder center of the planet Earth. We arrested over 8 million Americans in 1990. We have almost 800,000 people in prison, and we are forced to plea bargain hundreds of thousands of criminals because we have no courts left in which to try them and no prisons to hold them. Our capital, Washington, D.C., is the murder capital of the nation and possibly of the world, and meanwhile our infrastructure disintegrates, our roads crumble, our bridges rust and collapse. Let me give you an assessment of our present position from the German magazine, *Der Spiegel*:

> The Reagan revolution was not only an economic and social shock but also a political one. The motto was: a lid on charity and a free rein for Rambo. The dollar was the yardstick of political morality. The Reagan Mafia undermined the pillars of democracy: Three of the four political powers—the Presidency, the Congress and the press—coalesced into a cartel that neutralized any check on the government. . . . The Reagan revolution attempted to turn America into an oligarchy. It pushed for the vigorous leadership of an upper class: a form of rule by people who kept their money safe in numbered accounts in Switzerland. With catchy slogans about national pride, a future life of luxury, and anti-Communism, Reagan's circus of illusion branded every form of opposition by the notorious East Coast intellectuals as liberal (meaning crypto-Communist). No one who wanted to be re-elected spoke out against the dismantling of social programs. The media glossed over the creeping metamorphosis of the democracy into oligarchy. Not once did the television news stars Dan Rather, Peter Jennings or Ted Koppel, all experienced journalists, take Reagan on. Under such Byzantine circumstances, the administration of this popular President could do almost whatever it chose. (Translation from *World Press Review.)*

And it did; it certainly did; and this imperial Presidency is being continued, although whether the voice is George Bush or the very curious Mr. Sununu is still not clear; but whether the voice is of the one elected or of the other appointed, it is not the voice of a democratic leader, but a tyrant who has lost sight of reality and forgotten the agonies of the nation he purports to lead.

So ends 1990. The human condition is the struggle for peace—and that will be the text and circumstances of 1991.

January 14, 1991

Some Thoughts on Christmas

It was Mark Twain who said, "Christianity is a beautiful religion that has never been practiced."

Concerning practice and nonpractice, in 1898 Charles Monroe Sheldon published a book called *In His Steps: "What Would Jesus Do?"* It was the story told of a small town in what was still small-town America, where the local pastor proposed to his flock—the entire population of the town—that for one month they should live according to the simple teachings of Jesus, in particular, the Sermon on the Mount. The book in hard cover—there was no paperback mass market in those days—sold millions of copies.

When one recalls that the population of the United States at that point was about 76 million, the sale of *In His Steps* is totally incredible.

That was a simpler, perhaps a happier time, or perhaps not so different from today. We grow old and we tend to enshrine the past, because in the past of the old folks there is youth and vibrancy and the memory of a future where all things were still possible. I thought about such matters and of this forgotten book during the holiday season just past. Christmas is an odd bag of tricks, and something not to be put away with Tom Lear's cynical song, "Hark, the *Herald Tribune* sings, Glory to our lust for things," or with its manipulation of lowest and sorriest levels of greed. In a society that depends for its very existence on either war or feverish, maniacal consumption, Christmas has been turned on its head, and the media and the advertisers play on every base, piggish and selfish emotion a person has—with the warning that either you buy and buy and buy or our whole national house of cards will come down upon your head.

Yet a wise writer, a black woman, once said to me, "I revere the Christmas holidays. It's the one moment when I can forget that the whites are white and remember that they are also human."

And then a man pauses on the street and says to me, "I wish you a merry Christmas," without apology or explanation, and I, a Jew, glow with the very simple joy of an easy and harmless connection with another of the human race.

Of course on another day, a guy who stops people on the street to wish them well might get his head handed to him; yet you cannot put aside the fact that the brief lapse into decency that occurs around

Christmas time touches something very deep in our kind, a yearning for a state of being and a truth that is perhaps the most important thing in human existence and which is denied to us. We cannot be citizens of a killing machine, of an armaments factory—which is what we are as a nation—and still retain a sense of humanity. After three years of the crazy slaughter of World War I, there was a section of the trenches where, on Christmas Day, the British and the Germans climbed out of their muddy ravines and with cries of "Peace on Earth" and "Merry Christmas," crossed over the shattered no man's land to embrace each other. You can be sure that the generals soon put an end to that.

Hate is easy, but to function with hate, we must first divest the object of hatred of its humanity. When that takes place, the killing of human beings becomes as easy and as mindless as the killing of animals, but this does not happen simply, in and of itself. It is part of process, an enormous and complex process that exalts hatred and murder, that has made murder and heroism synonymous—the warrior as hero. The process is endemic to Jews, Christians and Moslems. And yet for a few precious days during the years, the masters of war and murders and death give us an interval of surcease and call it Christmas.

I remember reading *In His Steps* when I was very young. It was not a good book, as books go, sentimental, manipulated and in parts utterly ridiculous—yet it touched so deep a chord in me that I still recall it. In the part of the New York jungle I lived in at the time, a place where hatred and gang violence and ethnic viciousness flourished, its gentle suggestion that people could exist in harmony and love instead of hatred and viciousness was new and astonishing.

I have lived a long time since then, and aside from the few days of Christmas time, I am afraid that Christianity will remain untried. The hatred and slaughter and narrowness that has marked religion these past 2,000 years has little or nothing to do with Christianity or what we call the Judeo-Christian ethic, and if the dream of the author who wrote *In His Steps* is to come about, it will be through the eradication of hunger and unemployment and ignorance.

Meanwhile, the killing goes on, racism flourishes and another Christmas season fades into the past. For the months to come, we will stride by each other with set faces, the women aware that so simple a thing as eye contact can be dangerous in what we call civilization, the men engaged mentally with tension and fear. Serbs will kill Croats and Georgians will kill each other and in the Middle East terrorists will kill whoever is unlucky enough to be near one of their car bombs. In our inner cities, dope peddlers will kill any and all who stand in their way. And perhaps the best prayer we concoct for 1992 might go thus:

"Please, dear Lord, let not our elected officials concoct another war to get us out of this depression!"

January 20, 1992

What America Has Lost

At this writing, I am just back from a week in Paris. I went there to take part in the dedication of a public square to Dashiell Hammett. They do such things in France. They name streets after poets, musicians, novelists, painters, sculptors. For example, here are the directions given out to get to the place: "Inauguration de la place Dashiell Hammett à Bobigny: (entre la Maison de la Culture, bd Lénine et la Bibliothèque Elsa Triolet, rue de l'Union)."

At one side of the square, a great new library; at the other, a new theater. The library, as you see, was named after a beloved French poet. The occasion for naming, as the French proudly put it, the "first street in the world for Dashiell Hammett" was the 150th birthday of Edgar Allen Poe, revered by French critics and regarded there as the inventor of the modern detective story. I was invited along with 15 writers from various countries to take part in the ceremonies.

The French attitude toward the detective story is quite different from ours. Writing at the death of Hammett, Louis Aragon, the great French poet and novelist, said: "We owe to Dashiell Hammett the paternity of a highly criticized genre, but one which to my thinking dominates this century, even more so than Faulkner and Hemingway." Let me also mention that Hammett was hounded and persecuted by the Government of the United States—suspicion of being a communist, or just decent—and then put in prison for six months for his refusal to name names and become a stool pigeon. Yet his name and his work will outlast even the memory of the un-American committee.

On my first visit to Paris, 42 years ago, I walked into its streets one afternoon with Dr. W.E.B. Du Bois, the black historian, and I remember his saying to me, "Howard, should the Good Lord ever decide to create that paradise that Christians blather about, he could find a worse model than Paris."

A lovely fantasy, of course, yet each time I return to that incredible city I think of what Du Bois said. Its beauty is undiminished, and they refuse to follow our habit in New York of tearing down splendid old buildings to put up trashy high-rises. They cherish their past and they live with history, instead of forgetting it or turning it into a lie, as we do. One can walk the streets safely at night, and in all the time I was there I saw no panhandlers and not once was I cadged for a coin. There were no homeless people sleeping in the streets and there was no place to compare with the wastelands of the Bronx or Brooklyn. There was a sense of pride on the part of the ordinary citizen that we seem to have lost, and instead of victory parades for the demented Gulf slaughter, there was a celebration in honor of a French brigade in *World War I* that refused an order to fire on civilians.

Compared with the United States, France is a poor country, its density of population far greater than ours, its land in no way as beneficent as ours; yet it feeds its people and it manages in these difficult times to maintain its cities as civilized and functioning groupings of mankind. Above all, like England, France is a country that remembers. It lives with its history. It remembers the defense of Montmartre, not because of hundred-dollar tickets to a glitzy musical called *Les Misérables*, but because the sacrifice was sealed with the blood of their beautiful city and its people.

It's good to get home because home is what it is, a place with more possibilities than any other land on earth. After all, praise France or England as one will, only we, here in the United States, have put together nations from every corner of the earth and given them a common language and a common hope.

But in the process we have lost something. We have traded our ethnic memories for no memory at all, and we have sacrificed all the rich and beautiful ideals of the best of men to one simple goal, greed. It is not that the evil our government does—the slaughter in the Gulf War for example—is so different or worse than the slaughters done at one time or another by every government; it is simply that we appear to have lost any sense of either guilt or compassion. We do not apologize for the dreadful things we do, we exult in them. And because we refuse to see the reality of what Washington does in other lands, we close our eyes to the reality of what Washington is doing to us here at home.

Under the pseudonym of E.V. Cunningham, Howard Fast has published 21 suspense and detective novels.

June 17, 1991

Chapter 3

The Failed War Against Drugs

On Poisons Legal and Illegal

It is almost 30 years since I smoked my last cigarette, yet I remember—and will to my dying day—the taste of the first cigarette with the morning cup of coffee. It was beautiful, exquisite, heady and poisonous. Around that time, I switched to a pipe and cigars and, while I have not actually smoked a cigar for 10 years, the close of a good dinner still leaves me longing for a fine, illegal Cuban. According to a close friend of ours, a brilliant physician who has worked in the field, nicotine (a poisonous, colorless oily liquid extracted from tobacco, per Webster) is much tougher to kick than either cocaine or heroin—and more deadly.

The deaths from tobacco outnumber by the thousands deaths from heroin or cocaine, and those who peddle this death so flagrantly—as for example the Philip Morris Company, with its disgusting ads in *The New York Times* praising the Constitution—do so unchecked, the profits from their little bundles of poison running into the billions.

Yet for all of this, for all of the death and suffering, and agony of emphysema and heart attack and cancer caused by tobacco, I would fight with all my strength any movement to ban cigarettes and cigars. Such a prohibition would be so destructive that the very thought boggles the mind. Indeed, such a prohibition might well hold in itself forces that would bring an end to our society. I need only look back to the days of my youth when, say, a dozen people, all of them smokers, were in a room for a social gathering and the cigarettes ran out. Then the scramble for butts—straighten them, smoke them—the search through drawers, there was a cigarette somewhere, midnight and nothing open and I'd give my soul for a butt.

You know, we went through the whole shtick with a thing called Prohibition, a neat little plan cooked up by the same pious lot who consider abortion the work of the devil, and which forbade the consumption of wine or liquor or beer. Before Prohibition, we were a more or less relaxed society of some 70 million people with a minimum of crime. Prohibition—mandated by the 18th Amendment to the Constitution—created organized crime, elevated crime into a billion dollar industry, turned millions of decent, honest Americans into criminals, killed thousands with wood alcohol, destroyed the burgeoning American wine industry, put thousands of people out of work and, above all, increased the consumption of alcoholic beverages.

And again, if we face the facts squarely, we must admit that alcohol is a far more deadly poison than either cocaine or heroin, that it has killed during the past 12 months through drunken driving and alcohol-related disease more than 100,000 people, that it has destroyed homes and blighted the lives of countless women and children. It is also the source of unique pleasure, and the thought of life without wine or beer is bleak indeed.

The point in conclusion is that society is a group of people who must live together, and the conditions under which they live take various and historic forms. Our society is a democratic community of people who have agreed to abide by a common set of rules and values. So long as the set of rules and values remains reasonable, the citizens of our community—with the exception of criminals—will observe these rules and values. But when the majority—or even an assertive and powerful minority—disagree with imposed restrictions, then the community moves toward disintegration, and this disintegration, whether slow or quick, takes the form of an increase in crime, both victimless and with victims.

We see this very clearly in the case of abortion rights; when abortion is forbidden by law it does not eliminate abortion, it simply criminalizes it, with the result of infection, sometimes death, and at times prison and ruin for those who practice it. It also imposes a soaring cost on the process.

Until this point, I have carefully avoided any mention of the legalization of cocaine or heroin. That is very touchy ground, indeed, a sort of hornet's nest, where few indeed dare to tread. Interestingly, it is also a place of neither the right nor the center nor the left, but a position-mix of parts of all three. Yet the question must be faced. There is no way to interdict these drugs, no way to turn poor farmers from a crop that brings them wealth and security for the first time, no way to seal off our borders and remain a free country. And even if we could seal our borders with the Army and the Navy, that will not stop the flow of drugs but only raise the price, which will mean more crime and more destruction.

The only way is the way we took with tobacco: education and reason, and in the ghettos, jobs and jobs and jobs. So while I do not suggest the legalization of drugs, I do strongly suggest that the question must be faced and discussed. Get it out of the closet and discuss it openly and fairly.

April 16, 1990

A Different Tack in the War on Drugs

Again and again, during the past months, we have been witness to drug busts that yield millions of dollars. The money, bills of every denomination, is stacked up like so many bales of hay, yet what the cops grab is only the tip of the income generated by the drug industry. It is a multi-billion-dollar criminal enterprise that is sucking the life and energy out of this country, and it is also an irresistible force for corruption. We have seen national leaders of the highest rank bought and sold for a few thousand dollars; imagine the force of the drug billions.

It is a matter of historical experience that one cannot legislate liquor, tobacco or drugs out of existence. More than 350 years ago, James I tried it with tobacco and we know how successful he was. We had our own experience with Prohibition, and we remain one of the very few developed countries that makes prostitution a crime. And now, having succumbed to the Church's hatred of abortion, the new French abortion pill—which removes the threat of infection or sterilization—will soon become a bootleg product, another source of crime and money.

The harm we have inflicted on ourselves, our nation and our youth with this bluenosed dementia is beyond calculation, as are the deaths that have resulted from these attitudes; and instead of the reasonable and wise Judaic-Christian instruction *Do no evil to another*, we have proposed laws that say, *Do not do to yourself anything that we, the state, consider wrong or evil.* And the saddest part of it is that no matter how bitter and terrible our experience, we do not learn.

Now just suppose that drugs were legal, and along with that, we'll suppose that prostitution were legal:

Since the question of prostitution is less complex, let's look at it first. Legalized, it would be under local health control. That would help to stop the spread of AIDS and venereal disease. It would save lives and it would at least begin to undermine the tyranny of the pimps. It would protect both the woman and the john; it would limit the practice to certain areas; and it would free hundreds of cops to deal with real crime, and the practice would pay millions in taxes.

Now as to drugs. The first result of the legalization of cocaine and heroin would be to do away with the pushers. Since the price of legal drugs would be lower than the bootleg price, and the product cleaner, the pusher would be cut out of it, and without the large army of pushers, there would be no force exercised to hook new addicts.

Now whether or not this would increase the number of addicts, no one knows. In the aftermath of Prohibition, the use of alcoholic beverages did increase for a time; but then it leveled off and a decrease began. In recent years, the decrease is very considerable.

But let us suppose that an increase in the number of addicts resulted. The very fact of decriminalization would open paths for rehabilitation which do not exist today, and a publicity and educational campaign—with the pushers out of the scene—would have a much stronger appeal. If we add to this a valid and vital program of job opportunities for inner-city youth, we begin to restore the moral fiber of the nation.

And look at the other benefits:

An end to the drug lords and an end to the battlefield on our streets.

Billions of dollars put into savings or spent on commodities instead of drugs.

Elimination of at least 60 percent of crime nationally.

The easing of the prison situation. The pace of the increase of our prison population due to drugs is something no civilized nation can live with. We must either reverse it or cease to exist as a democratic nation.

A vast increase in the amount of Federal taxes collected. This is an area where I can find no figures or statistics, understandably, but the amount of taxable dollars has been estimated to be in the billions. The infusion of this huge amount of money into the bloodstream of our nation might indeed usher in a new period of growth and prosperity—and if one realizes how many addicted men and women spend practically all of their earnings on drugs, one begins to understand what is involved.

I have mentioned only a few factors; I have not gone into the number of lives that will be saved, the agony and life-shortening results of addiction done away with eventually, the salvation of our cities—and in the last analysis, the salvation of our country.

In the very small space I have here, I could only touch on aspects of this matter, nor have I tried to suggest how such legalization could be managed. But I believe this—that even if the immediate result would be an increase in users, it is a price that must be paid. We can work with new addicts and help them, but if we lose our nation to anarchy and terror, then we lose everything; and unless we act, we will lose it all.

October 29, 1990

Why We Should Legalize Drugs

Suppose tobacco were illegal, with the same injunctions against production, transportation, sale and use as are today invoked against cocaine, marijuana and heroin. And while entertaining this fantasy, we will accept the fact that tobacco is more habit-forming, more addictive and less easy to discard as a way of life. That is not a supposition, but a fact, attested to by every specialist I have consulted on the question.

So we'd have a situation where the sale or use of tobacco is a criminal offense. Two things would inevitably take place. First, the manufacture of cigarettes and cigars, formerly legal and subject to millions of dollars of taxation, would now be illegal and beyond the power of taxation. Second, the value of said products would increase so explosively that manufacture and use, illegal though they may be, would also increase.

You see, at this moment, the newsstand peddling of cigarettes is no more remunerative than the peddling of popcorn; but the day cigarettes become illegal, the price jumps, and he who has a pocket full of illegal cigarettes is very much in business, while his illegal supplier is on the way to millions. And the demand—well, there is one thing the seller knows, namely that if he is to increase his business he must increase the number of his customers. Each one hooked is a potential lifelong resource, same system as Philip Morris uses today. (Remember when the cigarette manufacturers used to give away small free trial packs?)

Another short jaunt on memory lane: Do you remember what used to happen back in our youthful days when all the cigarettes ran out, and it was late at night, and we used to go from ashtray to ashtray, straightening out crushed butts, trying to rescind a puff here, a thread of smoke there? You do remember. Translate that to the fantasy situation I propose above. It is twelve midnight. The cigarettes have run out. "No sweat," says our good host, and he calls his supplier. "I can let you have ten at ten dollars each." A sigh of relief from the assembled company. At that price, the supplier delivers.

In other words, make tobacco illegal and the number of smokers will double in a single new generation, and with it the stream of death that cigarettes produce. Most of us learned to smoke out of peer pressure when there was no money in it for the pusher; consider the situation with enormous financial gain to drive it.

There is history behind this supposition. Prohibition not only increased drinking substantially, it spread the consumption of alcohol to a generation that would not have rushed to it, were it not for the spice and adventure that illegality gave it. This will be hotly denied, but since drinking was illegal, no statistics could be kept. Yet speaking from what I saw and heard and read at the time, I have absolutely no doubt that drinking—particularly hard liquor—mushroomed during the Prohibition years. It is claimed that after the repeal of Prohibition, drinking increased; but since no statistics of the Prohibition period are available, this claim is groundless.

This I do know, having lived through it; in the field where my young life was lived, writing and publishing, the entire industry was in the grip of the Prohibition syndrome. To a very large extent, they drank themselves to death, and many men and women I knew died in their forties, fifties and sixties—done in by booze. The post–World War II generation drank much less, and their children even less. I go to literary parties today where wine is served and no hard liquor at all. In the Prohibition and post-Prohibition era, that would have been inconceivable.

Now the above, of course, is not by any means directed toward action on alcohol or tobacco. I would fight with all my strength to maintain the legality of both. I have simply used the facts above to illustrate my argument that the *only way* we will ever control and finally rid ourselves of the drug problem is to legalize drugs; and to make a point to those who cry out that disaster will befall us if we do legalize drugs, we must point out that for generations this country lived and thrived without the illegalization of drugs. Many a sick and despairing old citizen managed to make the last years of life tolerable through generous use of Lydia Pinkham's Vegetable Compound, liberally laced with opium; and no one closed the book in horror, reading that Sherlock Holmes sharpened his wits with injections of heroin.

There has been something maniacal in government's hunt for pot, jailing kids by the thousands, poisoning marijuana fields, sermonizing against it. Those kids were of my children's age and time; they smoked pot and then they put it away and forgot about it. It was illegal, but it was cheap and available and could be grown in a window box—and the net effect was the same as if pot had been legalized. It was available, and its use died down.

Meanwhile, we have turned our inner cities into battlefields, given the kids of the inner city over to slaughter, changed them into pushers and dealers, destroyed families and turned a large part of the *American Way of Life* into hell on earth. And so long as drugs are illegal and the distribution remains in the hands of the most malevolent criminal conspiracy this world has ever seen, the process will continue.

Have we no common sense? If no other argument hits home, don't we realize that enough tax money is lost to pay off a substantial part of the national debt? This is not simply an issue; it is the life and death of the American city.

April 15, 1991

Chapter 4

The Culture of Violence

The American Way

My friend, D'emas, is a savage, which is not to put him down but simply a description of his state as opposed to civilization. He comes from one of those forsaken South Sea islands, where television and even the radio are unknown—a background that explains his primitive and barbaric outlook. It all surfaced when I took him to a heavyweight boxing match. He enjoys the excitement of a crowd, so he was quite content until the match started.

"Good heavens," he exclaimed, "they're hitting each other!"

"Of course. That's the whole point of it."

"I had no idea," D'emas said. "You mean you and all the rest of these people paid $50 to watch two men hit each other?"

"Absolutely."

"They're hurting each other."

"They have to. It's the point of the game."

"They're trying to kill each other."

"Oh, no. No. They're simply engaging in the manly art of self-defense."

"But how," D'emas asked, with typically primitive obtuseness, "can they be practicing the manly art of self-defense when they're both attacking each other?"

"Precisely. That's what defense is. Every nation practices defense by attacking another nation."

"But these are men."

"Same thing," I assured D'emas.

"Oh, they must hate each other!" D'emas cried.

"Oh, no. Not at all," I explained. "They're boxers. They live to beat each other to a pulp."

"And they don't hate each other?"

"Of course not. If not for each other, how could they fight?"

"Why do they fight at all?" D'emas wondered.

"For money. Entertainment is one of the central facts of civilization. You wouldn't understand that, being a savage—I mean, I don't want to hurt your feelings, young man, but I know it's hard for you to comprehend why thousands of men and women should sit in this arena and watch a boxing match."

"Yes, but they keep screaming, Kill the bastards. Why do they hate the fighters so much?"

"They don't. They just want their man to knock the other man unconscious. It's part of the sport. Indeed, in our society these fighters are public heroes. Don't you have heroes in your primitive society?"

"Oh, yes. If someone saves a life, he's a hero. But when someone punches someone else, we put him in jail. Isn't this thing dangerous? I mean, they keep punching each other in the head, and they're both bleeding . . ."

"Oh, yes. And in time, the fighters become punch-drunk, as the sporting people put it. It means they become brain-damaged."

"Do they know that?"

"Oh, yes, but they're paid well."

"And all these thousands of people," D'emas wondered, "who have paid $50 to $100 each to sit here and scream and yell for the fighters to kill each other—are they true products of what you keep telling me is civilization?"

"Of course they are. They're Americans."

"And this is what you keep explaining as the *American Way?"*

"One part of it, certainly."

At this point, one of the fighters took a knockout punch and sprawled full length on the canvas. The crowd rose to their feet, screaming.

"I hope he's not dead," D'emas said, shouting above the joy of the crowd.

"It happens," I admitted.

"I don't enjoy this very much," D'emas said, as the referee finished counting and the roar of the crowd subsided. "I'm glad Mr. Bush was elected your President."

"Why?"

"He promised a kinder, gentler America."

How could I possibly explain to a savage what Mr. Bush meant? How could I possibly explain it to anyone, even myself?

February 6, 1989

The Pornography of Violence

When I wrote *The Immigrants* some years ago, a producer who worked for Dino De Laurentiis became intrigued with the story and begged Mr. De Laurentiis to buy it and produce it. Dino and I had a rather good personal relationship at the time, and he was interested enough to have it translated into Italian. Having read it, he said to me woefully, "Howard, how can I possibly make a movie out of it? It has no violence."

His was an honest, simple and direct statement. As an Italian film producer who had only recently—at that time—moved his business to America, his contemplation of the entertainment scene here could be summed up in a single word: violence. And while every so often a film is made without violence, and sometimes the very best of films, these are only the exceptions that prove the rule. Our film and television screens are flooded with death and violence. They slop over with gore; they are inhabited by demented men who punch each other at the slightest provocation; the hand guns and machine guns and shotguns beat out an endless tattoo; and every now and then, a brain-damaged cretin like Rambo fills the screen with more corpses than a year's count in the city morgue.

This is neither art nor drama, and for normal people hardly entertaining. It is what is so well described as the pornography of violence, and at this point, it is a national sickness. Children watch four to eight hours of vicious looniness every day—a process that has to dull their sensibilities and plant in them a belief that violence is the answer to most of life's problems. Never before, not even in the days when gladiators fought each other in Rome's amphitheaters, has a population been subjected to such an endless parade of brutality and murder.

It has been argued that this has not turned us into a nation of murderers, but rather into a population of sodden lumps who spend their evening hours on their couches, munching popcorn and sucking at the tube; and while this is true, it is also true that we are dulled to a parade of violence that moves in our midst and has turned the streets of our cities into a battleground. I am not saying that life is without violence; every moment of humanity's endless struggle for liberty and decency has been marked by violence, but such violence reflects reality and does not titillate but speaks of the suffering and agony of people who hurt when they are struck, who feel pain, and whose death brings grief, not amusement.

I have lived and worked for years in Los Angeles, and I know the television and film community and I know a good many of the writers who work for the industry. The average wage of the members of the Writers Guild West is not much above $5,000 a year, and many of them write to survive, and a single writing job can keep bread and butter on the table. They would gladly end the violence and write things they dream of writing, but the networks and the film producers—with some notable exceptions—will not buy it. The exceptions to this, the producers who fight for reality and decency in their product, cannot be honored enough; but this does not change the fact that sitting one long evening in front of my television, I counted 42 deaths by violence.

One can only hope and pray that network television, as we now know it, will give way gradually to public television and pay-cable. Laws and good taste have set some limits to the pornography that uses women, and 8-year-olds cannot turn on a TV set and watch men and women having intercourse, but they can turn that switch and watch a man's guts spill out, a man's head blown open, a woman beaten to within an inch of her life—and this, the pornography of violence, is totally legal and protected by the First Amendment.

Of course, there is something we can do. As Ralph Nader constantly points out, the consumer is not without power. The bottom line is that we get what we deserve. We watch an imbecile cartoon character called "Rambo" gunning down every human being in sight, and then we are treated to the pleasure of hearing the President of the United States admire him. We watch "Dirty Harry" spreading death and destruction, and pressing a "bad guy" to make his day by inviting suicide at the muzzle of Dirty Harry's gun, and then we hear the President, who never quite got the difference between television and life, offering the same choice in the same words to a nation.

Well, there's a new man in the White House now, and he talks about a kinder and gentler America. It's time, but I've also heard that water can flow uphill, and who was that man who promised to balance the budget?

February 22, 1989

Guns and Democracy

I came home the other day, and there was D'emas packing his small straw suitcase. "I'm leaving," he said unhappily, "providing I get out of here alive. I have just been reading a poster distributed by Handgun Control Inc. It says that in 1983 handguns killed 35 people in Japan, eight in England, 27 in Switzerland, seven in Sweden, six in Canada, 10 in Australia and 9,014 in the United States. That's only handguns. When you include shotguns, assault weapons, rifles and machine guns, the total in one year is 10 times as large as the death figure in the American Revolution."

D'emas, mind you, is a rather simple-minded, gentle native of one of those far-off lands, where they don't even have television. I have been trying to explain civilization to him. Now I convinced him that he was not in imminent danger.

"But tell me," he said wistfully, "please tell me. I do want to understand. Here your ex-President was struck down by a bullet from an assassin's handgun, yet he defended handguns vigorously after he was shot. I simply can't understand that."

"No, D'emas," I said soothingly. "Of course you can't. That's because you're a primitive. You see, we Americans have the richest pool of talent and creativity in the world, but we're very democratic, and when it comes to electing a President, we find us some semiliterate chap who can barely read and write. Ronald Reagan spent his life as an actor. Directors would dress him up either as a cowboy or as an officer in the U.S. Cavalry. He always had a handgun strapped to his belt, and when he got this part as President, he couldn't just pretend that he had never been a cowboy or an officer in the cavalry—now could he?"

"No, I guess not," D'emas admitted. "But take President Bush. He wasn't an actor, was he?"

"Oh, no. But, you see, he is compassionate." Puzzled, D'emas shook his head unhappily. "Yes, I keep hearing him say how compassionate he is. Then he should be filled with compassion for the thousands of people who are murdered by handguns."

"Yes, of course, but you must consider that even more thousands of people who own handguns have not yet murdered anyone. Mr. Bush has to have compassion for them, and since there are so many of them, the compassion for them outweighs his compassion for the murdered. That's democracy."

"I'll never understand democracy," D'emas said. "Never. Here's that terrible thing out West where a whole class of small children were slaughtered by a lunatic with an assault gun, and just a few weeks ago another madman walked into his place of work and shot everyone in sight with his assault gun, and I read that the police everywhere plead for a law against assault weapons, and yet Mr. Bush refuses to forbid the sale and manufacture of those weapons."

"Yes. You see, when he ran for President, Mr. Bush was supported by the National Rifle Association. The National Rifle Association is against laws against any guns, assault rifles or otherwise. Mr. Bush has great compassion for the National Rifle Association, because he wants their support when he runs for President a second time."

That silenced D'emas for a while, and I talked him into unpacking his straw suitcase. Then he said, nodding, "I think I understand. The whole country must be members of the National Rifle Association."

"Oh, no," I said, not desiring to confuse the poor primitive any further. "Only a comparatively tiny minority belong to the National Rifle Association. In all my life, I never met anyone who belonged to the National Rifle Association."

"But I thought that in a democracy the majority rules."

"Oh, yes, absolutely. That is the basis of democracy, the rule of the majority. Of course, you must understand, D'emas, that it depends on what majority we are talking about. Certain matters are decided by the majority of the staff in the White House, and then there is the majority in the Senate, and then there is the majority of the money that can be spread around, and then there is the majority in the House of Representatives, and then there are the lobbyists who work up their own little majorities, and then there is a majority of the Supreme Court, and then there is the majority of the Joint Chiefs of Staff, and then—"

"Stop! Please! Enough!" D'emas pleaded. "My head is splitting. I listened to your President Bush addressing the whole nation on the subject of drugs and crime, and practically every police force in America pleads for laws against handguns and assault weapons, and Mr. Bush is filled with compassion for the owners of handguns and assault weapons, and a majority is not a majority—I must go home to my primitive little island, where even the chief of police is so uncivilized that he doesn't carry a handgun."

October 16, 1989

Assault Weapons and Illusory Hopes

It cannot be said that there are not, in both houses of Congress, men of character and intelligence; yet they are so few and so powerless that one must specify the Congress, as a whole, as a body that is cowardly, corrupt and poorly informed—and without a shred of compassion. Possibly, there is nowhere in the Western world a legislative body so immune to the needs of the people it pretends to govern and protect.

Nothing illustrates the above more vividly than the attitude of the Congress toward rapid-fire assault weapons. These hand-held weapons are in effect machine guns; in other words, when the trigger is pulled, the gun fires automatically at great speed, literally spraying the target with bullets. Some of these weapons, like the Uzi, can be fired by one hand, becoming machine pistols with no ability for proper aiming, but spraying death as a hose sprays water and thereby creating a pattern of random killing.

We in New York have been witness to this lately, sacrificing children—and not the first time in America—to the altar of the gun lovers. In January of 1989, a man, emotionally disturbed, in Stockton, California, armed with an AK–47 assault weapon, let loose a hundred shots into a crowded schoolyard. Five children were killed; a teacher and 19 other children were wounded, and all in a few seconds. During the past two years, a dozen other such incidents took place, including the slaughter of a group of women in Canada.

These weapons are war weapons. They have no place or purpose in civilian life except when used by trained men in a police force—and even the police plead not for the use of these weapons but for their interdiction. These assault weapons have no place in hunting, and hundreds of districts throughout the United States have forbidden their use by hunters. However, they have become *de rigueur* in the drug trade, and in New York as well as in every other large city in America, drug dealers own and use these weapons—as we in New York have learned to our horror.

Now a New Jersey Democrat in the House of Representatives, William J. Hughes by name, sponsored a bill to ban all assault weapons. So completely is a majority of the House, Democrat as well as Republican, against this measure, that the sponsors are unwilling to bring it to a vote, knowing in advance that it will be defeated—just as all efforts to limit or legally define the ownership of hand guns have been defeated. But while even sane people can marshal a few arguments against the banning of handguns, no one in his right mind can bring forward any argument that makes sense against the banning of assault weapons.

Yet a majority of the Congress of the United States will vote against such a measure.

What are we to make of this? Here is a legislative body, sworn to serve the people of this country, that will not forbid the easy sale and purchase and use of the most deadly infantry weapon in the armaments of nations. Europeans writing on this subject are totally confounded, but so is every American I have ever spoken to. Apart from Congress I know of no one outside of the drug world who favors the sale and use of these dreadful weapons.

Then, looking at the Congress from the point of view raised by The Automatic Weapons Bill, we must say, as so many ordinary citizens are saying, that the only solution to the future and the awesome problems it will bring is to rid ourselves of incumbents, to vote new people into Congress with the firm belief that no matter how bad they may be, they cannot equal the mental lapse of the clowns who are re-elected as regularly as a clock ticks. Of course, another measure that would help would be to extend the Representative term of office to six years, as in the Senate. That done, a Representative might turn his attention and his wits—considering he has any—to something other than being re-elected. But these hopes are as illusory as the hope that George Bush might awaken to the fact that a large country exists outside and apart from Kennebunkport in Maine.

November 5, 1990

A National Icon

The question arises: Can we take back New York City from the people with the guns—or Los Angeles, or Washington, or Chicago or Boston? Take it back; a new way to think. The American Rifle Association says that guns don't kill, people kill, and a hall of craven sellouts, otherwise known as "The House of Representatives," backs up the American Rifle Association with a refusal to legislate guns out of existence. A six-year-old is found with a gun. A 10-year-old kills his sister by accident with Pop's pistol. Two nine-year-olds play with a gun and one of them is dead, and on and on and on, and during the past 12 months, over a thousand of man and wife, father and son, mother and son blew one or another out of this world with handguns.

We rarely consider a problem in other than surface terms; we rarely dig down deep, because digging down uncovers layers of horror that we deposited, and we don't like to see this and be reminded of it. But the gun is more than a gun; it is an icon, a symbol of what we so mindlessly call "the American way of life." Consider that the average American family watches six hours of television a day, six hours hooked onto that box that Harlan Ellison so aptly calls the "glass teat," and consider that no six-hour period ever passes without being punctuated with endless gunfire and violence.

In the idiot world of network television, a producer is not allowed to show a knife stuck into a dog or a bullet fired into a dog without a battle with the network over content, and even after such a battle, he is not allowed to film a dog beaten into unconsciousness. But he is not only permitted but urged to show an unending procession of men, women, girls, boys, infants shot, whipped, beaten, dismembered—and most often the shooting is so casual, so indifferent to the life of the slain, that an impressionable viewer must come to the conclusion that the taking of human life is a small matter indeed.

The child watches the most of television, and the child is the most impressionable; and the child who is not living in a structured home where a morality and a concern for pain is taught and tendered, is almost totally impressionable. All television networks operate on a license granted by the Government, a given from the people of this country, and yet to all our pleas, public and otherwise, that they subdue the violence and exercise some human values, their reply is that violence sells and that the Nielsen ratings are more important than the public weal. Yet their license does not give them the right to make endless millions in a demented competition with each other; it only gives them the right to exercise a public service.

And what does all this have to do with the proliferation of guns and gunshots? The guns and the gunshooting are a part of the fabric of society, and the minds that regard handgun murder with horror are all too eager to support the national outpouring of literary and television violence and brutality. Violence and horror sell, and a writer named Bret Easton Ellis was well aware of this when he put together a compendium of horror and mental sickness that turned the hardened stomachs of the editors of *Spy* magazine. They reprinted a few paragraphs from his opus, and as a result enough people recoiled to make the CEO at Simon & Schuster decide not to publish the book, titled *American Psycho*. No matter; it was eagerly snapped up by Knopf, once known as a house that published writing of merit. And, of course, for a big fat price.

As the telephone commercials say, we are all connected—and with much more than telephone wires. With tragic obsession, we are turning the United States, once the most wonderful social experiment in the history of man, into a nightmare. We wage war after war without reason or sanity. We herd our poor into ghettos and feed them an endless diet of mayhem and madness on a glass teat called television, and we take the billions of dollars that would give these same ghettoized people jobs and homes and proper education and clean streets and police protection, and turn it over to the munition makers and to the troglodytes at the Pentagon, who play with their visions of death with our hard-earned dollars. We are rich indeed as a country, but no one is that rich, as witness the implacable disintegration of our local and national infrastructure.

So we return to the thousands and tens of thousands of handguns on the streets of New York and try to see them not as the youthful fecklessness of wild kids, but as the fruits of seeds we planted and which we go on planting. You can quite legally buy a handgun in New York, but you cannot buy cocaine in a New York shop, and it's worth pondering on which kills most. The sick minds who display on a bumper sticker the words "LET'S NUKE THEM" are not so different from the exalted minds in five-hundred-dollar suits and Washington addresses who have already turned so much of the Western states into atomic hot spots.

The killing on the streets will stop when we cease to make killing a national icon and when we begin to look for the truth behind the sound bites and the catchwords. If the war begins in Saudi Arabia, the American kids will not be dying for their country; they will be dying for the oil moguls and for Mr. Bush's vanity. If we can get that through our heads and make it plain, it's a beginning.

January 7, 1991

We Are Not Protected

Fai Yeung, age 21, was the only son of Ping Yeung, a Chinese immigrant who opened a small Chinese restaurant in Waterbury, Connecticut. Fai Yeung was a good son, and he worked hard to help his father, making takeout deliveries as well as other things. On August 10, Fai Yeung was making a takeout delivery when he was allegedly accosted by five local kids, 13 to 18 years in age. The kids seem to have been bored teenagers, spending a hot summer in a depressed town where there were few if any job opportunities. According to the police, they had decided that they would commit a robbery, boasted about it, even invited their girlfriends to witness the robbery.

One of the five kids, a 13-year-old, brought a gun that had belonged to his father, police said. The father had died of cancer, but the gun was in the house and the 13-year-old took it and allegedly handed it to Gerrod Ellis, 17. According to the police, the five boys followed Fai Yeung when he left his father's store with the delivery, waited until they had him in a quiet place, surrounded him and took the takeout order and a few dollars he had in his pocket. Then, said the police, Gerrod Ellis, using the gun lifted from the 13-year-old's house, shot Fai Yeung in the chest and killed him.

As a result of those events, the lives of a Chinese family were shattered; the hope that a Chinese family places in a son was destroyed, and five kids who might have grown to sensible adults were charged with murder. The families of these teenagers will continue to experience the anguish that comes out of such an incident.

I am sure that you find this story commonplace. It is commonplace because it happens over and over, day in and day out, and there is no way in the world to communicate adequately what parents feel when the central meaning of their lives is taken away so cruelly and senselessly.

Now, not too long ago, an overweight "hero," named Stormin' Norman by that ever-inventive Barbara Bush, speaking on the occasion of putting aside his medals for civilian clothes, told us that we, in America, were "well protected," which, in a land where political lies and political inventions are second to none, hits the highest ground of duplicity.

No, Norman, we are not well protected. We are not protected, period. Your parting statement is as outrageous as any of the endless homilies delivered by your Commander in Chief, George of the Golf Cart. Nowhere in the world do people live in such fear of assault and violence and death by fire as here in the United States. We have spent more money on our Army and Navy and Air Force during the past 50 years than has been spent by any other country in the past thousand years. We have taken the wealth of our country and spent it on military killing machines, and yet after dark the people who rule this land and make our laws are afraid to walk on one-third of the streets of our national capital—which is, incidentally, known as one of the 10 most dangerous cities on the planet.

No, we are not off track. This killing in Waterbury, Connecticut, and the destruction that flows from it are typical, not atypical, of the situation in America's cities. Death, violence and murder have become a way of life—and the vilest part of this lunacy is performed by the politicians, who throw up their hands in despair and say that they can do nothing about it.

If one-quarter of what is spent each year on this wasteful, pointless lunacy called the Pentagon were spent on ridding this country of guns, we would be rid of guns. When a spineless and corrupt Congress allows the gun lobby to turn every city in America into a killing ground, then we have lost all right to boast about American society.

And the saddest part of all is this illusion that we are being protected, that our armed forces make it safe for us to live in the United States. I know personally at least 20 families in New York City who will not leave their apartments after dark. We are afraid of the streets. We are afraid of addicts. We put four, five, seven bolts on our doors, and then reinforce them with steel rods. We are warned by the police of New York not to leave windows open at night. Is a little fresh air worth the chance of being robbed, raped, murdered? During the Gulf War, the number of many men, women and children murdered here at home was 10 times the number of soldiers of our armed forces killed by enemy fire. The field hospitals of the Army in Saudi Arabia were almost empty, while our trauma teams in New York hospitals worked through the night and the halls of the hospitals were filled with beds, for want of place to put the wounded.

And the mothers and the fathers of the city casualties weep into the television cameras and plead: "Why my child? Why did my child die? Why was my daughter raped? Why? Why?"

The answer is not complex. There is no real big money in making our cities decent and safe places to live. The big money is in doing business with the Pentagon. As the song says, "Money makes the world go round," and there's no one, not in Congress, not in the White House, not in the Judiciary, who gives a damn about anything else. If there were, they would begin the process of ridding America of the guns.

September 3, 1991

The Unfortunate Case of Mike Tyson

In the act of rape, there is neither love nor decency nor desire. It is a brutal act of malignant hatred, turning the most intimate thing of our species into its opposite. And having said all this, I still retain a shred of sympathy for Mike Tyson. Rape, a crime with which he is charged in Indiana, was neither in his blood nor in his genetic makeup; it was a learned act of horror, with our so-called civilization as his teacher.

Consider his profession—what we call, so stupidly, the manly art of self-defense, and which is neither manly nor defensive. In our society murder is punishable by either imprisonment or death, but when a fighter dies in the ring—as many do—or later as a result of his injuries, it is not considered murder but a necessary part of the "sport." And this in spite of the fact of a legal ruling that a fighter's fists are lethal weapons. Yet when a fighter steps into the ring, his aim is to destroy his opponent, either by beating him to a point where he can no longer fight, or beating him while he can still fight back, or knocking him out, that chef-d'oeuvre of the game, as it is called.

And what of Mike Tyson? From the age of 14, he is fed, trained and taught to be both a brute and a killer. (Not to kill? Come on, what else do they pay $100 a ticket for?) His whole life is to hit and be hit, to step into a roped square with another man and to damage him as much as humanly possible. Love, gentleness, compassion—the sense most of us have, that to strike another human being is degrading, and that for a man to strike a woman is most degrading, this sense and conditioning are denied him. Then is it any wonder that he should feel hurt and indignant at the accusation of rape? He is accused of being what we trained him to be, and what we trained him to be is exalted the country over, the champ who makes headlines in every newspaper in the land and who is "illuminated" on the screen by none other than that anointed apostle of brutality, Sylvester Stallone.

But then we have taken both of them to our hearts and set them up as symbols of *civilization-USA-current.* They are what we are, at least what we are somewhere inside of us, and they serve to define the naked fact of our existence.

The fact that we have set up the most complex system for the judgment and punishment of lawbreakers that the world has ever known, and the fact that we spend millions of dollars for the trial and punishment of some besotted brute who has committed unspeakable murders and then sentence him to death—and then organize committees and pleas and marches and prayer meetings to void this death sentence—serves to give us a mantle of compassion as phony as any of the thousand pious lies we delude ourselves with.

Certainly, decent people have agitated for years against boxing, but, as with everything else, there are intrenched interests, and while we have managed to make dogfights illegal and cockfights illegal and bullfights illegal, we draw the line at boxing—and the whole sham is without a shred of validity. In the tradition of American filmmaking, you can show men and women being decapitated, gutted, torn to pieces, but if you show a dog killed—well, then you're in trouble. There appears to be in our society a total indifference to the act of murder, providing that the act of murder takes place within the framework of what we call permissible murder. When President Bush sent his warriors into Panama to get Manual Noriega and in the process caused the deaths of somewhere between 3,000 and 4,000 civilians, the murders were permissible—and therefore no indictments, no trials, no punishments. We wept over the dogs and the scam perpetrated in the dog cemetery, and day after day the media spilled their crocodile tears over the misburied pets; but the dead in Panama? Sweet forgetfulness.

You know, I really don't give a tinker's damn about what happens in a dog and cat cemetery. I love dogs and cats, but I love them when they're alive, and I had thought that funerary veneration of animals had gone out of the picture with the ancient Egyptians. We exercise neither balance nor real compassion in our tears, and we have taught ourselves so many lies and legends that no handle on the truth remains. We have lost all sense of shame, and our so-called religion is an embarrassment.

And then, we beat up on Mike Tyson because he is accused of raping a woman. We made him, shaped him, taught him and exercised him.

An old saying of mine, but let me tell it once again:

Davy Crockett sees this man aiming up at a tree. "What're you aiming at?" Davy asks. "Baar," the man says. "Baar?" says Davy. "Hell, ain't no baar in that tree. You're aiming at a louse on your own eyelash."

October 14, 1991

Chapter 5

Anti-Semitism and Racism

The Sickness of Anti-Semitism

The bitter and sometimes vituperative discussion that has arisen out of the placement of a Carmelite convent on the edge of the Auschwitz death camp cuts to the root of truth in history. The Jewish position is that this awful place, properly called Auschwitz–Birkenau, an institution designed and built as a state-of-the-art murder machine, should be left alone, a monument to, and a reminder of, man's inhumanity to man. This was an institution created to kill Jews, and in this institution three million Jews were put to death, man, woman and child. This is not to be confused with the adjoining Auschwitz, where many others of various nationalities were put to death.

By and large, the Jewish point of view is that Hitler's decision to make Europe *Judenrein* (free of Jews) was the final, cumulative result of almost 2,000 years of anti-Semitism. It is also a fact of history, indisputable, that anti-Semitism has been fostered, preserved, nurtured and maintained through the centuries by Christians, and while nurtured by all branches of Christianity, the central and most powerful and consistent purveyor, until very recently, has been the Catholic Church. This is an unavoidable fact of history, painful to thousands of compassionate Christians, but so plainly a fact that no one can deny it.

Thus, when the Carmelite nuns, a Christian institution, decided to make a place of residence alongside of Auschwitz, with the explanation that they were there to pray for the souls of the murdered Jews, Jews received the macabre horror of this enormous non sequitur either in hopeless silence or with understandable anger. In *The New York Times* of September 13 we were shown a very large cross silhouetted against the wall of the Auschwitz death camp, with a caption informing us that the cross stands on the grounds of the Carmelite convent.

What is a Jew to make of this huge cross standing at Auschwitz? For 2,000 years, it has been the symbol of the anti-Semites, and isn't it understandable that a Jew should see it as a statement of triumph, a declaration of the final solution?

I know that sensitive Christians will recoil in disgust at the very suggestion; but think about it. The notion is loathsome, and the fact that it may be true does not make it less loathsome. In Poland, in that same country in which Auschwitz stands, not so long ago there were almost six million Jews. They gave to Poland zest and laughter and literature and art and music, and their houses of worship, which dotted the land, lent elegance and style to Polish architecture. Now they are gone. A handful of Jews remain in Poland, a few thousand at most, yet the Polish Cardinal Glemp spits out the same vitriolic hatred of Jews that has been the sum and substance of anti-Semitism since the disease began.

The Cardinal is annoyed by what he calls "Jewish interference." What business is it of theirs what goes on in Auschwitz? The good nuns are praying for their dead. Why can't they accept the prayers and be quiet?

I would like not to be angry. I would like as a Jew to accept the whole thing with equanimity. It would be so very comfortable and pleasant to be indifferent to the fact that one lives in a Christian world where a stupid and insensitive churchman can insult the dead and degrade the living. But I am not that comfortable nor have I any hope at this late date ever to be that comfortable. I think that what is happening now in Auschwitz is a part of what happened there half a century ago, a continuation of one of the most unspeakable and vicious attitudes of so-called Western Civilization, and I think that it calls for apologies from the Holy See and down from there.

And one thing more. Through my life I have known and worked with Christian church people who were among the best and bravest and most selfless men and women I have ever known. I have written about them and paid homage to their courage and their work among the poor and the suffering. I have worked with the Catholic movement for Central Americans' freedom and known the warmth of being with them, and I consider the role of the church in Central America and South America to be a testimony to man.

I cannot entirely agree with Mark Twain, who said that Christianity is a splendid religion that has never been tried. I have known those who tried and succeeded, and the world is better for them. But they remain a handful in a world that still fosters the ancient and awful sickness of anti-Semitism.

October 2, 1989

The Merchant of Venice

I have seen, over my lifetime, four presentations of *The Merchant of Venice*. I saw the role of Shylock played by Joseph Schildkraut, who vowed that he would present Shylock as a sympathetic character. He failed to do so, just as every other actor who attempted to play the role sympathetically failed. It simply cannot be done. *The Merchant of Venice* remains a passionate exercise in anti-Semitism, as vicious a document of the kind as exists.

And why? Why did the noblest of all English writers pen this vicious document, when it has been pretty well established that William Shakespeare could hardly have seen or ever spoken to a Jew?

Let me try to shed some light on that aspect of it. Roderigo Lopez, a Portuguese Jewish physician, settled in London in about 1550. A man of knowledge and great charm, he soon became a member of the College of Physicians and was the first House Physician at St. Bartholomew's Hospital. Lopez had close relations with important people at the Spanish court. At that time, England was on the edge of war with Spain. Lopez, physician to Queen Elizabeth of England, was paid a large sum by the Spaniards to try to persuade Elizabeth to turn a friendly face to Spain. The British party that was anti-Spain and pro-war discovered this and concocted a charge, backed by false witness, that Lopez was plotting to poison the Queen. Although Lopez had been baptized, he was arrested, denounced as a Jewish devil and executed on June 7, 1594.

Londoners were deliberately worked up to an anti-Jewish, anti-Spanish fury by the story of this plot to poison their beloved queen, and Shakespeare, ever responsive to the political currents of his time, took an old Italian demonology tale and used it as a basis for *The Merchant of Venice*.

I think we have come to a point in history where almost every intelligent and educated member of the human race understands that anti-Semitism is basically a political tool, manufactured and used for many different purposes, most of them vile. The Italian demonology stories of the 13th, 14th and 15th centuries were created in some measure to aid Italian bankers and ship owners in their war against Jewish bankers and ship owners, virtually wiping them out of existence and leaving the field clear for usury to the extent of 100 percent a year. Another part of these demonology tales originated in the Catholic Church in its drive against the Jews, whom they always regarded as a barrier to total conversion and therefore a constant threat to Christianity.

But I have no desire here to attempt any history of anti-Semitism. I simply want to make my views about *The Merchant of Venice* clear, and to say that I see no reason for its presentation to any civilized society. It is defended as a work of high art in terms of and with constant reference to the glorious speech on the quality of mercy, but one such speech does not confirm a masterpiece. It must be looked at as a whole, and as a whole it is clever and vicious anti-Semitism. I am not saying it should be suppressed. When Sigourney Weaver chose to do it Off Broadway a couple of years ago, I asked her husband why. Why this play of all plays?

"She wants to be Portia," he told me.

As for Dustin Hoffman, I cannot guess why he lends himself to this or what "Jewish" guilts drive him. He can give no greatness to Shylock. Coming from a people known through the ages for their gentle acceptance of all fate, from their exile to the Holocaust, Shylock is a lie, a vicious lie and a burden Jews have borne for centuries. Mr. Hoffman's choice of Shylock out of the great panoply of Shakespeare enlightens no one and can only do harm to Jews—who, God knows, carry enough of a burden already.

About 25 years ago, a Hollywood producer sent me a copy of Gogol's novel *Taras Bulba* with the suggestion that I read it and perhaps think about doing a screenplay for a film based on the book. I read it for the first time and discovered it to be as viciously anti-Semitic as any novel I ever read—indeed, perhaps more so. While I refused the job, the film was made with anti-Semitism expunged. I then brought up the subject with a Russian diplomat, asking him whether the book was still printed and sold in the Soviet Union.

"Of course," he replied. "Gogol is one of our great classic writers."

"But the book is naked anti-Semitism. I have been given to understand that the promulgation of anti-Semitism in the Soviet Union is a crime."

He shrugged and smiled. "You would not expect us to suppress Gogol?"

Nor to suppress anti-Semitism, as the world discovered.

March 5, 1990

Two Stories in Black and White

Every so often, some professorial type eager for publicity announces that he has been working with intelligence tests and has concluded that blacks are less intelligent than whites. Without remarking on said professor's intelligence, I might mention that the validity of "intelligence" testing as a mark of what we like to think of as intelligence has been put in doubt so often that it's pointless for me to belabor the case. However, there is one incident in testing that I find fascinating.

This was many years ago, and the Binet-Simon method of testing was then in use. A teacher friend of mine brought me two tests to look at, both a part of a class of age-twelve public school students in New York. In this test there was a printed circle representing a field and an opening representing a gate. The test asked the student to describe with his pencil how he would go about looking for a baseball lost in this field. One test was taken by a white boy, the other by a black boy.

The white boy, middle-class, test-wise, from a home where there was an endless list of specifics, knew what was expected: He carefully drew in a crisscross, a gridiron covering every inch of the field. The black boy, out of a much poorer background with limited specifics but with the driving force of survival calling upon inventiveness and originality, drew a haphazard, wandering pencil line that drifted senselessly—apparently—here and there around the field.

By the rules of grading, the response of the black boy would have designated him as of subnormal intelligence, but my friend, the teacher, knew that the black boy was unusually bright and inventive, and his reaction to the question caused the teacher to question both boys about their response.

The white boy admitted that he knew what was expected. He was expected to create a pattern in the circle that would leave no part of it unexplored. As for the baseball, he never gave it a second thought.

The black boy reacted quite differently. He dealt not with tests or lines, but with reality. He was imaginative; he had to be to survive. So he thought back to the last time he had lost a baseball in a grassy field and he remembered how he had looked for it—as anyone looks for a lost ball in reality—wandering here and there, kicking the grass, hoping that eventually he'd come to the ball. Thus, when he answered the question, he simply re-created the situation in his mind, abstracted it, studied the memory and then drew in as honest a re-creation of looking for a ball as he could.

Who was more intelligent? What is intelligence?

A wise old black man, professor and philosopher, W.E.B. DuBois by name, talking about the complexity of racism, told me the following story:

In the old days, before the civil rights movement, a salesman came to a small Southern town. There were two hotels. The salesman, who was white, went to the white hotel, but every room was taken. Tired and desperate for sleep, he then went to the black hotel, where the room clerk informed him that while they had a room, the clerk didn't dare rent it to a white man. As much as the salesman pleaded his exhaustion, the room clerk stood firm. This was a racist town. He could take no chances.

Finally, in desperation, the salesman asked whether the clerk had a can of shoe polish. The clerk grinned and handed him a can of black shoe polish, and the white man took it into the lavatory and blacked his face. Then he returned to the desk, and the clerk, smiling appreciatively, said, "Yes, sir. Now I can give you a room."

The white man thanked the clerk and asked to be given a wake-up call at seven in the morning, so that he might catch the early train. The clerk was as good as his word, and at seven o'clock the following morning, the salesman's phone awakened him. But he had slept soundly and he awoke lazily, and as a result when he reached the railroad station the train was already beginning to move.

Carrying his sample case, the salesman raced for the train, managed to swing up onto the last car, only to face the grim glare of the conductor, who pointed to his face and said, "This is a white car, mister—only whites."

Dumbfounded at first, the salesman then remembered the evening before, grinned and said, "Give me a moment in the bathroom and we'll solve that." And he pushed past the conductor and into the lavatory, where he soaped up his face and rubbed it briskly. But when he washed off the soap, he saw that nothing had changed, that he was still black. Wildly, he soaped and scrubbed—and remained black.

And then he realized that the room clerk had awakened the wrong man.

Having told me this story, the old philosopher smiled, and when I asked him what it all meant, he said gently, "The meaning, Howard, is for you, not for me."

May 14, 1990

The Fire That Does Not Dim

On Chapultepec Heights in Mexico City, there is a small museum—or was when we last saw it, 40 years ago—that celebrates the gallant defense of Mexico against the invading Americans. One wall was given over to a map of North America, and on this map, firmly drawn, the national boundary of Mexico included Texas, New Mexico, Arizona and California. These are lands which we took from Mexico by military conquest, legalizing our larceny by having them taken over by armies of freebooters, Anglo Saxon freebooters, and then turning them into fictitious republics that joined the United States.

Mexico never accepted this, howsoever the maps and treaties were drawn. It was only 150 years ago, not very long on the tracks of history. There were other choice pieces of real estate that we acquired one way or another, as for example Alaska, the state of Washington, Puerto Rico, etc. Some of our territories were acquired by the simple process of genocide, murdering the native population, as in New England, or through war with the Indians, the mighty force of the United States against handfuls of poorly armed tribesmen. Some territory was acquired by expelling the native population and other land was gained by forcing its occupants into large concentration camps, which we called, euphemistically, reservations.

We were not alone in this: The British in Australia learned well from us; the Germans destroyed 50 million people to take over land they wanted; the Japanese were hot for the game, but johnny-come-latelies with the odds against them, and so forth and so on, and all was fair in real estate and war.

Until the Jews came along and organized the State of Israel. (Let me make my own position clear. I believe that the Palestinians should have the West Bank. I have no argument on that score.) But let us also remember that the Palestinians and the Jordanians are the same people with the same language. The King of Jordan nonetheless drove the West Bank people—and a good many of the East Bank Palestinians as well—out of his country into Lebanon, mercilessly, making a killing of Palestinians that the media for the most part simply ignored. Arabs killing Arabs—why bother?

And now Jimmy Carter, enthroned on the only achievement of his dismal four years, the brokering of the agreement between Israel and Egypt, is making a new career out of the New Fashion of Jew-baiting and the condemnation of Israel for resisting the intifada and not giving back the West Bank immediately.

Whatever one may say about Israel, it is the only constitutional democracy in the Middle East. It sits alongside of Jordan, which slaughtered the Palestinians without mercy; and Syria, where President Hafez al-Assad murdered 35,000 of his countrymen in cold blood; and Iraq, which conducted a genocidal slaughter—by nerve gas and other means—of thousands of Kurds. But for these demented murderers, Mr. Carter has no strong words. It is only Israel that he actually attacks, equating it with the countries around it.

Now I have as little regard for Jimmy Carter as I have for Yitzhak Shamir. It was the sour taste left by Mr. Carter that gave us Ronald Reagan, and Mr. Carter's cowboy expedition into Iran was as crazy an act as any President ever pulled off and could have drawn us into a major war. But for Mr. Carter to indict Israel without even a reference or a memory of his own country's practice when it came to taking over the land of others, speaks very poorly for his integrity and his education.

When this country became as one mind and developed one purpose, namely the destruction of Adolf Hitler and all he stood for, the young Jews of my generation poured into the armed forces, convinced that anti-Semitism would be slain along with the Nazis.

But anti-Semitism had deeper roots. Not only had the Jews given the West Christianity and the East Islam, but Jewish doctors conquered some of the worst diseases of mankind, Jews created the science of the mind, and Jewish scientists opened the universe and began the process of solving its mysteries. Yet for all of that, hardly a tear was dropped by the Christian world for the horrors of the Holocaust.

If Mr. Carter and his associates in the Israel-bashing business would only examine the direction of their thinking, they might understand that this new process is no different than the old manner of anti-Semitism, elevated now to the national scene.

It spreads like a fire in the sagebrush. Bishop Desmond Tutu, coming from a land where the Government murdered untold thousands of his people, has criticism only for Israel. Pope Paul, coming from the most viciously anti-Semitic land on earth, has no words of condemnation for the murder-orgies of the Arabs, only for the Jews. Senator Robert Dole, who has never uttered a word against the millions we give to the murder squads of El Salvador, speaks out against the funds we provide Israel. In Europe, in countries bereft of Jews, the same crazy shouts of anti-Semitism are heard, and in Russia, that country that once preached the socialist brotherhood of man, the anti-Semites pledge death to all Jews.

A wise man once said, long ago, that the degree of civilization of any Western country could be judged by its attitude toward the Jews. Something to think about.

May 21, 1990

Defenders of Law and Order

On September 21, a woman named Judith Regan, a senior editor at Simon & Schuster, hailed a cab in midtown. Moments later, three cops pulled over the cab for some minor infraction. She says the cops began to hassle the cab driver. Ms. Regan, with the sensitivity that any decent person would show, reportedly asked the cops whether they didn't have something better to do than to put down her driver. Whereupon, she claims, the brave defenders of law and order yanked her out of the cab, handcuffed her and, according to *The New York Times*, "subjected her to a torrent of threats, lewd insults and anti-Semitic slurs." Ms. Regan is half Irish, half Sicilian, but she says one of the cops cried out delicately, "This bitch lives on Central Park West." She said she believed "the mostly young, Irish cops" figured she was Jewish.

Ms. Regan said she was then taken to the midtown precinct, locked up, held incommunicado for five hours and subjected to "sadomasochistic games."

(A week before the above incident, quoting *The New York Times*, " . . . a 23-year-old college student was held for nearly two days on charges of assault and riot after he asked officers to go easy on a New Jersey woman who began sobbing when she discovered that her illegally parked car was about to be towed.")

Odd coincidence? Off-chance happening? Not by a long shot! Through my years of living in New York City, I've seen this again and again and again, from a cop berating my 10-year-old daughter for riding a bike on the Central Park grass to cops going berserk at a peaceful demonstration and beating bystanders with their nightsticks. And if they did what is described above to a middle-class white woman simply because they had decided that she was Jewish, can you imagine what a black woman would have suffered in a similar situation?

Now I am not going to suggest that this even begins to equate with what happened to the jogger in Central Park, and no suggestion of sexual molestation on the part of the cops is involved. It was, after all, a busy midtown street, and sexual molestation would have played hell with their pensions. At the same time, what allegedly happened on September 21 must be faced.

Here was a woman alone, sick as it happens, unable to defend herself, guilty of no crime, not even the merest misdemeanor, who claims she was suddenly attacked by policemen. If true, there is no other word for it. She was allegedly attacked in a manner that was so disgraceful, so uncalled-for that the very telling of it commands disbelief.

Now it occurs to me that what Ms. Regan says happened to her must happen day in and day out on the streets of the New York City ghettos. White people puzzle over the antipathy that the blacks hold for the police, and thereby we do a mind-set that wipes out their endless protests as a sort of racism in reverse; but we should be able to understand that since the black neighborhoods are the scene of most of the city's crime, it should be expected that the blacks would hold the police in reverence, regardless of the color of said police. The fact that they almost universally regard the police as their enemies is, I believe, the most telling indictment of the police that could be put forward; and may I add that this hatred that exists between the people of the ghettos and the police can only feed crime and, in the end, increase it.

If Lee Brown, the city's new police commissioner [he has since left office], is serious about law and order on the streets of New York, then he'd better pay deep and serious attention to the two incidents described here. They are by no means the most dramatic of police forays in a city that increasingly resembles a battleground, and they don't make headlines as vibrant as a Dodge City shootout, but believe me, they go deeper into the heart of the city's pain than drug busts. Better than most people, Mr. Brown should realize that this is a city of ethnic groups, the source of its endless vitality and excitement and achievement, and that while most of the nations of the world are represented in this wonder-polis, the two major groups are the blacks and the Jews. For better or worse—and for better indeed in my book—these are the two strong anchors of the city, and they give it so much of its verve and character. The cops should know this, and if they still do not know it, then it should be hammered home to them.

As for the case of Judith Regan, it should be taken as seriously as the case of the jogger in Central Park; and if the cops did what Ms. Regan claims, they should not come off with a grinning slap on the wrist. If they do, then our trust in the police will sink even lower.

October 8, 1990

It Is Indeed an Interesting Thing

Some 30 years ago, my wife and I had dinner with two of the most remarkable men I have ever met. It was at the home of Hy Brown, the art collector, and we sat entranced, listening to the tales of these two men, who for the previous 20 years had been in the business of buying Jews. Oh, yes—you read correctly, buying Jews. The two men worked in Europe for a group of Americans who were able to save hundreds of Jews from the Holocaust, the mass graves and the crematoria by purchasing their lives from the corrupt officials who oversaw the death trains and the death camps. Most of their dealings were in Hungary and Romania. They were able to make a few purchases from Germany, but it was very difficult to set up with the war in progress. They had a deal set up with Nazi officials to trade 4,000 trucks for 4,000 Jewish lives, and, though the Allied Command felt the trucks would not be of significant military help to the Nazis, Churchill rejected it.

When the war ended, the business of buying Jews continued to flourish—particularly in Romania. Of all the Communist parties in Europe, the Romanian Communist Party was certainly the most corrupt and opportunistic, and the party leaders in Romania closed their doors to the Jews who had survived the war and let it be known that they were ready to do business. The two men we dined with that night made the deal, signed the contracts and paid the money—a significant footnote for those future historians who review the so-called civilization of the 20th century. But while those exchanges have been noted and written about elsewhere, so far as I know, the following detail has not appeared in print.

The exchange of Jews sold into freedom took place at a bridge across the Danube. The two men I met were at one end of the bridge, the Romanian exit station at the other end. As the Jews began to cross the bridge, my dinner companions noticed a very odd thing. The purchased and liberated Jews were dressed as no other people on earth were dressed. The men: Their coats fell in half-inch ribbons from their collars; sleeves in ribbons, jackets in similar ribbons, trousers in ribbons half an inch wide, shirt in ribbons. The women: Their coats, as with the men, were in long ribbons, their dresses in ribbons, their hats sliced into strands, their shawls in ribbons.

At first, the men who had bought their freedom were horrified, puzzled and amazed, but the explanation was quite simple. The Romanians, to make certain that no departing Jew should take with him a coin or paper money that could be sewn into clothing, made each Jew, man, woman and child, disrobe completely so that men with razors could slice their garments into ribbons.

It is indeed an interesting thing to be Jewish.

There is a very small country called Israel, where the Jewish people have made a nation. After 2,000 years of being slaughtered, degraded and demeaned by a world that calls itself civilized, the Jews took up arms and said: "Enough. We have been murdered enough."

This was after the Holocaust, after one of every three Jews on earth had been murdered by the Nazis and their allies. And for this bit of land called Israel, the Jews paid a terrible price. And now, countries that have been at war with the Jews for more than 40 years are willing to talk peace—if the Jews give up half their land.

One of these countries is Syria, a dictatorship ruled by a man called Hafez al-Assad. Morally, this gent makes Saddam Hussein look like a nice guy. There was an Islamic uprising in a town in Syria called Hama. Mr. Assad dealt with that uprising by putting the entire population of Hama, some 20,000 people, to death. He then added a new wrinkle to genocide by paving over thousands of graves. This same worthy has provided haven for the worst of the terrorists, has been the force behind the taking of hostages and now occupies Lebanon with an army of 40,000. He is also our new ally, bedfellow and helpmate in the Middle East.

The second gentle neighbor of Israel that will talk peace if Israel gives up part of its land is Jordan, a bastion of civilization that dealt with its own Palestinian *intifadeh* by murdering more than 2,500 Palestinians in little more than a week.

And the third party willing to talk peace in exchange for Israeli land is Saudi Arabia, an enormous country a hundred times as large as

Israel, ruled by barbaric families of desert chieftains who will permit no church to be built in their vast territory, who rule by fiat, amputate the hands of thieves and put women who have committed adultery to death.

And behind those three countries are the great and powerful nations of the "civilized" West, telling the Jews to chop up their tiny land and give it to their good neighbors.

It is indeed an interesting thing to be Jewish.

August 19–28, 1991

The Willie Horton Syndrome

Let's try this one for size: Marijuana is a fairly mild drug, and its effect in most cases is a mellow state, the very opposite of violence. Doubtless many of you have smoked a little pot in the past, and you will recall being high and agree that it rarely incited to violence. Add to this the fact that marijuana can be grown in any backyard, any empty lot, any patch of ground, and that it is not addictive in the sense that cocaine and heroin are addictive.

Then, in the light of the above, how is it that the Federal Government has managed so well to inhibit and indeed destroy most of that native production of marijuana, interdicting its import successfully, while allowing an ever increasing river of cocaine to flood the United States?

One can argue that the Government's anti-drug program is inefficient. One can also argue that inefficiency in a Government program is more often than not the result of indifference. And one might even say, recalling the role of the CIA in the past, that the drug-running itself may, at time, be a tool of high-level policy.

Let's shift gears for a moment and move to one of the wealthiest and best-policed suburbs of New York. Its local symphony orchestra was giving a concert at the high school. A woman, alone in her car, drove up to the school parking lot. As she stopped, the car door opposite opened and a black man with a knife tried to climb in. She pushed him away and accelerated. He fell out of the car and she got away with only a cut finger. In this suburb, as in every other suburb around New York, there is a solid Democratic Party core, middle-class people who pride themselves on being liberals. Those with whom I have spoken translate this incident into a fear of blacks—a fear that has become so pervasive that it overcomes all their reservoir of rational understanding.

Such middle-class people—and I believe there are millions of them—often have no relationship to the vast numbers of blacks who work for a living, who act in every profession from college presidents to physicians to carpenters. There is no social intercourse between black and white; most of the suburbs—peopled by urban flight and fear—are white. They read about, and see on their television screens, a world where crime by poor blacks goes on without end, where a drug culture has made death by violence the largest cause of death in the ghetto, and where prisons are built to house a criminal population that is 90 percent black.

Is it any wonder then that many of these people should regard every black man with fear and suspicion, and that the association of blacks and crime should become a fact of their thinking?

The media, the same media that parade this endless show of black violence, deny this. They talk about Magic Johnson and other successful and distinguished black men and women, but no amount of such talk can hide the other side of the coin, as Mr. Bush proved so well when he based his Presidential campaign upon a black man named Willie Horton.

Let's come back to marijuana and cocaine.

Marijuana has been more or less eliminated, yet cocaine flows like a river. Cocaine means violence. Cocaine is destroying the black population of America.

And how does one end it? Well, first of all, one must want to end it. One must ask who benefits from this methodical destruction of a whole population. The alliance between the black population of the United States and the Democratic Party is traditional, and traditionally the Democratic Party has held out a hand to black Americans. The grim political fact of the matter is that the Republican Party has made much use of an accusation that exploits this tradition. It goes like this: Vote Democrat, and you vote for the party that supports a weak position on crime. Vote Republican, and you vote against the poor black and the black criminal. The poor black has destroyed our cities. He is a dope addict and a criminal. Vote Democrat and you foster him. Vote Republican and you will hold him in check.

Call it the Willie Horton syndrome.

And to sustain this way of being and thinking, one needs an unending flow of cocaine into the United States. *Ah*, you say. *You* tell us how to stop it.

That's not impossible. Let the Army do something constructive—let them cover every inch of our border. Let the Navy stop playing games in other oceans and patrol our coasts until a fish cannot get through. Let the Air Force interdict every unlicensed plane in the American skies—and in six months we would stop the flow of cocaine. And more: We must pass a national gun law. Disarm the dealers, imprison them. End this sick gun-worship that pervades our nation.

At the same time, we should make jobs for every unemployed black or white in the inner cities. Put them to work. Rebuild the rotting infrastructure. The work is there. Do it.

There's nothing new or even inventive about these ideas. They could be realized tomorrow. We have the energy, the money, the way, everything but the will. We can do anything we desire—if we have the desire. But so long as the Willie Horton syndrome pervades the thinking of our political leaders, nothing will be done. We will remain victims of the unending, clawing struggle for power between two corrupt and impotent political parties.

November 25, 1991

The David Duke Syndrome

[David Duke, a neo-Nazi and KKK sympathizer, was the Republican candidate for Governor of Louisiana in 1991.]

It seems rather euphemistic to speak of the David Duke affair and his defeat as interesting, yet in a historical sense that is perhaps the best word to describe it. We are weak on history here in this country, and that is a condition that most often leads to confusion—and not infrequently to tragedy. It is not that history repeats itself, but that threads and roots run very deep in history, and to know and understand these threads and roots is to be able to deal with them.

The necessity to eat is most basic to the human condition; without food we simply die. Whenever the economic system breaks down in a complex society, explosive forces are let loose, as they were in two extreme examples: the Nazi movement in Germany and the fascist movement in Italy. Here in the United States, at the time of the Great Depression, a whole tribe of David Dukes arose and a swarm of fascist hate movements took the field. In 1938, in New Jersey, a man called Pelley organized amateur storm troopers, dressed them in silver-colored shirts and announced himself as a native Adolf Hitler. Much more numerous, the German-American Bund put 20,000 German-born and native-born Americans into Nazi uniforms. On June 5, 1937, they built a huge bandstand in Yaphank, Long Island, in imitation of the monster bandstands that served as background for Hitler's speeches, hanging enormous Nazi flags and banners all over the place and telling a screaming, hysterical, hate-filled crowd that the day of reckoning for "Jews and Niggers" was here.

Another type of precursor to Mr. Duke was the "radio priest" who took to the air in 1936, and sent shivers of fear through every decent American. His name was Charles E. Coughlin. He seized upon the radio the way current politicians seize upon television and, like columnist Patrick Buchanan, he used innuendo to cover a full battery of hatred and anti-Semitism. Father Coughlin was only one of a whole tribe of radio hatemongers, and while they addressed the unemployed, the hungry and the hopeless, on the other side of the coin were those who addressed the part of America that still possessed money and power.

The most flagrant incident among the latter occurred in 1939. Marian Anderson, the black singer, whose golden voice was describe by conductor Arturo Toscanini as "a miracle that happens once in a hundred years," was denied the right to sing in Constitution Hall in Washington, D.C., by the Daughters of the American Revolution. Eleanor Roosevelt thereupon resigned her membership in the DAR and arranged for Miss Anderson to sing for thousands at the Lincoln Memorial.

I have only touched on the David Duke syndrome during the Depression years. The important thing to remember is that each and every one of these movements is self-serving, putting not even a crust of bread on the table of anyone except the handful who manipulate the show. Thousands of good Americans worked with all their energy to put Franklin Delano Roosevelt in the White House to provide jobs for the unemployed, to build the tiny labor movement into a mass work force, to rebuild the infrastructure of our nation, to feed the hungry and care for the sick, to create for the first and only time a people's theater here in America, a people's art and a people's literature out of the Works Progress Administration—while all this went on, the David Dukes of the time sowed only hate and anger.

We are an amazingly complex society, perhaps the most complex social structure on the face of the earth. I am constantly astonished at the outsiders who come here, stay a few weeks or months, and then explain us to the rest of the world. I have spent a lifetime trying to understand and comprehend America, and still I only scratch the surface. But that bit of surface scratching has taught me a great deal.

We are a combination of what is best and what is worst in the human condition. We have brought together ethnic groupings of every nation on earth. We have provided a living standard for most of our population higher than any other, and we have led the world in concepts of democracy.

On the other hand, we evolved a theory of Manifest Destiny that led to a bloody rape of a continent and the mass extermination of the native people. We enslaved millions of Africans so that a handful of planters could live in luxury beyond measure, and we are thoroughly tinged with racism.

The story is complex beyond measure. At a terrible cost, we freed the blacks we had enslaved. We aided and abetted the rise of fascism, and—again at a terrible cost—we helped to destroy Hitler and the Nazis. We embark on brainless, idiotic military ventures such as the invasion of Panama and the Gulf War, and then the whole nation joins to pray for the life of a single sick child. We are confused and perverse and wonderful and terrible, and our long historic journey to the brotherhood of man is as agonizing as one poor Jew's journey to Golgotha. But be it said and underlined that never in all our history have we gone the way of David Duke! Behind the easy smile of this good-looking young man is the unspeakable horror that cost mankind 50 million deaths in World War II. Make no mistake about that. Once born or twice born, David Duke is a fascist—a petty little fascist now, but a fascist nevertheless. Like all his predecessors, he knows only one path, the path to hell.

December 9, 1991

David Duke, Populist?

Speaking of David Duke and what he stands for, a writer in *New York* magazine described him as being part of "a grand, nauseating populist tradition that goes back to Georgia's Tom Watson and a slew of others who could always convince the rubes that if it weren't for the jewboys and niggers, they'd be living on easy street."

Not a very pleasant description, and certainly one that has no connection with reality. The writer is into catchword thinking, cute constructions that are as vapid as they are meaningless.

In other words, the man who wrote the above-quoted paragraph has not the vaguest notion of what populism is or how it came into our history and what place it fills in history.

In that, he is not alone. Words catch on; they become fashionable and soon everyone who is too lazy to find out what a word means is throwing it in the hopper. We read that Boris Yeltsin is a populist, that Jerry Brown of California is a populist, the Governor Cuomo has populist tendencies—yes, and David Duke is not a fascist but a populist.

Well, let's see what populism means and how it became a part of the American tradition. A year before the election of 1892, there was a widespread—and not unfamiliar to us today—feeling in the United States that neither the Democratic nor the Republican Party spoke to the needs of the working people and the farmers. The plain people felt that they were ignored and taxed and pauperized by a corrupt and indifferent national government. In response to this growing conviction, various groups—the Greenback Party, the National Farmers Alliance, the Grangers and other state groupings—held a national convention in Cincinnati, Ohio, in May 1981 and organized the People's (populist) Party of America.

Among other things, the original convention platform called for the following changes: national ownership of all means of public transportation and communication; a graduated income tax; popular election of United States Senators; the adoption of the initiative and referendum in legislation; a 2 percent ceiling on the interest on loans to farmers who dealt in perishable crops; and the prohibition of alien ownership of land.

The fact that, in the 100 years since then, so many of these radical demands have been effected and have become a given without question testifies to the soundness and validity of the Populist movement.

Their demand for a "national money" issued by the Federal Government, and doing away with the chaotic bank-money of the time, was not only valid, but had to come about as a precursor of the industrial-financial system of today. Their demand for unrestricted silver coinage became an object of mockery in financial circles. William Jennings Bryan, the populist candidate for President in 1896 (the Vice Presidential candidate was Thomas Watson of Georgia), subsequently allowed himself to become a defender of creationism in the famous Scopes trial.

Nevertheless, Bryan's ringing statement that mankind should not be crucified on a cross of gold was also an interesting anticipation of events to come. Today, more than ever, with a government in Washington interested only in bloody foreign war and a Congress made impotent by a cold and unfeeling and heartless President, the populist movement becomes increasingly important. Bryan fought the gold standard, today the gold standard is gone. The idea of a canal to connect the Atlantic Ocean and the Pacific Ocean was a populist idea, and they worked for it until it was taken over by the other parties. The safety and security of postal savings was also a populist demand—a desperate demand at a time when banks were even less secure than they are today. When the populists called for a secure paper money, such as we have today, backed by the full weight and integrity of the Federal Government, they were told that their demands were insane; nevertheless, today the whole world has turned to such a monetary concept. When the populists put forward their demand for a graduated income tax, "We demand a graduated income tax, to the end that aggregated wealth should bear its just proportion of taxation," a wild outcry exploded. Were these madmen who would destroy the country and all that it stood for?

Such is a brief—indeed painfully brief—recollection of the great populist movement of the turn of the century, and it should be remembered and studied and understood— even by political magazine writers.

No other Western nation dumps its history into the scrap heap as we do, and no other Western nation manipulates the truth of the past as we do. Our failure in the teaching of history is a national disgrace. We have substituted an idiotic Hollywood charade for the actual past of this country, perpetuating myth and fable and nonsense and simply dismissing the historical truth. As I remarked a few years ago in this column, when Ronald Reagan compared the leaders of a scurrilous band of mercenaries called the Contras to George Washington and the men around him, we touched the bottom rung of the ladder of ignorance. Since we elect men like Mr. Reagan and Mr. Bush to public office, it is understandable that we have no historical memory—understandable, but terrible.

As for David Duke, he is no part of the populist tradition. He is a latter-day fascist, a Nazi in the tradition of Adolf Hitler.

December 23, 1991

Patrick J. Buchanan (A Bad Dream Come to Life)

Patrick J. Buchanan strikes me as a bad dream come to life. He is so perfect a combination of all the dreadful terrors of the 20th century that it would be almost impossible to invent him. Consciously or unconsciously, he has designed himself into a careful composite of a clutch of nasty dictators—to a point where, as with the character in Chaplin's wonderful film *The Great Dictator*, he becomes a caricature of himself. It is all there, the innuendo and then the denial, the low voice, insinuating, engaging, the suggestive hint that he is giving voice to your own nasty secrets. "Come on, come on," he whispers, "am I not saying what you always thought but never had the guts to say? Isn't it time someone got it out into the open? Blacks—do you really like them? Jews—oh, I am not an anti-Semite, but Jews—think about it."

In an article by my favorite *New York Times* reporter, Maureen Dowd, we have the first major unveiling of this new aspirant to the Presidency of the United States. Ms. Dowd writes of a ". . . brawling teenager from Northwest Washington, who grew up in a 'world of clarity and absolutes' where his father's 'political holy trinity' was Francisco Franco, Joseph R. McCarthy and Douglas MacArthur."

The affection for McCarthy appears to be genetic, for Mr. Buchanan apes him in tone, gesture and sullen malevolence. The absence of the communists as whipping dogs after the collapse of the Soviet Union has robbed Mr. Buchanan of the favorite targets of his predecessors, but he has ample replacements among the Jews and the blacks. The darts come slowly. As Ms. Dowd points out, Mr. Buchanan denies that he ever stated that AIDS was God's punishment upon homosexuals, but on the other hand he has written that AIDS was "nature's retribution."

He handles the question of blacks being admitted as immigrants or refugees to the United States by asking quite reasonably whether we—his listeners—would not prefer a white majority in this country. And concerning Jews, he is even more delicate, separating—at least in his own defense—hatred of Israel from anti-Semitism. He chooses Dartmouth, a campus where the most misbegotten racism flourishes, for one of his most trenchant talks.

He was a brawler and, according to those who knew him in his younger years, a bully. Before dignity became a political necessity, he liked to throw a punch on occasion. His "America First" slogan is by no means an unconscious repeat out of a pro-fascist historic past; it was chosen quite deliberately, so that a proper echo might resound.

Being a good deal older than Maureen Dowd, I can only stare in amazement at what I have just written. It simply seems impossible. We have heard everything Mr. Buchanan has to say; we heard it all half a century ago, and for hearing it the world paid a terrible price. The power that was put into the hands of men who spoke as Patrick J. Buchanan speaks and who programmatically carried out those notions that Mr. Buchanan has begun to whisper and imply—that power given to them cost the human race 50 million lives. In the years between 1933 and 1945, in those 12 years, as many people as the entire population of the United Kingdom were slain in the struggle against Nazism and fascism.

Mr. Buchanan calls himself a conservative, a right-wing conservative; but be it said that if one thinks like a fascist and talks like a fascist, one is a fascist, regardless of what one calls oneself.

We are at a precarious moment in our history, sliding into a recession quite different from anything we have experienced during the past 50 years. As of this moment, no one knows quite how it will end, whether it will stop and reverse itself, as previous recessions have, or whether the slide will continue and perhaps turn into a repeat of the Great Depression of the 30's. We created the focus of and the reason for our despair: the 11 years of Reagan and Bush. For eight years, a second-rate actor, witless on his own and moved by a set of strange advisors, looted this country as it had never been looted before, piled up a national debt of hundreds of billions of dollars and created a military monster. It was handed over to George Bush, who having control of this terrible toy saw no reason not to use it in two senseless and dreadful wars.

Our despair rises out of the fact that we have no leaders who are concerned with the ordinary people of America. They offer no path that has meaning, no hopes, no dreams. The money that could be used to create millions of jobs and to educate our youth is being thrown away, to pay for the crimes of a set of swindlers—the President's son among them—who destroyed our banking system and who go unpunished, and a military-industrial complex that is utterly insatiable.

The cure is neither unknowable nor impossible; the cure can be summed up in four words: jobs, homes, schools and hospitals. There is no cure in racism, anti-Semitism, hatred and war. There is no cure in what Patrick J. Buchanan will offer us.

January 27, 1992

Chapter 6

Crimes and Punishments

Oliver North

Colonel Oliver North was indicted for conspiracy to sell weapons illegally to Iran. The funds received for the weapons were to be used to support the Contras, an army of mercenaries organized and supported by the Reagan administration to conduct war against the legal government of Nicaragua. Colonel North testified at length before a Congressional committee. His ultimate sentence included no jail time.

I feel sorry for Ollie, and I am downright tired of everyone dumping on him. Here he stands, a tall, handsome all-American boy, a Marine officer, loyal and true, with a fine wife and family and a most beautiful secretary who makes a million male mouths water when she walks across the TV screen; and if that isn't what everyone in this fine and democratic nation of ours dreams of and desires, I'm a monkey's uncle.

And now we're punishing him for doing what he's doing, which is what every handsome all-American boy has been taught is the true and rightful path of honor.

Take Commies, for instance. Didn't we train and arm the death squads of El Salvador, who murdered 60,000 citizens of all ages and both sexes, because odds on, if you kill 60,000 people, there's sure to be some Commies among them? And nobody's been indicted for that.

Why Ollie?

And didn't we grab the defeated National Guard of Somoza, a retired-to-Miami dictator, and arm them and train them and instruct them to move into Nicaragua and kill anything that moved, because who knows but that some innocent 6-year-old may grow up and become a Commie, and isn't it better to blow his head off now than to wait 15 years and have to do it then?

Why Ollie?

You know, it seems to me that all Ollie ever wanted was a few bucks to make his life a little easier, and what's wrong with that? And didn't that cheerful raconteur of the American Way among the upper echelons, Adam Smith, replying to an indignant query about the junk-bond millionaires, state, "That's the name of the game, isn't it?"

Why Ollie?

According to *The New York Times,* Ollie was utterly besieged with cash-flow problems—and who isn't, come to think of it? " 'He [Ollie] would run by and his face was red and he was very upset with my staff if for some reason they didn't have money,' " *The Times* writes. This from Mary A. Dix, the National Security Council's Administrative Officer; and she goes on to say, according to *The Times,* that " 'he [Ollie] would say that he didn't have enough money to buy gas to get home.' "

It happens to all of us, doesn't it? And who knows but that Mary A. Dix was getting her licks in for what Ollie said about co-workers at the National Security Council? After all, Ollie, who was saving democracy practically single-handed, was paid only a lousy $50,000 a year. A New York cop with some decent overtime can make almost as much.

Again, according to *The New York Times*, Ollie would pursue Ms. Dix through an office corridor, yelling, "Mary! Mary!" But that happened only when he was out of gas. "When he submitted travel expenses to her office for reimbursement," *The Times* goes on to say, " . . . he would immediately seek payment. 'He would be frantic that we turn them around as fast as we could because his credit cards were charged to the max.' "

Well, who isn't in that same situation? What do they hand out credit cards for, but for us to go over the maximum, and why should Ollie be zapped for maintaining our economy? He knows—as you do—the dire consequences that would arrive should we ever stop buying and consuming like crazy. Should Ollie be faulted for desiring to avoid another *Great* Depression?

It might appear a bit strange that Ollie—according to his own testimony—should keep a steel box bolted to his closet floor and keep in that box $15,000 in cash, but, considering the condition of the banks these days, he really should not be questioned on that score. As for the money being in cash, Ollie explained that he kept the cash in order to buy a GMC Suburban. Anyone knows that you can make a better deal if you shove a fistful of cash in the dealer's face.

The same goes for the $7,000 horse Ollie bought for his daughter, and anyone who has a daughter these days knows how cantankerous they can get about horses. Then with Ollie there on trial, actually on trial while half a hundred bums, free-loaders and other varieties of Washington officials walked around free as birds with never even a teensy-weensy indictment pushed their way, he is faulted for accepting a gift of a $13,800 home-security system. Well, if I had been pushed around and condemned and indicted the way Ollie has been, for the sin of trying to live the American Way, I'd want some security too.

May 1, 1989

Equal Justice

It took my friend, D'emas, some days before he thought his way through the Ollie North affair, but D'emas comes from a far-off land, and his understanding of democracy and civilization is primitive at best.

"What I can't understand," D'emas said, "is why this Judge Gesell didn't give Ollie the 10 years his crime called for."

"The judge felt it would harden his misconceptions if he went to jail."

"Oh? But it seems to me that the essence of Ollie's misconceptions was that he did not agree that the United States was a country where Congress makes the law of the land. It seems to me that 10 years in prison might knock that notion out of his head."

"D'emas," I said tiredly, "sometimes I'm ready to give up trying to explain democracy to you. It's true that most of the people in the United States believe that Congress makes the law and that we are a nation of law; but the executive branch of the Government feels that Congress is a nuisance that exists because some thoughtless gentlemen long ago slipped the notion into the Constitution. They have a thing called the CIA that breaks the law day in and day out, and they have another thing called the FBI, also very good at breaking the law, and there's the National Security Council, and they don't even admit that Congress exists, and then there are all the other odds and ends like HUD, where nobody ever bothered to tell them that there were laws or that it was wrong to steal—"

"Oh, hold on—please!" D'emas cried. "You are confusing me."

"Exactly," I said gently, unwilling to undermine the poor man completely. "That's how the country functions. Confusion. If we stopped being confused, heaven only knows what would happen."

"But you still haven't answered my question."

"Ah, yes—but it is so obvious. No, forgive me, D'emas. You haven't had our advantages. You see, Ollie is a hero. He wore a uniform. He salutes at the drop of a hat. And he always appears at the point of tears, which makes the public sorry for him. We are a compassionate and emotional people. Look what Richard Nixon did with a small dog and a tear or two in the Checkers affair."

"Yes, but Jesse James and Bonnie and Clyde and Al Capone were also heroes of a sort, and no one ever suspended their sentences—"

"D'emas," I said severely, "that's a horrible comparison."

"Well, yes, I guess so. But take Mario Biaggi. He served for years in Congress, and he was a good Congressman and kind and decent to people in his constituency, and just because he picked up a few dollars on the side, the judge really dumped on him."

"Yes, of course. Mario Biaggi doesn't sound like Ollie North—does it? He was not in the club and he didn't wear his uniform."

"What club?"

"D'emas, how can I explain that to a primitive?"

He squirms a bit when I call him a primitive. That's because he has a very dark skin. He understands that in America, people with dark skin are not considered good candidates for explanation—unless of course the coloration is the result of sunshine at Palm Beach.

"But," he said, really trying to understand, "take the case of Stanley Friedman. All he did, when he was running the Bronx, was to pick up a few thousand dollars no one really missed, and the judge dumped on him even worse than Biaggi—"

"D'emas, think! Was he in the club? No way. Did he wear a uniform?"

"No, he didn't. Are you trying to tell me that equal justice for all is just an advertising slogan?"

"Oh, no," I assured him, unwilling to fill the poor savage with misconceptions that might match Ollie's misconceptions. "Equal justice exists. It must simply be seen in the full sense. There is equal justice for those in the executive branch of Government, and there is equal justice for those in the Wall Street branch and equal justice for the folk in East Harlem and there is equal justice for the 75,000 homeless New Yorkers who mostly sleep in the streets. It's just that justice is more equal for some than for others, as a wise man once said. And after all, the judge did slap a fine of $150,000 on Ollie."

"So he did," D'emas agreed, "and that shows that people like Ollie can't just go around breaking the law whenever the thought takes them. And his Navy pension may be down the tubes."

"He'll survive that," I assured D'emas. "With all the publicity, his lecture fees are up to $25,000."

"It's a remarkable society," D'emas admitted.

July 31, 1989

In Greed We Trust

The *American Heritage Dictionary,* a very American product, published by Houghton Mifflin Company, which defines each word in modern terms, has a short, succinct, single-sentence definition of *greed:* "A rapacious desire for more than one needs or deserves, as of food, wealth, or power; avarice." In its definition of *greedy*, the adjective, the dictionary adds: "Wanting to eat or drink more than one can reasonably consume, gluttonous, voracious."

According to *The New York Times,* Leona and Harry Helmsley are worth $11 billion; and for folk like myself who deal uneasily with such numbers, it translates into $11,000,000,000. That is larger than the yearly gross national product of at least a dozen Third World countries. Now suppose the redoubtable Leona M. Helmsley were to swing into action with all that eager energy and anger that she has a reputation for, and manage to blow $500,000,000 a year. Of course, such a buying spree might daunt a lesser woman, but let's just say that Leona might pull it off. If she did, and if her base fortune were invested even very conservatively, she still could not lessen the $11,000,000,000.

Well, let's not get too righteous about that. When it comes to stiffing the Government over a few bucks of tax money, what Mrs. Helmsley is charged with, the line can form to the right and stretch unbroken from New York to Los Angeles. But the scams don't stop with beating the Treasury. Years ago, John B. Connally, millionaire, Governor of Texas, and on his way to becoming President, was accused of taking a bribe of $10,000. Petty money, play money. Mr. Connally beat the rap, but the accusation and evidence presented destroyed his political career. The financial crimes in the indictment of Ollie North were so petty and picayunish that one had to wonder at the falling price of dishonor; and the deep instinct for larceny landed most of Richard Nixon's Government in jail and himself in total disgrace.

And during the eight years of Ronald Reagan, one couldn't toss a pebble in the White House without it bouncing off someone bound for indictment, under indictment or on his way to jail.

The recent revelations about the Department of Housing and Urban Development underline this, but in a curious way. What we have been witnessing is not simply a parade of thieves, but rather a gang-rape of Government money by smirking, insolent middle-class crooks who have stolen our money. Let me underline that again, our money. If someone came into our homes and stole money from us, we'd be properly aggrieved. But it appears to me that very few people have this sense of personal funds being taken from them. When a beautiful, blue-eyed, blond lady indignantly denies wrongdoing, the media treat her very differently from some black kid being dragged into a station house by a couple of cops; and the pudgy, round, bespectacled gentlemen who have hooked onto hundreds of thousands of HUD money are handled with courtesy and respect. But HUD money is our money.

The Government produces no money. Not the White House, not the enormous staff that inhabits it, not the Congress, not the Senate, not any of the swollen bureaucracy that inhabits Washington—not one blessed one of them produces a dollar of money. They use the money we earn. They swill from a trough we fill and refill and refill endlessly. They live out of our labor, our creativity, our intelligence, and it's never enough and they ask for more and more and more. And then, to add the ultimate insult to this very real injury, they grow a crowd of goniffs unmatched in any country on earth.

So we return to the beginning of this piece, the question of greed. What are we to do about it? The smart-ass answer is to change the slogan on the dollar bill from "In God we trust" to "In Greed we trust." That would be a sound confession and sturdy beginning in the practice of honesty and integrity, but I truly doubt that the present Congress would go for it. The concept of integrity is apparently as difficult for the Congress of the United States to swallow as the concept of common sense. For 45 years, we have wasted enough money preparing for a war with Russia that will never and can never take place to pay off the national debt five times over and to rebuild every major city in the bargain and to provide jobs for every unemployed man and woman in America. And all of it, every last penny of it, has come out of our earnings. A hell of a note, isn't it?

And aren't we lucky that we have Leona M. Helmsley to gloat over!

Not a nice woman, not a pleasant woman—and every woman-hater in the country is getting his jollies out of beating up on her. Perhaps she deserves every bit of it; on the other hand, I'd like to see the media put on the gloves with the real bums. You don't have to look very far.

August 14, 1989

Mrs. Helmsley was accused of avoiding taxes by charging her business for personal expenses. She is now [1992] serving a four-year jail sentence.

The Rewards of Betrayal

A man called Paul Janszen told reporters that he was a friend of Pete Rose. As far as I can find out, being a friend of Pete Rose is the only distinction that this man Janszen can lay claim to. According to *The New York Times,* "Paul Janszen, who told baseball investigators that he had placed baseball bets for Rose, the Cincinnati Reds' manager, said he had provided Federal agents with evidence that Rose had tried to hide income."

Before you decide to cheer this public-spirited "friend's" action, I must tell you that, like most betrayals, this one did not go unrewarded. This creature called Janszen sold his betrayal to *Penthouse* magazine for the tidy sum of $25,000, together with a neat residual agreement that would pay him 25 cents for every copy of *Penthouse* sold over 2 million. No part of the media appears to be particularly disturbed by this obscenity—certainly not sufficiently disturbed to sound a judgmental note.

There is an ugly little joke about an ugly little man who is sitting next to a beautiful woman on an airplane. After a few words of conversation, the ugly little man says to the beautiful woman, "Lady, would you go to bed with me for two million dollars?" They are flying first class, and the beautiful lady does not reject the notion immediately. She broods over it for five minutes or so, and then replies in the affirmative. The ugly little man says, "How about ten dollars, madam?"

Furious, she turns on him and snaps, "What do you think I am, you ugly little man?"

He replies, "Lady, what you are we decided before we took off.

Now we're bickering about price."

Not a nice story, but one that might underline a new credo. I have always regarded Ted Kennedy as one of the few bright spots in a very dismal Congress. For years now, Ted Kennedy has fought and argued and voted on the side of the angels. To my knowledge, no one in the United States Senate can equal his record. But a man called Leo Damore decided that it was time to trash Senator Kennedy for a tragedy that happened 20 years ago. When my wife asked woefully why he had done it, I could only reply that there was a neat buck in it. Why not? Our country has been turned into an institution where every value has gone by the board. Certainly it is less vicious to go after a stranger than to give evidence against a friend.

It's not so much that these things are done; what is much more discomfiting is that the public and the media which purport to reflect the public will—embrace these betrayals and trashings. A generation that talks about the positive good of greed is something new on the face of the earth. The betrayal of Pete Rose by this Janszen creature is one man's betrayal of another, and so it is with the trashing books. Since I was a child—or perhaps I should say, When I was a child—we taught our children that the betrayal of one's country was a grim and awful thing indeed.

But how now? We have seen Army personnel and Navy personnel and diplomats and even an FBI agent sell out their country, not for an ideology or a belief, but for cold cash—and seen it passed over with hardly a snort of anger out of the media.

Perhaps honor and betrayal have gone out of our language. When a whole parade of loathsome Russians sold out to us and sold their country for that blessed United States dollar, no one ever hinted that they had betrayed their country. Instead we hailed them as defectors to the home of freedom, with never a word about what perfect swine they were! Not one of them came over to our side without a nice pile of dollars or a cushy job to soothe his presence in a new land.

And not one of our own sellouts did it for ideology, but only for the buck.

It may well be that Mr. Janszen will be much bemused by this column and say, "Well, doesn't everyone?"

September 4, 1989

Let the Punishment Fit the Crime

Let all of us stand up and cheer: A wretched little con man, name of Jim Bakker, has come to what many will call his just desserts, 45 years in prison with some possibility of parole at the end of 10 years. Lo and behold, the courts have spoken and justice has triumphed.

But in all practical truth, let's look at what the body politic has done. We have made a commitment; for 45 years, we have contracted to supply him with clothes and shoes and the services of a physician, and we guarantee that hospital space will be available to him if and when he should require it. And since most work-prisons pay some very small wage, we have also contracted to pay him.

Does it make any sense at all? Are we punishing Jim Bakker? Of course, there are the violent criminals, the thugs, the murderers, the dope sellers, the armed thieves—and these must be removed from civilized society, and since we have learned nothing in the past 2,000 years about how to deal with such people, they must be locked up.

At the same time, they are being punished. To remove men from the company of women, to take them out of society, to confine them for years in an enclosure—this is a terrible punishment, far more agonizing than any person who has never been to prison can imagine.

Yet how does punishment profit either the punished or the punisher? We gain nothing from it; society gains nothing, and except for those curious people who gloat and squeeze pleasure from another's anguish, punishment of criminals returns nothing to us. The whole concept of punishment is barbaric, vicious and beyond defense. It is the opposite of teaching, of love and forgiveness, and rarely if ever do the punished benefit from it. The reverse is more likely, that punishment leaves scars that can never be erased.

So what about Jim Bakker? I have no statistics to back me up, but I would imagine that perhaps half of our prison population is there for non-violent crimes, and among these, thousands perhaps for white-collar crimes. Their incarceration brings no benefit whatsoever to them or to the community. So let us look at Jim Bakker in another light. He is a small-time con man who found a way to put his hands on millions. He is apparently devoid of any standards of right and wrong, ethically a neuter, and possessed of only the vaguest concepts of Christianity. Is there any hope or salvation for him? (I use him only as an example who is very much on page 1.)

Suppose that instead of prison, Jim Bakker were sentenced to spend 10 hours a day for 10 years in a hospital for those dying of AIDS.

Suppose that in such a place, he washed floors, emptied bedpans, and did other necessary hospital work. We are desperately in need of people to do such work in such places. The community would profit and, as for Jim Bakker, he would perhaps learn something of the humility and compassion that come to those who help the fatally stricken—and some do learn—and who knows but that he might not achieve some deep sense of God and the universe.

The point is that we must come to grips with the problem of crime and the punishment—as we have it—that fits the crime, or surrender our society to chaos. Some 4,000 years ago, at the dawn of civilization, someone invented the cell and the locked door. We have really never improved on the original concept, nor have we ever actually tried to examine it. We read in the newspapers of some benighted mother who locks her child or children in a closet and keeps them there for years, and we sense the horror of the situation, and we nod approval at the state's solution, which is to lock up the mother.

I have no answers that go further than what I have put down here, but questions are very important, and sometimes if there are enough questions, the people who run governments will set about finding the answers. Usually in our society, a solution is found or sought only when the condition becomes utterly untenable, as witness the desperate search for a solution for nuclear waste. We are at a point where jailing has become equally untenable.

And as one small afterword, the judge who sat on the ridiculous Zsa Zsa case was unable to resist giving Zsa Zsa three days in jail; and one wonders what went through his so-called "judicial" mind. Did it give him some measure of satisfaction? Or was he so drunk with his petty power that he had to send the silly lady to jail? If he had a shred of common sense, he would have sent her over to the Beverly Hills police station with a mop and a pail of suds and told her to clean it up. A practical solution.

November 13, 1989

Who Pays the Price?

A gentleman called Stanley M. Friedman, a political sleaze who bilked the people of New York City out of thousands of dollars, was sentenced to 12 years in a Federal prison. He began serving this long and senseless sentence in 1988, and now he is fighting a desperate legal battle to have his sentence shortened. In this, former Mayor Koch has become his ally, which makes it news.

I have little sympathy for Mr. Friedman. I think he should be punished as severely as possible, if only to set some sort of example for the endless army of political crooks the people of America must endure; but the mode of punishment is totally senseless. It costs about $5.20 a day to feed a Federal prisoner, more than $200 a year to keep him in clothes, bedclothes and linens, and more than $1,000 a year to house him and guard him—and damn it, that money comes out of your pocket and mine.

Why? Why should I be taxed for the criminal antics of Stanley M. Friedman? Why should I have to pay that enormous maintenance for 12 years? He's no danger on the street; he's not a mugger or a housebreaker or a killer. Punishment?—of course he should be punished. Put him to cleaning the floors of city hospitals. Make him pick up the godawful trash that lines the city parkways. Put a radio attachment on his leg that will monitor his movements day and night. Put him under house arrest and rout him out at dawn to do eight hours cleaning sewers too nasty for paid workers to touch. Give him 10 hours a day collecting garbage in Harlem and the Bronx and other places where the garbage sits undisturbed month after month. Let him feed and clothe himself. He has ample funds, and if a similar criminal is broke, pay him enough to survive.

But take him off our backs. We are not called to account to pay for Stanley M. Friedman's crimes.

On the other hand, in that place on the Potomac, a place I feel to be a foreign country, which has cognizance of neither our pain nor our needs, criminals like Mr. Friedman do not go to jail at all, even when juries find them guilty to the extent of 25 years of possible punishment according to the legal code. Of course the problem is different, for while we have had our cluster of crooks, down there whole administrations, one after another, have been indicted. Their crooks are heroes, for while our local con men have taken us for thousands, the crowd in Washington—those indicted—have taken us for millions. I speak only of those who have been caught; others in that golden playpen have taken us for billions. And when each criminal on trial emerges from his particular courtroom, he is greeted with cheers and hurrahs.

Now I do not for a moment think that anything would be gained by sending either the pink-eyed Ollie [Oliver North] or the dashing John Poindexter [both of Iran–Contra fame] to Federal prison. I'm sure their food and conditions would be better, which means that we, the taxpayers, would be shelling out even more. I have done nothing to be sentenced to feed Mr. Poindexter his three meals a day. And it's worth keeping in mind that the whole lot of idiots indicted for their part in the Iran–Contra affair have been sold down the river by Ronnie, who has taken shelter behind those immortal words "I just don't remember."

Nevertheless, they are criminals and they should be punished, or equality before the law becomes a farce. There are enough garbage-ridden blocks in the Washington ghetto to give employment to every White House crook since the unspeakable Nixon, and there are enough hospitals underserviced to restore some shreds of morality and honor to men who have forgotten the meaning of the words.

Our prison system is as hopeless and antiquated as the thinking of the men who operate it. Defined properly, it must be seen as no more or less than a vast university of crime. We stuff our jails with kids who never had a chance to learn much else than crime, and by this we proceed to hone the edges, heighten their skills, so that the amateur becomes the professional. This is both unreasonable and stupid, but to populate our jails with the white-collar malefactors who present no physical danger on the street compounds the stupidity.

Behind this, of course, lies the unwillingness of people we elect or appoint to office to think. Thinking is dangerous. We have enough atom bombs to depopulate the earth 20 times over—don't think about it. Make more. We have a national debt that is rushing us to destruction—don't think about it. Borrow more. And we are increasing the criminal population at a rate that will, in not too long a time, force us to imprison one out of every 10 Americans—don't think about it. No, never think about it. Just close your eyes and it will all go away.

April 23, 1990

Chapter 7

Rights, Values, and Religion

The Right to Protest

When I was a kid in grade school, "The Star-Spangled Banner" was not our national anthem, and the principal of our school asked that it not be played. He regarded it as warlike and un-Christian. At assemblies, "America the Beautiful" was sung, and we were given to understand that it was the national anthem. For those who may have forgotten, the first few lines go as follows:

O beautiful for spacious skies, for amber waves of grain,
For purple mountain majesties above the fruited plain!
America! America!
God shed His grace on thee,
And crown thy good with brotherhood from sea to shining sea!

I loved the song. It brought to us, as children, an image of a good and gracious land, a place of peace and love. It was easy to sing and it was like no other national anthem in the world.

Then, in 1931, Congress, which then as now was always out to lunch with their heads at the cleaners, decided to replace this sweet and gentle song with another—a song written by a drunken lawyer and put to music in a barrooom by a company of drunks to the tune of an English barroom ballad called "Anacrion in Heaven." This is the song known to us as "The Star-Spangled Banner." It's a silly song, impossible to sing, and if you think about the words, utterly meaningless today. Far from being poetry, it can hardly even be called doggerel. It was written by Francis Scott Key after he stood as an envoy on the deck of a British warship that was bombarding Fort McHenry. Its refrain, "Oh, say, does that star-spangled banner yet wave o'er the land of the free and the home of the brave?" is as inane and meaningless as the rest of it.

Now, having written the above, have I committed a punishable crime? Is this silly, unsingable song we are forced to try to sing over and over, ad nauseam, sacred? Has it taken on a holy resonance beyond the smell of beer in the saloon where it was put together?

I ask this in terms of the recent Supreme Court decision that it is not a criminal act to burn the flag of the United States—my analogy being that if the flag is holy then the national anthem should share in that holiness, and what I have written is criminal. But Congress, that same company of curious folk who watched the CIA overthrow governments and train murder squads with hardly a murmur of protest, who watched our fisheries destroyed by Exxon with scarcely a whisper until it was too late, who sat almost mute as our air and water were poisoned and who mumble inanities as our youth become drug addicts by the millions—this same Congress exploded with rage and a cacophony of inane speeches when our conservative Supreme Court said it was not a punishable crime to burn the flag.

Ah, well! I thought I would wait until the patriotic fury cooled a bit before I made any observations of my own. To my way of thinking, nothing is sinful that does not hurt a human being, and the same may be said of crime. It can be argued that animals should be included in that injunction, and perhaps that is so, but symbols are neither alive nor holy, and if a flag can be criminally damaged then so can a cross or a six-pointed star or a scimitar and there goes the First Amendment. The wisdom of the Supreme Court in this decision is quite extraordinary—in fact, one of the wisest and most searching decisions in many years, and if there were some brains and perception floating around the halls of Congress, they would have greeted this decision with cheers.

Ideas change. The flag of the United States is a symbol. In itself, it is neither holy nor sacred; it is simply pieces of cloth dyed and sewn together. When it appears as a symbol on bags of food sent to a famine-stricken area, it represents the best in man, the holding out of a hand to those in need, the charity that is given freely. When it waved over men who fought against the horror of Nazism, it was the symbol of freedom; when it was printed on bombs that tore Vietnamese children to shreds, it was the symbol of mindless destruction. In the 60's, it became the symbol of brainless thugs who beat up on kids with long hair, and, traveling through certain Western states, those kids would paint flags on their cars to protect them from the hoodlums who considered the flag to be a symbol of their own brutality and brainlessness, and therefore entitled one who displayed it to be greeted as a friend.

The explosion of fury that burns a flag is part of our right to protest, and the vitality and hope and ultimate decency of the United States of America are fed on protest even as a plant feeds on nutriments in the soil. Take away or cut into that right of protest, and the body will begin to die. Something for the "patriots" in Congress to remember.

July 16, 1989

Traditional American Values

Robert S. McElvaine, professor at Millsaps College, in Jackson, Miss., working on a book about American values, sent me the following three questions: What concepts do I believe are the most important "traditional values" in the United States? Have these values been, on the whole, beneficial to our society? And what changes, if any, have these values undergone in the last quarter-century?

A very tough nut, that one. On the same day, writing in *The New York Times,* William Safire nibbled at the edge of the question. With a disclaimer that this was not his normal journalistic practice, Mr. Safire wrote: "But it struck me that this was no ordinary peccadillo. The President of the United States was sleeping with the mistress of the head of organized crime in Chicago. . . . That was not all: Sam Giancana (the crime boss) was identified as the Mafia leader chosen by the Kennedy Administration to arrange the assassination of Fidel Castro after the failure of the Bay of Pigs invasion."

Thirty years ago, but one is still impelled to say, "Wow! That was something!" But traditional?

Further along in the same column, Mr. Safire lists some sexual judgments of the lady who divided her bedroom hours among a President of the United States, a mob boss, and a singer: "She considered Mr. Giancana kind, Mr. Kennedy cold, Mr. Sinatra—who called her a hustler and was later awarded the Medal of Freedom by President Reagan—cruel."

I give Mr. Safire credit that though he occupies the position of right-wing anchor on *The New York Times*, he often speaks his mind more plainly and willingly than any of his left-of-center colleagues. To what he has said above, however, I might add that Mr. Sinatra was kiss-kiss with Nancy Reagan all over the White House, an honored guest of both Reagans.

So what do I say to Professor McElvaine? Here he's hard at work in a book about traditional American values, exemplified without question by the highest office in the land, and I quote Mr. Safire. He asks, almost wistfully, what has changed in the past 25 years, and I give him the Reagans. I could say that Mr. Bush, our current knight in white armor, upholds traditional American values by treating the Panamanians, the Nicaraguans, and the Salvadorans precisely as we treated the Mohawks, the Sioux, and the Cheyenne—and so proves that nothing has changed very much. The trouble with history, as Professor McElvaine will surely discover, is that it depends on who is writing it.

It's always the question that determines the answer, as many a TV interviewer has learned. What is traditional? When the American people were suckered into electing Warren Gamaliel Harding as the 29th President of these States in 1920, he made an inaugural address that was described as "the most illiterate statement ever made by the responsible head of a civilized government." The quote is from the writing of the historian A.J. Hanna. You'd have to scrape diligently at Mr. Nixon's skin to find a value, traditional or otherwise; and when Stuart Rosenberg, the director, was called down to Washington to try to teach Lyndon Baines Johnson some television manners, he wailed, "How does one tell the President of the United States to stop picking his nose and lifting a leg to fart in front of the camera and using chickenshit in every other sentence?"

I will give it to Professor McElvaine that Mr. Rosenberg exaggerated, and a British journalist did write at the time: "When Mr. Johnson puts on that Stetson of his, he becomes the very image of his native state." There you are—we've found ourselves a traditional value—of Texas if not of the whole country.

Writing in this space a year ago, I spoke of a value, and I will gladly pass it on to Professor McElvaine: It happened many years ago, when the people who created this country were fighting for their very existence. The general of their army, George Washington, had left his beautiful home on the Potomac—it still stands today—to lead his troops. He had put his cousin in charge of the estate. The British came up the Potomac and wanted to burn Washington's home. His cousin bought them off.

When Washington heard of this, he was furious. The homes of some of his fellow officers and many of his troops had been burned. He was enraged that his cousin had prevented the British from destroying his place as well. He wanted to suffer what his people had suffered. This is not a cherry tree story, but a fact. I suppose it might underline a rather decent set of values.

But traditional? I simply don't know. We are blessed with the most wonderful piece of real estate on earth, with a Constitution that is unmatched in history, with a heritage of English common law and with a work ethic handed down by iron-willed Puritans. We also inherit the fruits of slavery and racism and greed. We have done decently, but it has been an uphill battle every day of our lives. I suggest that the good professor forget traditional values and think about the decencies we have fought for and died for.

April 2, 1990

In the Name of Religion

In the most recent issue of a wonderful little magazine called the *Underground Grammarian*, published in Glassboro, N.J., by my friend Richard Mitchell, appears the following letter:

> 1699
>
> To ye aged and beloved Mr. John Higgenson:
>
> There be now at sea a ship called *Welcome*, which has on board 100 or more of the heretics and malignants called Quakers, with W. Penn, who is the chief scamp at the head of them. The General Court has accordingly given sacred orders to Master Malachi Huscott, of the brig *Porpoise*, to waylay the said *Welcome* slyly as near the Cape of Cod as may be, and make captive the said Penn and his ungodly crew, so that the Lord may be glorified and not mocked on the soil of this new country with the heathen worship of these people. Much spoil can be made of selling the whole lot to Barbadoes, where slaves fetch good prices in rum and sugar and we should not only do the Lord great good by punishing the wicked, but we shall make great good for His minister and people.
>
> Yours in the bowels of Christ,
> Cotton Mather

Is there nothing new under the sun? Somewhat less than 300 years later, the Catholic bishops of America join together to hire a public relations firm, Hill & Knowlton, known as hotshot top-of-the-hill flaks, who also represent Playboy Enterprises and certain other less than elegant clients, and to pay said flaks $3 million to $5 million to convince the American public that American women should not have the right of choice or control over their own bodies.

Eugene Kennedy, former Catholic priest and professor of psychology at Loyola University, has let us know by way of *The New York Times* Op-Ed page that he feels that this is a sorry mistake and that the money could be better spent on the poor and homeless. Of course, a young woman of 13 years, poor, homeless and pregnant might never get to read Hill & Knowlton's product and be persuaded that she should bring into this overpopulated world another child destined to the same ghastly fate that is hers. She might—if the bishops succeed—go to a $20 illegal quack and have the fetus torn from her womb by some filthy fraud—as happened thousands of times before abortion was legal in the United States, and then die of blood poisoning, which also occurred thousands of times.

But lest it be thought that I am too selective or perhaps prejudiced in my comments on religion, I propose that we should not ignore the recent actions of Rabbi Schneerson, that "holy" leader of the Hassidim in Brooklyn. So far, the press has been loath to do more than tell the circumstances straightforwardly, without even a trace of the judgmental, with not even a whisper of such on the editorial or Op-Ed pages. Let me recall the circumstances.

A few weeks ago, at long last, Shimon Peres was able to put together a majority in the Knesset in Israel, which could install a Labor Government and finally deal with the Palestinians and bring peace to the Middle East. He managed this by persuading two members of a tiny religious party to join with him. But Mr. Schneerson, on the grounds that God had informed him that not one foot of ancient Israel was to be given away, reached out across the world and persuaded the two religious-party members to withdraw their support from the peace party.

A great many Jews live in New York, and a proper observation of contempt and anger can too easily be read as anti-Semitism. Does the good Rabbi Schneerson sleep well? I wonder.

The bitter nugget of this tragedy—a few moments plucked from the history of three great religions—is what it does to that wonderful sense of the mysterious beauty and connection that unites all human beings and which in the beginning gives rise to everything we call religion, and which religion forgets so quickly. When, as a little girl, my daughter asked me about Hell, I replied that it was an evil lie, invented to frighten people. I reminded her of the pain that came when she burned a finger, and asked her what kind of lunatic god would do that to a person's whole body and maintain it forever? The image shocked her, but it also reassured her.

I have no desire to rant on about the unspeakable horrors that have been done through the ages in the name of God and religion. These are the doings of people with twisted minds and ghastly obsessions. But it is now 1990, and we are being forced to face the fact that we must grow up, that our beautiful blue planet is on the verge of extinction; and that either we will recognize that we are connected, that all mankind is connected, and that we must stop visiting horror and pain on others in the name of religion, or we shall all perish.

As for the bishops, ministers, assorted prelates and Rabbi Schneerson, I call to their attention that old story wherein a heathen came to the blessed Rabbi Hillel to learn the Law of God. "Stand on one foot and I will teach you God's Law," Rabbi Hillel said. And the heathen did so.

"Love thy neighbor as thyself. That is the whole Law. All the rest is commentary. And now, standing on one foot, you know it."

May 7, 1990

Credentials Made of Sealing Wax

Some 40 years ago, during the time we remember as the McCarthy era, when this country trembled under the terror-dictatorship of J. Edgar Hoover, chief of the Federal Bureau of Investigation, over a dozen writers were imprisoned for refusing to testify as informers, and hundreds more were denied work in the film industry and publication in the publishing industry.

In spite of the obsessive and very often cruel measures taken against these writers, never did PEN come to the defense of any of them. In fact, the cowardice and slavish conformity of PEN frequently tended toward supporting the censors, the blacklisters and the terror created by the Federal Government. It must be said and remembered that the American Civil Liberties Union, so boastfully projecting itself today as a defender of the people, also turned a deaf ear to what was happening in America during that time, refusing under the specific instructions of its leader, Roger Baldwin, to defend any man or woman of the left who might in any way be associated with communists. Like PEN, the civil liberties union built careful perimeters around its actions.

When it came to defending the rights of a malignant covey of Nazis to march through a suburb of Chicago, a Jewish neighborhood where many concentration camp survivors live, the civil liberties union was right there. The Nazis were denied a permit. The civil liberties union fought for the Nazi permit.

I thought about this as I read the stories in recent issues of *The Observer* concerning the strange union of PEN and the rich. It had hardly occurred to me that the union was a curious one. Forty years is a long time, and there'll be voices to cry out that the PEN today is not the PEN of 40 years ago. I think the coming years will disclose whether or not that is so.

The editor of this paper observed to me the other day that I took many positions that were not liberal positions. I explained that this was because I am not and never have been a liberal as it is understood; and I think this becomes very apparent as one watches the liberals of America—with a few notable exceptions—leaping to support this abominable and idiotic adventure in Saudi Arabia. The credentials of your liberal have always been made of sealing wax; a little heat and they can be stamped out of a totally different mold.

That, throughout history, has been the tragic practice and fate of the liberal. He is against all the evil things that a person of good will should oppose—war, hunger, poverty, injustice, inequality, tyranny—until push comes to shove, and then suddenly a dirty, shameless and murderous venture to control the major oil deposits of the world is turned into a noble crusade against aggression and a part of the *new order* that will make the world a civilized place; and the liberals leap into line, clapping their hands, and shouting that the Butcher of Baghdad must be taken out, even if we have to nuke him and a million others.

Conceivably, there is no such thing as humanitarian consistency apart from the handful of people who cannot compromise their beliefs—a very small handful—and having lived to see a "socialist" country, the Soviet Union, leap onto the dismal bandwagon of Saudi Arabia, I am ready for anything. Yet I refuse to give up hope. People are people, and while we're not very much to boast about, we have been given minds—and perhaps if the liberals have sold the future down the drain, there will be a new generation ready to face the practical matter of survival; and if the liberals have neither the will nor the understanding to fight each line of defense as it appears, it may just be that the businessmen of the world will come to understand that a world without breathable air will be short on customers.

That's still in the future. The problem today is to get ourselves out of that Arabian bear-trap the incredible Mr. Bush has put us into. It's still not too late to pull our junk out of that desert and say, "To hell with you and your oil! We'll suffer a bit, but we'll make our own forms of energy without polluting the world." What a proud, independent thing that would be! To say—we made a mistake. We did it the way it's always been done, and that doesn't work anymore. So we're going to try something else.

I know that's dream stuff. A man I knew and loved, H. L. Mencken by name, said, "The government I live under has been my enemy all of my active life. When it has not been engaged in silencing me, it has been engaged in robbing me. So far as I can recall I have never had any contact with it that was not an outrage on my dignity and an attack on my security."

I deeply wish I could say otherwise. The liberals who fled for cover in the McCarthy period argue that the past is dead and these are different times. But this oil adventure may herald a time as mindless and reactionary as the years of Harry Truman—and I have yet to see a response from PEN or any other association of "liberals."

October 1, 1990

Keep Freedom of Religion Free

Many years ago, my wife and I were frequent guests at the home of Herbert Steinman, a film producer and a generous host. Herbert delighted in gathering around him on Friday nights a group of interesting people, men and women, Jews and Gentiles, most of them in the arts or the theater. At these Friday night dinner parties, Herbert would make the traditional Hebrew blessing over the wine and the bread, and for this he would hand out yarmulkes, small silk skullcaps, to all of the guests.

On one of these evenings, Artie Shaw was present, and he refused to don the skullcap. When Herbert pressed him to do so, Artie replied that he at least attempted to live by the laws of reason, and that while he was Jewish, he was a totally secular Jew, and he felt that to observe what he considered to be a mindless superstition was to degrade his own intelligence.

As a totally secular Jew myself, I reasoned with Artie that life was filled with ancient and meaningless rituals, such as shaking hands, and that it did no harm, indeed made life colorful, to observe them when the occasion arose. I persuaded Artie, an old friend, and he put on the skullcap, and dinner began.

I thought of this incident when I read that Prime Minister Yitzhak Shamir of Israel had signed a coalition agreement with a small religious party called Agudat Israel. This deal with Agudat firmed up Mr. Shamir's shaky hold on the government and made a Labor victory in the next election very unlikely. In return for Agudat's support, Mr. Shamir agreed to force the passage of four bills: The first would ban the sale or production of pork in Israel; the second would eliminate public transportation on the Sabbath; the third would forbid abortion; and the fourth would forbid public advertising that featured the charms or bodies of women.

To the Orthodox Jew, these laws may appear only nominal; to me, a secular Jew, they are intimidating and horrible, and bring up visions of a fundamentalist Moslem state. It might be argued that these few laws exact no great toll from an irreligious citizen, that they are easily lived with and that even here in the United States, we have strong forces pressing for the illegalization of abortion. On the other hand, approval of these laws opens the gate to additional laws of Orthodox Judaism which a person like myself or Artie Shaw could no more live with than we could live with the laws and injunctions of the Ayatollah.

Artie Shaw's resistance to wearing a skullcap was, whether reasonable or not, an act of religious freedom. But if the police forbade Herbert Steinman and his friends the wearing of skullcaps, that would have been an act of religious tyranny, and to make it even plainer, for me to eat a ham sandwich in Israel would be an action taken under the umbrella of religious freedom, but to jail me for doing it would be tyranny indeed. Freedom of religion is only partially applicable to the right of any group or sect to practice the religion of its choice; the rest of the concept deals with the right of any citizen to refrain from the practice of religion and, if he so desires, to oppose and denounce it.

We need not reach out to Israel; we have learned here in the United States that the extension of orthodoxy to the unorthodox can lead only to misery, crime and a diminution of democracy and civil rights. Israel has held on to the banner of being the only true democracy in the Middle East, but if these four laws come into being, Israel will take the first unhappy steps toward the end of democracy.

Two thousand years ago, during the lifetime of Jesus, the Rabbi Hillel said that the essence of Jewish law was to refrain from doing to others what you would not wish them to do to you; but orthodoxy is the antithesis of such teaching. Until we learn that no one, no man anywhere can speak in the name of God or tell us what God desires, we will remain an uncivilized lot. Governments have the right to make laws in order to protect their citizens and to establish and maintain an orderly and peaceful society, but no government has the right to establish any law based on religious belief. No government has the ear of God or hears the voice of God, and isn't it time at long last to do away with this kind of idiocy? When Jesse Helms, the tobacco Senator, presumes to tell us what is right and what is wrong and what is ethical and what is unethical, all in the name of religion, then one can only throw up one's hands in despair.

And so goes it for the Agudat Israel. They are a greater danger to Israel than armed enemies, and if they and their orthodox followers come to rule Israel and direct the laws and fortunes of Israel, then only a great tragedy can ensue.

December 3, 1990

Chapter 8

The Right to Life

The Right-to-Life Movement

Of course there is nothing new about the anti-abortionists' concern for the unborn fetus. The new head of the right-to-life movement, a physician and, if I am not mistaken, the first male leader of that organization, fairly oozes emotion and pity when he speaks of seven-week fetuses that undergo abortion. He describes them as small people, and his voice quivers with horror and indignation when he describes the murder of these small people.

Murder is his word of choice, as it is the word of choice for the entire anti-abortion movement—not *killing*, not *terminating*, but the totally judgmental *murder*.

Well, if one says nothing else about these people, one must admit that they appear to consider the taking of a human life—as they define the fetus—an abomination beyond forgiveness; and one might just be lulled into accepting this as a high moral position. But then one is struck by a very odd factor in this moral position; the right-to-life people raise thousands, indeed millions of dollars in defense of the unborn, they picket clinics and hospitals, they endure arrest, they stare out of TV screens ad nauseam, they lobby legislators and they plead for right-wing Supreme Court justices to reverse the law that makes abortion legal in the United States. But, in all of this great and earthshaking effort, their moral position is limited to the unborn. When that embryo is born—well, then everything changes.

Once that little creature leaves the womb and enters the world of living human beings, the right-to-lifers fold their tents like the Arabs and silently slip away. The outrageous and unspeakable putting to death of men, women and children does not even elicit a flutter of protest or indignation from these anointed enemies of abortion. They're just not interested, nor is the taking of a human life outside of a woman's womb considered to be murder. No indeed. It's quite permissible and very often the "American Way."

You will find in their ranks some of the sternest advocates of capital punishment, but there we deal with people, not fetuses; and they will tell you that here is a criminal, as opposed to the innocent unborn embryo. On the other hand, I have never heard a right-to-life voice raised in protest against the 60,000 innocents murdered by the death squads of El Salvador, death squads trained and armed by the United States, trained by our West Point–educated officers—officers and gentlemen always—and done to death with weapons our tax dollars paid for.

But can you imagine the wild and holy squeal of horror that would have come from the right-to-life people if they had learned that their tax dollars had paid for abortions in El Salvador rather than hand grenades and carbines! Said squeals erupt periodically when there is talk of our Government underwriting population-control programs in some of the terribly overpopulated third-world countries.

The awful truth of the matter is that the anti-abortion movement has nothing to do with fetal injustice and genocide practiced against innocents who cannot resist. I have been active in one part and another of the peace movement over the past 40 years, but never have I seen in our ranks or on a petition against war and genocide a banner or even an indication of the right-to-life movement. I am not saying that there are no individuals among the anti-abortionists who support the various peace movements; there may be many; but never have I seen any trace of the organization that calls itself the right to life.

So what are we to conclude about this very strange movement that fights so passionately for fetuses and is so indifferent to the fate of those already born, the thousands of children doomed to die of AIDS, the millions doomed by radiation and deadly waste and hunger and war? What are we to think of an organization that is ready to doom 14- and 15-year-olds who have become pregnant by forcing them to come to term and bear children unwanted and equally doomed from birth? What are we to think of religion that curses abortion but is silent and indifferent to the unending slaughter of the innocents in war and famine?

I have no answers. I simply don't know. I have lived my whole life in a world of lunacy, and when I begin to prod at such demented goings-on as this above I feel the lunacy choking me. I used to believe that a reason—apparent if not sane—could be found for every action of people, but aside from being a useful instrument for the election of the most brainless and reactionary candidates for public office, I find the right-to-life movement defies comprehension.

January 23, 1989

A Very Compassionate Man

Those of you who have been reading these columns for more than a few months will remember D'emas, a simple soul from a forgotten, far-off land where a handful of people live quietly, not vexed by the irritations of "civilization." D'emas has made a number of visits to New York, obsessed by his desire to understand our ways; and after a long absence, he turned up a few weeks ago just in time to read Cardinal O'Connor's statement that Roman Catholic politicians who support the right of choice in abortion face the threat of excommunication.

"Isn't that rather severe?" D'emas asked me.

"Oh, no," I told him. "The Cardinal is deeply concerned about human life."

"But the fetus—well, you know, they don't teach very much biology on our island, but I did learn that the fetus at two months is not very human."

"But it has a soul—that's the Cardinal's deep concern."

"And he feels," D'emas said, clinging to the point as he always does, "that this tiny shapeless thing is as human as a grown man, and that it would be as much of a crime to kill this fetus as it would be to kill a grown man or a grown woman?"

"Absolutely."

D'emas sighed and said that the Cardinal must be a very compassionate man.

"You can bet on that."

"Then the Cardinal must be against killing and murder?"

"Of course!" I snapped, and then feeling that I did not want to hurt the poor savage, I explained that I was short with him only because he sometimes misses what is obvious.

"Yes," D'emas said, "but sometimes what is obvious to you is not obvious to me. I mean—well, I don't want to press the point, but I read about those six Jesuit priests—we do get *The Times* on our island—who were murdered in El Salvador, and the authorities seem to know who murdered them, and I just can't remember that Cardinal O'Connor ever threatened the murderers with excommunication."

"He did express his sorrow and regret."

"Oh, yes—yes, of course, but when they murdered the Catholic Bishop of San Salvador—well, I don't remember that the Cardinal even mentioned excommunication."

"D'emas, do you think the Cardinal can just devote himself to threatening excommunication everywhere a Catholic commits a crime? My word, he'd never get anything else done. And I'm not even sure that he has the power outside of his home ground."

"Well, yes, sure," D'emas said uneasily, "and I don't want to give the impression that I am disrespectful or anything of that sort, but when the Catholic nuns and lay workers were murdered in El Salvador by army men who were Catholic, I can't remember hearing more than a faint whisper from the Cardinal."

"Nonsense! Of course the Cardinal was upset. But all of these people were tinged."

"Tinged? I don't understand."

"Tinged by Communism," I said.

"And does that mean it's all right to kill them?" D'emas wondered. "You must be patient with me, because I never can get a grip on what you call civilization. How can a bishop and priests and nuns be tinged by Communism?"

"Because they associate with Marxists. They talk to Marxists. They even listen to Marxists."

"And does that mean they have no immortal souls?"

"D'emas," I said firmly, "no matter how hard I try, I simply cannot get through to you. Do you really expect Cardinal O'Connor to threaten to excommunicate everyone who kills people who are tinged by Communism? We supplied weapons to El Salvador and we sent our people down there to organize death squads to kill people and to teach them the best way of killing—and do you want Cardinal O'Connor to become angry and make threats against the death squads just because the 60,000 people they killed were Catholics and the death squads were composed of Catholics?"

"You mean all 60,000 were tinged by Communism?"

"Absolutely."

"But," D'emas said pleadingly, "you told me that the Cardinal is filled with compassion for any human beings and all human beings—"

"D'emas—"

"Then it's not wrong to kill Commies and people tinged by Marxism. I can understand that. But suppose one of these tinged women has an abortion. Must she be excommunicated?"

"D'emas," I said severely. "You are impossible, and I refuse to go on with this conversation."

July 2–9, 1990

Life Is a Mixed Bag

This is a special story, addressed to the right-to-lifers, with carbon copies to the Cardinal and the Pope. It's the story of Susie, who is 14 years old and is hooked on crack, because most of the kids she knows are hooked on crack; because she needs the crack so desperately, she buys it with the only exchange she has, her body; and being penniless most of the time, she has no money for a pessary or condoms. So at age 14, Susie is knocked up. That's street talk for pregnant. Those who do it to her really don't give a tinker's damn whether she is knocked up or not.

Susie discovers that she is pregnant. She is never sure of her periods and the drugs sometimes interfere with the rhythm. She is in her third month by now, afraid to go to an abortion clinic since she's under-age. She lives in a home without a father, and she is too terrified to tell her mother, so she puts the future off, continues to trade for crack, and one day she discovers that she is in the process of giving birth. She endures this agony alone in an old shed and, in utter terror and despair, not knowing what else to do, she wraps the infant, undersized and premature, in newspapers and puts it in a garbage can. A garbage collector, hearing a faint whimper, finds the newborn child, takes it to a hospital, where the quick, skillful work of the doctors saves the child's life, and thus another crack-infant comes into the world. There is no way to trace the infant, so it is institutionalized and will live in that manner, never loved, never caressed, never wanted.

And just in case you think I invented the above, I assure you that it is a moment in a doleful truth that happens not once but a thousand times, over and over and over, and sometimes the child lives and sometimes it dies. But let's see what happens to the child when it had the "good" fortune to survive. The following is from *The New York Times* of May 25, 1990, a paragraph out of a long story detailing the fate of children of mothers on crack:

> But some common threads are clearly seen by psychologists and neonatologists who have tracked such infants from birth. The most severely affected children suffer from seizures, cerebral palsy, or mental retardation. Most children have an array of symptoms that include hyperactivity, sudden mood swings, extreme passivity, apparent lack of emotion, slow language acquisition or mild speech impairment. Many

> are overwhelmed by stimuli like noise or piles of toys, have trouble interpreting nonverbal signals, are easily frustrated, find it hard to concentrate and learn something one day only to forget it the next.

This heartbreaking picture deals only with children in their fifth year. One can imagine the hell and horror that will dog these children as they grow older. Can they be helped? Opinions differ on that score, but to help these children of crack-hooked mothers will require billions of dollars and the creation of an entirely new and different educational system. Only a dreamer could imagine that happening, when our regular educational system is so inadequate.

In New York State, where the law does not require parental permission, thousands of pregnant children do have abortions; and thereby some degree of torment and unhappiness is avoided; yet forces in the legislature are fighting to reverse this.

When I watch the angry demonstrations of the anti-abortion people on television, I don't see Susie—in fact I don't see any half-starved, poverty-ridden children demonstrating for the right to life. Instead, I see bright white faces, blond hair, blue eyes, well-fed middle-class people, well-dressed, the sort of people one would find in any prosperous suburban community. If Susie were to ring a doorbell or two of these people, she would hardly find open arms ready to embrace her, and if the hospital were to offer the infant rescued from the garbage to these bright-faced anti-abortionists, I doubt that many or any of them would open their arms to receive and raise this poor, distorted, sickly infant. If I am wrong in such a suspicion, then why are the foundling homes filled with thousands of children that no one wants?

So I say to all of those who proclaim the right to life, that life is a mixed bag. Regard Susie's paper-wrapped child, and consider whether you want every pregnancy of children aged 12 to 15—and they number in the thousands—to carry to term. Think about it.

June 11, 1990

Chapter 9

New York City

The Race for Mayor, 1989

Serving a prison term for refusing to name names, in the old times when people went to prison for such things, I became friendly with the warden, who was a very decent man. I spoke to him about the insults and slanders directed at the black prisoners by some of the guards. "Fast," he said to me, "did you ever hear a kid say he wanted to be a prison guard when he grew up?"

It made his point, and recently I've been asking myself whether I ever heard a kid say he wanted to be a politician when he grew up. John F. Kennedy was quoted as saying, "Mothers may still want their favorite sons to grow up to be President . . . but they do not want them to become politicians in the process." The dictionary defines politician as "One who is interested in personal or partisan gain or other selfish interests" (*American Heritage Dictionary*).

Long ago, when Tammany still ran New York, the local neighborhood captain would visit us before Primary Day and Election Day. My father, Barney, had three sons, four votes in all, potentially at least, since we were teenagers. The captain's name was Jack Hennessy, and he was charming and on occasion would leave a fifth of bootleg booze; and while Tammany was stealing the city blind, we were at least connected with the political process in some vague manner, and while Jimmy Walker was a crook, he was sort of our crook.

Today, the definition of the politician still stands, and the gentlemen who run New York City have collected almost as many indictments as that sorry band of genteel hoodlums who run the Federal Government in Washington, but Mr. Hennessy is gone from the political scene, and not even the thinnest spidery web of a thread connects the average citizen with the community of goniffs who run the country and the city. Whereby, this very peculiar primary situation that we have in New York becomes even more puzzling.

The only candidate I have the slightest real knowledge of is Mr. Koch, who, whatever else may be said of him, cannot be accused of hiding his light under a bushel. Of Mr. Koch, we know the following: He is insensitive, thoughtless, loud-mouthed, argumentative, brazen and most often wrong. He does dumb things that defy explanation. Against enormous protest from black citizens, he closed down Sydenham Hospital when it would be most needed. In a city with a great black population, he advised citizens not to vote for Jesse Jackson. In a city with a very large Irish population, he spoke out for the British side of the struggle in Northern Ireland—and as for the firemen, perhaps the best in America, he tossed them overboard in a manner so dumb that it defied explanation. Most of what he does defies explanation—which seems to relieve him of the need to explain, and his most recent gaffe, the notion of blowing Lebanon into a graveyard, outdoes his earlier ones. He had surrounded himself with a gang of now-convicted crooks worthy of the days of Tammany.

Yet he comes out of it as an honest man who lives like an anchorite and who keeps the city running. That is nothing to sneeze at!

I like David Dinkins. He is a gentleman and a pleasure to talk to, but the business of forgetting to file his tax return stops me cold. Such an act spells gross indifference to reality and a lack of foresight that could play hell with a thing as complicated as New York. I hate to say that, but I know nothing more of his character than this.

Neither Harrison Goldin nor Richard Ravitch give me any sense of a presence. I do believe that Mr. Ravitch is a brilliant manager and executive. He has a splendid record, but he appears to be without vitality or even a touch of the charisma that one must have in a contest like this one. I can see no possible way that he could be elected, although I wish he could be the people's choice.

Which leads us to Rudolph Giuliani and Ronald Lauder. I simply do not think Mr. Giuliani comprehends New York and I cannot see him as mayor of this city. I may be wrong, and that is only a very personal opinion; I just do not see him paired up with New York. I don't believe that the women in New York will accept a candidate who accepts *choice* as a necessary piece of opportunism that election calls for. *Choice* does not stand by itself; the abortion issue cuts to the heart of the very shaky proposition that we live in a democracy. It has become symbolic of the whole defense of the people's right, and I have seen no evidence that Mr. Giuliani is or ever has been a defender of that right. His indictment and prosecution of Bess Myerson and Judge Hortense Gabel was a disgrace not soon forgotten, a shameful abuse of the power of the law. So I cannot envision Mr. Giuliani as mayor of New York City, notwithstanding his "Liberal" endorsement, which is only another bad chapter in the unappetizing record of what calls itself the "Liberal Party."

And thus we come to Ronald. Ten million dollars worth of what? Not printable at all.

So where are we? With Ed Koch? I wish I knew some answers.

August 28, 1989

The Name of the Game

The first column I wrote for *The New York Observer*, almost a year ago, concerned the trial of Judge Hortense Gabel and Bess Myerson. [See page 2.] In America, no bit of history seems to survive 24 hours after the last headline; so to refresh the memories of those who will ask, Who on earth is Hortense Gabel? I'll review it briefly. Judge Gabel, 76 years old, had a record for integrity, decency and compassion matched by few occupants of the bench. She also has a rather eccentric daughter.

Bess Myerson, a beautiful woman, once Miss America, has been whipped mercilessly by fate. She was in love with a man who was paying a very large alimony. Judge Gabel reduced the alimony. Miss Myerson gave employment to the daughter. Rudolph Giuliani, mounted on his steed of "legal morality," decided that there was collusion in this, had the Judge and Miss Myerson arrested and placed on trial, and then gnashed his teeth in anger when the jury delivered a not guilty verdict. Mr. Giuliani, who had persuaded the child to testify against her mother, denounced the verdict. But what jury, composed of people of flesh and blood, could have decided otherwise?

At that point, Mr. Giuliani had not announced but had only titillated reporters with the possibility that he might put himself forward for consideration as the next mayor of New York City. Now I am an old citizen, and my memory of New York mayors goes back to John Hylan and Jimmy Walker, and what a galaxy of different types they make! Think of Jimmy Walker, Fiorello LaGuardia, John Lindsay and loud Ed Koch; we had colorful mayors, crooked mayors, ridiculous mayors, explosive mayors and even a small fistful of honest mayors; but in all the history of this city I cannot think of a mayor who would have brought Hortense Gabel and Bess Myerson to trial for an exchange of favors.

The action was so devoid of understanding and compassion that one must try to probe the porcelain exterior of Rudolph Giuliani for some shred of insight. I find none. "Scratch my back and I'll scratch yours." "Reward your friends. Hurt your enemies." These are the blood and bones of American politics, and no one in his right mind talks of indicting George Bush because he rewarded James Baker with the post of Secretary of State after Mr. Baker managed his election. Yes, I realize that this case concerns judicial integrity and is thereby somewhat different; yet this sort of thing does go on day and night, and in this particular instance the evidence was so frail and the circumstances so sorrowful that even to watch the trial or read about it was a heartbreaking affair.

Thus, since the walls of City Hall were not shaking and the foundations of the commonwealth not in danger of crumbling, and since the prosecutor in question is now a candidate for mayor, it behooves us to examine the matter once again. Why did Mr. Giuliani bring this case to trial?

Surely not to see that no courtroom remained unoccupied, since we already have 10 crimes for every available courtroom. Surely not to keep this 76-year-old judge and Bess Myerson off the streets for the safety of our citizens. Or to demonstrate to the world that American law is swift and merciless, sparing no evil-doer. Come on, Mr. Giuliani! The answer is hardly that mysterious; for the publicity it brought him, Rudolph Giuliani destroyed the life and career of a good and honorable public servant.

Well, why not? People lie, kill, jump off bridges and slap policemen for publicity. It's the name of the game, isn't it? But do you know, I cannot imagine David N. Dinkins doing such a thing, not in a year, not in a hundred years, not even if it brought him the mayoralty.

And I wonder whether I am alone in seeing a philosophical connection between Rudolph Giuliani and Ronald Lauder, in spite of all the name-calling. Both have been embraced by Senator D'Amato and both have called out for the death penalty and both put themselves forward as crime-fighters, without a nugget of understanding about what causes crime in New York. In that first column I wrote about the Gabel case, I referred to Mr. Giuliani's dream of the mayoralty as "future shock." It was an apt phrase. You don't frighten or deter criminals with a death penalty; it only adds to murder, since with nothing to lose, certain killers will go on killing; and if ever the New York legislature is foolish enough to pass a death penalty bill over the Governor's veto, I shudder for the future of this city. The same shudder is my response to a Giuliani victory.

October 9, 1989

A Vote for the City's Survival

Among other things I am tired of hearing is the notion of a "Jewish vote." This phrase, used endlessly by smart-ass reporters and commentators who never pause for a deep breath before sinking their teeth into the nearest cliché, evokes a vision of a mass of united, controlled, mindless Jews, ready to vote whatever way some mysterious force compels them to. The fact that this is hogwash and proven hogwash again and again, does not serve to lessen the commentators' use of the phrase.

Jackie Mason, a comic whose brain and mouth appear to have only occasional and fuzzy relationship, makes a silly remark about blacks and, lo and behold, we are given a Jewish point of view, as if the senseless gibbering of Jim Bakker were to be paraded as a Christian point of view. There is no Jewish point of view; there is no Jewish vote; there is no Jewish philosophical concurrence. Orthodox Jews live by a set of beliefs that are as far from my thinking and the thinking of many other Jews as the myths of ancient Egypt, and thousands of Jews condone the actions of the Israeli Government, while thousands of others, myself included, look upon the incidents of the West Bank with horror and heartbreak.

The prejudices of Jerry Falwell have as much relationship to the thinking of Mark Twain as the ravings of Rabbi Meir Kahane have to the thinking of Noam Chomsky. For my part, the thought that gentlemen like Elliott Abrams or Henry Kissinger could have even the vaguest connection with either my thinking or my genetic inheritance fills me with nausea.

So much for the "Jewish vote" and the "Jewish voice." But other commentators, who deal in more mystical nonsense, have taken up the notion of "Jewish guilt," as a reason why Jews might vote for David Dinkins. I have never really understood this business of "Jewish guilt," and friends of mine who are psychoanalysts tell me that if there is a syndrome called "Jewish guilt" it doesn't hold a candle to "Catholic guilt" or to "Protestant guilt."

Jews will vote for David Dinkins. Thousands of Jews will vote for David Dinkins, and thousands of Jews will vote for Rudolph Giuliani. Jews will vote for Mr. Dinkins because like sensitive non-Jews, they see him as a non-violent man, a gentle and reasonable human being who might bring some hope and healing to this wonderful, tortured city. They will not be swayed by the fact that Jesse Jackson embraced David Dinkins. How on earth could Jesse Jackson continue as a political figure if he had not given his support to this decent man who is a candidate for mayor of the most important city in America? And other Jews will vote for Mr. Dinkins because they love New York and they understand that its condition today calls for compassion, not for punishment.

But this will not be the Jewish vote, even though enough Jews may vote for Mr. Dinkins to put him over the top. This will be part of a *white* vote by white people who are thoughtful enough to understand that the condition of New York today needs a man like Mr. Dinkins, rather than a man like Mr. Giuliani.

Mr. Giuliani's approach to crime is doomed, not only to failure, but perhaps to the potential of a situation so worsened that it becomes beyond repair. It calls for more police, more courts, more jails, more punishment—a condition that very soon becomes unsupportable within the framework of a democracy. Whether Mr. Giuliani understands this is questionable, and if he does not understand it and pushes it aside for a simplistic approach to crime, then he is engaging in a bit of obscurantism for which the city will some day pay dearly.

Truly, there is only one issue in this campaign—the fate of New York City—and we should forget about the Jewish, Italian, Irish votes, and begin to think about the city. Only two paths hold out a direction of hope for this city: One is jobs and more jobs. A very simple proposition; people who work hard all day do not do dope; and if they try to do dope, it will turn around and bite them. Unemployed people have their reason to exist torn away from them; they lose pride and manhood and womanhood, and they turn to the small piece of joy that dope grants them.

The other path is education. You can educate people not to do dope, not with Nancy Reagan's childish "Just say no," but with the kind of education that will give an addict a past, a pride in that past, an understanding of where he is today, and the conviction that he can make it. I would advise David Dinkins to forget about the Jewish vote or the Irish vote or the Italian vote. Present this city with the program it needs to survive, and white citizens will vote for you.

October 23, 1989

Mayor Dinkins

Now that Mr. Dinkins is our mayor, my last few words on the [1989] campaign. I love this city. A hundred years ago, my father, age 16, worked in the open iron sheds on the East River, beating the hot iron into the shapes that festooned the whole city then. I rode to school on the wonderful yellow streetcars and the Public Library gave me the world and its knowledge. The possibility that Rudolph Giuliani might become mayor of this still marvelous city filled me with trepidation—more so than in any local election I can recall. Now Dave Dinkins is in there. He's a good and decent man, and I wish him the best.

November 20, 1989

America Without New York City?

We are not much good at history, and therefore when something happens, we have no frame in which to set it. This national amnesia can be troubling at best and fatal at its worst. Do we surrender New York? How absolutely insane that would be, and we may thank God it is impossible. Let's try to remember that history undulates, that a body-polis sickens and cures itself and sickens again and cures itself again—and that this has been the course of every great city throughout history. Think of Rome when goats grazed for forage in its streets, of Jerusalem when it lay in ruins, of Tokyo burned to the ground, of San Francisco in ashes in 1906 and then so ridden with crime that no person could walk the streets alone after dark, of Victorian London with its footpads and murder-gangs—or indeed of New York during the Civil War, when Irish hoodlums murdered blacks by the hundreds, when no man or woman could walk safely on Tenth Avenue in Manhattan, or when "Gyp the Blood" spun his own web of terror, or Prohibition times when the mob introduced the "pineapple" (read homemade grenade) and the "chopper" (read hand-held machine gun) to the streets of New York.

It comes and goes, it waxes and it wanes. I have seen a little of this and that in my time, and I will go out on a limb to state that 10 years from today the drug scene in New York will have dwindled to a facet of city life of small importance. This will not happen in and of itself. In a way, a city is a living entity, a unity of its citizens determined to live in peace and raise their children in peace, and that entity will in good time enforce its desire for a decent and civilized way of life.

Can one think of America without New York City? I can't. To me, New York is the essence, the ultimate distillation of America's promise to mankind.

I am sick to death of those who say New York is not America. What is America? In *The New York Times*, September 8, page 11, there is the following bit:

> TOCCAO, Ga., Sept. 7 (AP)—Officials in this northeastern Georgia town have canceled a government-sponsored yoga class, bowing to pressures from protesters who contend that yoga invites Devil-worship. . . . Phillip Lawrence, a local chiropractor who has been leading the protests that he said included Baptists, Lutherans and Church of God members, asserted that people who relax their minds by performing yoga are opening the door to the devil . . . walking into it like cattle to the slaughter.

Is this America? Is this kind of thing, by no means confined to Toccao, Georgia, the symbol and meaning of America, stupidity embalmed in ignorance? Or have we perhaps another message to send?

Where else in all the world has a body-polis, as New York, shown that nations can shed their nationalistic and tribal fears and hatreds and live together in peace? What other place has taken whole nations into itself, black and white and brown and yellow, and given them a community of home and interest? What a wonderful, incredible mixture of mankind we are!

Easy? Good God, no! We have taken upon ourselves, we who are New York and love and understand New York, the most complex and difficult task on earth, and we have accomplished it and we have made it work. Here, in these five boroughs, is the greatest explosion of talent and creativity that man has yet produced, whether it be in the field of drama, or medicine, or dance, or literature, or song, or economics, or science.

And give this up to the drug dealers? Hell, no, not to them, not to any force or terror!

So what do we do? For one thing, we stop beating up on Mayor Dinkins. The other day, the Port Authority of New York decided to resurface the George Washington Bridge traffic lanes, not during the cold, quiet hours of the night but during rush hour when commuter traffic was at its height. The traffic jam and backup broke all records, and motorists sat for more than an hour at the access to the bridge. A TV news camera zeroed in on one Jersey driver who exploded with rage at Mayor Dinkins, called him all the names that we are permitted in our society to pin on our politicians. It never occurred to him that the Mayor does not run the Port Authority.

But of course, there he is, a black man elected to the leadership of the world's first city—and why not dump on him? If anyone in this metropolitan area is free of racism, would he or she please get in touch with me and teach me?

On the other hand, we have the good fortune, after suffering Ed Koch all these years, to have a decent, sensitive and intelligent man at the helm. He deserves time and support. He can't work miracles. He can only keep his head and do what has to be done as best he may.

September 24, 1990

Chapter 10

Our Friends in Washington

The Great Communicator

Ronald Reagan read his farewell address, and we are given to understand by the media that he wrote part of it himself. On all three major networks, this information was presented to the American public in tones of awe, as if the writing of a few words in the English language was a miracle to be set alongside the tablets Moses brought down from the mountain. We were also informed that the use of his own words by any public figure was unusual, which proves that there is a certain amount of obsequious honesty in the most puerile observations of the average anchorman.

Of course, bits and pieces of information leaked to us during the past eight years would tend to cast doubt even on so modest an attempt by an American President to match the ability of a high school graduate. In order to set up even a few cue-cards by himself, Mr. Reagan would have to possess at least a modicum of literacy; but no time during the eight years he played the role of President was there evidence that he ever read a book. His knowledge of American history was displayed when he compared the murderous thugs who call themselves Contras to Washington, Jefferson, and Adams. That he can read is plainly evident, for he has functioned with cue-cards written by others since he became Governor of California. But whether this trifle of literacy extends to more than writing his own name is yet to be proven.

Then what have we come to? The past eight years are a testimony to the strength and vitality of the American people, for they have as a nation survived not only this curious mindless actor, but all the dreams of Armageddon and the *second coming*, urged on him by such prime nuts as Jerry Falwell and Jimmy Swaggart and Pat Robertson and their moral majority, as well as a looting of the poor and the middle class to create an army of millionaires and billionaires beyond even the wildest dreams of Calvin Coolidge, who held that business was the business of America.

Still, it was to this man, Ronald Reagan, that the 45 percent of the American public that bothers to vote gave the Presidency of the most powerful and potentially wonderful national entity on the face of the earth—a man whose hold on reality was fragile at best, who often thought of himself as Knute Rockne and begged the country to "win one for the Gipper," who believed—and likely enough still does—that the people of earth had to be atomized in a final battle in the north of Israel. You will recall that the Armageddon fixation was behind Secretary of the Interior James Watt's indifference to the destruction and give-away of public lands, holding that after the "second coming" it would make no damn difference who owned Yellowstone Park and similar places.

Gore Vidal, the most gifted political commentator we have, in an essay on Armageddon, held that "The Great Obfuscator has come among us to dispense not only good news for the usual purposes of election but Good News. Reagan is nothing so mundane as an American President. Rather, he is here to prepare us for the coming war between the Christ and the Antichrist."

Fortunately, God or Billy Graham or Nancy spoke and this prediction that Gore Vidal made two years ago did not come to pass. This President who, again to quote Mr. Vidal, "was hired to impersonate, first, a California governor and then an American president" apparently decided that the *second coming* was not within his term of office. He decided that the *evil empire* was not quite so evil. Or, as one of those White House leaks, so abhorrent to him, put it, there was outside intervention.

The rumor has it that God was getting very disturbed at this Armageddon business that Jerry Falwell and Pat Robertson were putting out, and that God sent the Angel Gabriel down to earth to knock some sense into the Great Communicator's head. Thus the end of the *evil empire* and the birth of detente; but as Gabriel was preparing to return to heaven, Mr. Reagan grabbed him and begged for some hint of what God was really like.

At first the good angel protested that it would be impossible to convey such knowledge, but the President argued his own importance as leader of the earth's greatest nation, clinging to Gabriel's wings, until finally the angel sighed and said, "Well, let's say just a hint. To begin with, She's black . . . ."

January 30, 1989

Our Poor, Underpaid Government

The embarrassment of members of Congress as they pushed for their pay raise becomes quite interesting when one reflects that they exhibit no embarrassment whatsoever about all the other measures they have passed that are an affront to the American public. But money makes the world go 'round, and how can we expect a man to live on $89,500 a year? And the perks, the free plane trips, the staff—you know, those of us in the private sector, as they call it, would have to put out $30,000 for a researcher, $30,000 for a secretary—and what about the rest of their enormous staffs?

The Progressive, an honest and venerable magazine published in Wisconsin, has come up with an interesting name for, and explanation of, our poor, underpaid Government. The name is "kak-is-toc'ra-cy, n. (Gr. *Kakistos*, superl. of *Kakos*, bad, and -kratia, from *kratein*, to rule) government by the worst men in the state." In other words, we are a kakistocracy, and before we have a good laugh over it and dismiss it as a smart-ass notion, let us have a look at the case as it stands.

First, is it conceivable that any corporation on earth would hire 435 specimens such as inhabit our House of Representatives, and pay each of them $89,500 a year and the millions of dollars of perks that go with it, and be satisfied with the results we get—an enormous debt, closed factories, heavy industry surrendered to Germany, Japan and Korea, our auto industry handed over to Japan, our steelworkers frying hamburgers, our infrastructure rotting, our youth ridden with drugs, our schools a shambles, our foreign policy maniacal? And that's only the beginning. And it's not a Republican House, mind you, but a Democratic resting place.

I'm not at all sure that President Bush ($200,000 a year, plus $50,000 for expenses, plus $100,000 a year for travel) and his Vice President—what's his name—($97,000 plus $10,000 for expenses) and the Cabinet members ($86,200) are the worst people we could have in government. I am sure there is an ample supply of people more stupid, more venal, more ill-equipped; but, on the other hand, there must be thousands of Americans who are wiser, better educated, more compassionate and more concerned with the welfare of our nation and more skilled in the art of government than the motley crowd—Boyden Gray, John G. Tower, to mention only a couple—that Mr. Bush gathered together.

Since the death of President Kennedy, we have survived a crew of Presidents and a series of Governments that only Suetonius could do justice to, and I think there is no doubt but that *The Progressive* is right to this extent: If we do not have a government of the worst, we certainly have endured a pack of unique gonifs and even more unique misfits and dumbbells.

We have become amazingly gifted in what the psychiatrists call denial. We brush away our national debt, and we refuse to even think about the bag that goes everywhere with the President—the football, they call it—and that gives him the power to instantly eliminate all life on earth; and in that passel of "underpaid" legislators we call the House, there isn't a quorum *ever* to say that every two-bit demented dictator on earth—some of them both our creations and our clients—will soon have the atom bomb, and then there will be no way of putting the genie back into the bottle.

Quorum?—my word, there isn't a member with the guts to stand up and say, "Gentlemen, the Pentagon, with the help of this Congress, has brought us to the edge of destruction." Sooner or later, there will be an accident, for Murphy's Law is inevitable, an accident that can happen will happen, and our ex-President's nutty notion of a star shield is as nutty as most of his notions, and all the star shields in the world will not prevent a small motorboat loaded with an atom bomb from slipping into the harbor of New York, Boston, San Francisco or any other seaport and blowing our cities to kingdom come.

So when it comes to that raise Congress had pleaded for, my solution would be to let every one of them who can't make it on what they get resign—and then give us a chance to replace them with some intelligence, guts and honor. Simply asking for the raise was an insult to every citizen of these United States.

February 20, 1989

Interpreter Wanted

Neither can his mind be thought to be in tune, whose words do jarre; nor his reason in frame, whose sentence is preposterous.

—Ben Jonson, 1630 or so,
and a goodly time before that august body
the United States Senate came into being

A member of that body, Steve Symms by name, elected by the people of Idaho, says, "It's unfortunate that the nation suffers while we dally, because of the importance of national security issues—the

President's Administration is being given a spike in its heart by the partisanship here on the Senate floor."

Lest you protest that I have taken this bold attempt at the English language out of context, I hasten to add that this and other bits and pieces that I may refer to are part of the debate—not on the homeless or drugs or AIDS or the national debt, but on John G. Tower, who stood up as bravely as any repentant sinner at a revival meeting and gave his pledge to the people of America—"I will never touch the devil's brew again!"

Saluting this grim resolve, Senator John W. Warner, Republican from the state of Virginia, tossed his hat into the King's English ring with "We cannot let—and I hope it will never be characterized—this debate as a power grab of the power of the President to make his selection, given to him by the people of this country, and reposed in him in writing by the Constitution of the United States."

Ms. Rosalind Schissling, who holds the position of the *official translator*, asserts that the above means that Senator Warner hopes Congress will not lessen the power of the Presidency.

Senator Tim Wirth, who represents the residents of Colorado, evidently relieved to get off the hot seat of radiation, which, they tell me, is beginning to *permeate* his home state in a very alarming manner, found a new use for the word. In the venerable chamber of the Senate, he stated resolutely, "Let me make a comment. On the subject of appearance. There have been those who said this is not important, we shouldn't be thinking about appearance. Well, of course we should be thinking about appearance. And that appearance is permeating, rapidly permeating, and I think permeating very negatively. Those perceptions are now permeating, and they are important . . . ."

Ms. Schissling says the good Senator means that Mr. Tower's sins are coming home to roost, but another explanation might be that *permeation* might be obsessing Senator Wirth to a point where some small voice inside him might be shrilling, "Why are these nitwits wasting millions of words on a jerk who is obviously not the kind of a man you'd want your sister to date or your mother to buy insurance or a used car from, when my state is being destroyed? Do you know what is permeating, you brainless mandarins? I'll tell you what is permeating. Radiation is permeating one of the most beautiful and valuable places in these United States, and instead of doing something about it, you talk about Tower."

"But," says Senator Sam Nunn, that bastion of gun lore and pistol politics, "I would say there are a number of very significant differences between the committee's proceedings on the Tower nomination and the events in Salem—starting with the fact that the poor souls who were burned in Salem did not have the entire apparatus of the Federal Bureau of Investigation assigned to check out and, if indicated by the evidence, rebut the accusations. And indeed they did rebut numerous allegations in this report, and they did it very effectively on a number of specific occasions."

In the case of the above, Ms. Rosalind Schissling became very defensive. While some of the younger reporters raced to the Congressional Library to look up "Salem" to see how it ties into the Tower investigation, some of the older hands put it to Ms. Schissling flatly:

"Is Senator Nunn telling us that the FBI was involved in the Salem witch-hunts and the subsequent executions? From what he has said, that would appear to be the case," one of the old hands demanded, while another, a grizzled old journalist with a reputation for telling it as it is, demanded to know whether the Senator was a closet advocate of Revisionist History. "If he is, then, by God, he should let his constituents know and not travel under false pretenses. And is he prepared to bring this interpretation of Salem to the American people?"

At bay, Ms. Schissling became angry now. "What you need is an interpreter. I'm only the translator." And taking a cue from Alice, "Anyway, they're all a pack of cards."

March 20, 1989

She Tells It Like It Is

Sometimes, I don't believe it either, but here it is, right from the pages of the January 20 *New York Times*: "Peggy Noonan was sitting on a couch in a West Wing office at the White House two weeks ago, her black fake crocodile notebook in her lap. She was tired and drained. She had just finished working on Ronald Reagan's farewell speech, and now she was beginning to scribble notes for George Bush's inaugural address."

What? You thought Mr. Reagan was our ex-President, and that Mr. Bush had replaced him? Silly you. You thought that the "words" and "ideas" that issued from their mouths originated in what physicians and such call their "brains"?

"It felt like a new breeze," quoting Ms. Noonan. "There was a literal movement of air. A new history beginning today."

Do you see? She tells it like it is. "When you traveled with Reagan," Ms. Noonan told Maureen Dowd, correspondent for *The New York Times,* "it was like traveling with a God. People were struck by his radiance and looked at him with slack jaws. With Bush it was cuter."

No, I did not invent that. I did not invent Peggy Noonan. I am sick and tired of people accusing me of inventing the very ordinary day-to-day happenings in this democracy. No, sir. Peggy Noonan exists, and she trained for the job of being the mind and voice of two American Presidents as an adjuster for the Aetna Insurance Company, and damn it, if you don't believe me, call Aetna yourself.

Of course, you must not believe that President Bush just mindlessly mouthed Peggy Noonan's words. "It felt like a new breeze," Peggy Noonan recalled, and not to be upstaged by this bright little lady, Mr. Bush said, "A new breeze is blowing."

Of course, I by no means resent Peggy Noonan's being right there in the box and pitching a no-hit game. How often, reading the day's proceedings of our Government, I have said to myself, "Dear God, please give us at least 50 women in Congress, so that the human race may have half a chance of survival." There's no question in my mind which is the superior sex; and if the real brains behind these two elegant WASPish gentlemen is a pretty—and she is as pretty as a picture—Irish-Catholic lass, I am not one to complain. Now just listen to this, again from that fine journal, *The New York Times*:

> She [Peggy Noonan] provided some of Mr. Reagan's most moving moments, including his speech in Normandy to mark the 40th anniversary of the D-Day invasion and his remarks in 1986 after the explosion of the space shuttle Challenger. So moving were her words that she was dubbed "La Pasionaria," after Dolores Ibarruri, whose fiery speeches in the Spanish Civil War rallied the communists against Franco.

No sir—if you're so damn sure I sit at home and invent these things, write a letter to *The Observer*. Don't snarl at me. Snarl at *The New York Times*, because when I quote *The New York Times*, I do so with proper reverence for a journal I have read and pondered every day of my life since I was 10 years old, as follows:

> For those who watched Mr. Bush talk with his own words and then talk with Ms. Noonan's, the effect was eerie. Pre-Noonan, if Mr. Bush wanted to talk about drugs he would talk about "narced-up terrorist kind of guys," not, as he did today under Ms. Noonan's influence "deadly scourge."

I like that, and I credit Ms. Noonan. What does narced-up terrorist kind of guys mean? No images there. But "deadly scourge"—wow! Every time we switch on the TV we confront the deadly scourge. It's the real thing.

Ms. Noonan does not have a low opinion of her own work, and that's all right. Credit should be given where credit is due. She says of a major speech that "it makes people less lonely. It connects strangers with simple truths."

There are some spoilsports who, never content with anything the way it is in these remarkable times, will tell you that Abraham Lincoln wrote his Gettysburg Address with a pencil stub on a sheet of brown wrapping paper, while on the train that was taking him to the Gettysburg battlefield. But I'm sure if Ms. Noonan were handy, he would have turned the job over to her.

April 3, 1989

Yes, Peggy Noonan is real, a living, breathing, and very pretty woman. I insert this note for the possibility that this book may outlast my time—few books today have a life of more than twenty minutes, but there are some exceptions—and readers may suspect some chicanery on my part.

No, absolutely not. Ms. Noonan was employed as a speechwriter for both President Reagan and President Bush. She is credited with turning Bush from a "wimp"—rhetorically speaking—into the "aggressive" leader of armies he subsequently became. She is also credited with inventing some of the most successful clichés, such as "read my lips" and "thousand points of light."

We will encounter Ms. Noonan as these essays continue.

People in Glass Houses

Now that all pious folk are having a great hoot dumping on Jim Wright [formerly Speaker of the House of Representatives]—as if the politician ever existed who did not goniff a bit here and there—it's time we pinned down a thing or two. Mr. Wright has been cited by an *ethics committee*—God be praised—of the House of Representatives, an organization that occupies a glass house on the banks of the Potomac River. He is charged with unethical conduct.

Now just what is this thing called *ethics*? The media, which not only judges but frequently oversees the crucifixion as well, are never quick to explain; but one would think that with all this talk of ethics bandied about, some explanation of what the word means is due. So let's take it word for word from the Second Edition of *Webster's New International Dictionary*:

> ETHICS: The science of moral duty; more broadly, the science of the ideal human character and the ideal ends of human action. The chief problems with which ethics deals concern the nature of the *summum bonum*, or highest good, the origin and validity of the sense of duty, and the character and authority of moral obligation. The principal ethical theories are: First, such as consider happiness to be the greatest good; these may be egoistic, as is usually the case with hedonistic and eudaemonistic theories, or altruistic, as utilitarianism. Second, theories of perfectionism or self-realization. Third, theories resting on the relation of man to the universe or to divine law, as Stoicism, abolitionism, Christian ethics. Intuitionism and empiricism in ethics are doctrines opposed with respect to the character of the sense of duty. Absolute ethics affirms an unchanging moral code; relative ethics regards moral rules as varying with human development.

Ethics in Congress? Ethical Committee? Ethical judgments in the House of Representatives? Who was it who said, "Let he who is without sin cast the first stone!"

Ethics in Congress?

Are these the same lot of clowns who clapped hands and danced a jig of approval when Mr. Bush decided to send millions of dollars more of our money—remember, it's always our money—to the Contras, so that they might continue to murder women and children and threaten to overthrow a legal government?

And do I hear even a whisper out of that great chamber of ethics as the murder squads, which we train and equip, continue their grisly work in El Salvador, where they have already put more than 60,000 people to death?

And when the Exxon oil spill threatened the ecology of one of the richest fisheries in Alaska, did I hear that august "ethical" body we have been discussing, call for immediate Government aid to clean up the water, or did they vote to punish Exxon—or, for that matter, have they ever passed one meaningful bill that would reverse the destruction of our air and water and lakes and forests?

And when our President—Mr. Gentler and More Compassionate himself—endorsed the nuttiest and most frightening idea of the century, to put our most powerful atomic warheads on railroad cars and keep rolling them around the country, did our keepers of the *summum bonum*, namely that "ethical" body called Congress, come up with even a whisper of outrage?

Ah, well, I could go on and on, and that won't change one of those curious characters who live to be re-elected and only to be re-elected, and who year after year go through their charades of being the representatives of the people of the United States.

(But Jim Wright, they say, is unethical, and they're going to get him or know the reason why. They're going to make an example of him, all right, they're going to show these Democrats that they're just as damn well crooked as the other side of the House.)

It's not that these low-lifes we elect to public office are not, with very few exceptions, crooks of one magnitude or another, with little in their heads other than to milk the public. We've known that, and did you ever hear a kid say that he wanted to grow up to be a politician? Both Mark Twain and H.L. Mencken put themselves on record to that effect, and we've survived Boss Tweed and a hundred thousand like him. It's part of being a democracy, and a thousand times better a small goniff than some fascist bastard who calls for honesty according to his own lights. But what troubles me is when a group like the House of Representatives closes its eyes to the filth and deception and cowardice and insane military and foreign policies that are destroying our nation, and fixes on Jim Wright for the kind of thing every politician does to one extent or another; and then claims virtue. And that's not new either.

May 15, 1989

The Fuzzy Boundaries of Ethics

Twenty-five hundred years after Socrates, a large part of what H.L. Mencken called "Boobus Americanus" refuses to accept that a significant part of the human race is homosexual; and now it is suddenly stimulating news that Barney Frank, Congressman, is homosexual. Usually, news is of the fact, but Mr. Frank had already admitted to the fact of his sexual choice some time ago, and what now brings the media to excited attention is the revelation that he dallied with men. Well, what on earth did they expect of a homosexual?

This is all a part of what the House Ethics Committee considers its province, and they are beginning to sound like a parcel of deacons in old Salem. Congressman Donald E. Lukens was accused of contributing to the delinquency of a minor by having had sex with a 16-year-old. Well, by my measure, she already had sufficient of what they choose to call "delinquency" when she popped under the sheets with him; and if every male over 21 who had sex with a minor were to be lined up shoulder to shoulder, they'd reach from City Hall to Albany and maybe to Buffalo too. Congressman Gus Savage is accused of fondling a peace worker, and if she was indignant enough to be traumatized to the point of going public, why couldn't she just give him five across the face, which many thousands of women have been known to do in similar situations?

It all comes out of a thing called "ethics," and that's what confuses the situation so—at least for me. I frequently go to the dictionary to see what a word meant before the media bent it entirely out of recognition, and in this case, we have a definition of ethics as so: "That branch of philosophy dealing with values relating to human conduct, with respect to the rightness and wrongness of certain actions, and to the goodness and badness of the motives and ends of such actions." That, according to *The Random House Dictionary*, Second Edition.

And what a thorny path that leads us onto. When you raise the question of ethics, where do you begin and where do you end? The point is, does ethics, as seen by Congress, apply only to the sexual mores of the human male, or does it, as the dictionary would have it, reflect a general concept of *rightness and wrongness*? If the latter is the case, Congress should turn an angry and sour eye on the past 30 years, both in the Congress and in the White House. It should reflect on the malignant idiocies of Vietnam, Nicaragua, El Salvador and Afghanistan, on the thousands of lives lost, on the maimed and those made mad—for no reason that any sensible person could comprehend.

If, however, the ethics bunch in Congress is interested only in sex, they should become retroactive and recall that Thomas Jefferson took a black lady out of wedlock—whom he loved deeply—and had a number of children by her. Then there are the affairs of Benjamin

Franklin, famous in France and England, as well as in America, and his diverting essay on why young men (presumably minors) should bed down with older women, thereby enlightening themselves and bringing a bit of joy to older citizens. (Or is there no delinquency when the male is the younger?) And John F. Kennedy? Well, if even half the women who go around claiming to have bedded down with him are telling the truth, he was a man of singular accomplishments. But before we pin any medals of that sort on his memory, let's think about the father of our country, a fine and wonderful man whom I have loved all my life.

We go back to 1938. My new bride and I are in the Genealogical Room of the New York Public Library. It is filled with paper boxes of personal letters, hundreds of thousands of historic letters that have, for the most part, never been read or catalogued. We choose at random, and Bette, my wife, finds a letter that makes her cry out in delight. We copied it, of course, but the words are engraved on both our memories. It was dated 1818, and it was written by one of General Washington's staff officers in reply to a letter addressed to him.

The letter he was replying to came from a lady in New Jersey, who desired to know whether General Washington had ever slept at her mother's house. In answer, the staff officer wrote, in part:

"I do not know, madam, whether the General ever stayed the night at your mother's house, but since he [bedded down] every lady of quality in the Jerseys, he must have spent at least a few hours there."

An exaggeration, no doubt, but what a noble one! Truly, the father of our country, and as for Barney Frank, God give us a hundred like him in the Congress of the United States, and I don't give a fiddler's fig who or what they bed down with. A hundred like him, intellectually and ideologically, would give the whole world a chance to breathe more freely.

As for the ethics committee, sniff around HUD and the rest of Mr. Reagan's cheerleaders in Congress, and leave honest men alone.

September 25, 1989

It's No Joke

There's an old saying that you can't saw sawdust; it's been done already. Can you joke about a joke? But the joke is already a joke, which makes it pretty hard for an old gadfly who tries to say something about society. In an amazing picture in *The New York Times* of June 14, Mr. Quayle is shown holding a huge rapid-fire junior cannon of some kind, while he gibbers about human rights in a country [El Salvador] where American-trained murder squads have already killed some 60,000 people.

At the same time, a foolish old man accepts the Order of the Bath—a sort of quasi-knighthood—from Margaret Thatcher. This man, of course, was for eight years President of the United States, during which he did his best to wreck a country so strong that even his nutty notions could not quite push it over the edge. How do you do the joke? Well, you could guess that he forgot that he was President and believes he was king. But that makes a crummy Order of the Bath too small potatoes, unless perhaps Margaret Thatcher really believes that she is the queen, and since the Empress of the Indies went the way of all flesh, Empress of all the Americas will do. Perhaps this line of thinking led Mr. Quayle to assert that he was "glad to be in the Honduras," when he was actually in El Salvador.

How do you joke about a joke? It's true that the image of Ronnie kneeling to receive his O.T.B. will provide cartoonists with ammunition for the next 12 months or so, but can we go on with cutouts from *Mad* magazine? We are not a collection of goons here in the United States; we are the most astonishing and marvelous society ever put together, and the men who wrote the Constitution were a collection of the noblest intellects ever gathered together on this planet. We are a family of nations who live together in peace within our borders, and nowhere else on earth is this true. Yet this preposterous, stupid, uneducated little fool named Quayle wanders around the earth, spouting his idiocies in our name. It's a black, black joke. How can we joke about it and let it go at that?

He urges Roberto d'Aubisson to respect human rights; does he know who Mr. d'Aubisson is? The most casual reading of *The Times* or the *Washington Post* or *The New York Observer*, for that matter, would tell him about Mr. d'Aubisson and the death squads in El Salvador. Does he know anything? I wouldn't dare to charge him with ever having read a book, but one must ask whether he ever read a newspaper. He talks about Marxism–Leninism constantly, but I bet a fat bag of potatoes that he doesn't know whether Mr. Marx is alive or dead, and that if you told him that Lenin was once mayor of Carson City, he'd agree. If he can read, which is a moot question, I would guess he never read a page of what Marx or Lenin wrote, but then neither did most of the folk in government, so I don't know what that proves.

It all comes down to jokes. The old fool who got his O.T.B. appointed a gentleman to look over and care for our parks and woods, and the bespectacled idiot he appointed, a born-again fundamentalist Christian, believed, body and soul, that Armageddon was just around the corner and, that being the case, his job was to sell off the public forests and parkland just as quickly as possible and make quick bucks for his friends before doomsday. (And for those of you who haven't dipped into your fundamentals, Armageddon is the last great battle between good [us] and evil [Soviets], where the good, merciful God that these folk worship is going to make a killing that will make Hiroshima look like a picnic.)

Again, the joke–but it is also absolutely crazy, as crazy as the story that goes around that Mr. Bush chose Mr. Quayle so that he could not be impeached if all the stuff about Iran came out.

Do we actually live in a total loony-bin? One could breathe a sigh of relief as the various and sundry embezzlements, frauds, swindles and outright thefts at Housing and Urban Development under Mr. Reagan begin to emerge. This is good, solid, old-fashioned thievery, a proper concomitant of American politics. It gives one the feeling that there is ground under our feet. Not even Jimmy Walker would have complained on a trip to Latin America that he was sorry he had never learned to speak Latin, and not even Boss Tweed would have apologized for the vigorish that flowed through his hands with an excuse like Armageddon.

You may argue that case and tell me that nowhere in the American Constitution is there an article that calls for an I.Q. over 80 as a requisite for public office. You'd be right. Nobody thinks of everything.

July 3, 1989

Nobody Is Without Sin

A few weeks ago, writing in *The New York Times*, Harrison Salisbury reflected on the incidents in Tiananmen Square and put forth his opinion that the Chinese were deficient in such "democratic" qualities as compassion and respect for human life. With his wealth of experience, Mr. Salisbury should have known better, but his opinion is widely shared. It is very difficult for some to imagine that people whose facial features and skin color differ from ours are really human at all, and because we are willing to rob these people of their humanity and reduce them to the status of intelligent, slightly subhuman animals we have been able to kill them in great numbers without troubling our "democratic" conscience.

Not only have we killed untold numbers of Asians and Africans, but as late as 1920, guides for hire in Northern California would lead hunters to where a frightened remnant of an Indian tribe lived or existed, so that these brave hunters might slay the biggest "game" of all, defenseless, terrified Indians.

We are a most remarkable people. Here in the West, in North and South America and in Europe, the prevailing religion is Christianity. Since most wars in this area were fought in the name of the God the Christians worshipped and—of course—with God on their side, regardless of which side that was, the concept of "compassion" becomes a bit slippery.

We really are not very interested in the religion of others, but anyone who will take the time to read a little about Buddhism cannot help but understand that of all religions, this is the most gentle, the most forgiving. The religion of the Compassionate Buddha preaches the love of all things that live, and simple, ultimate forgiveness. Nowhere has this religion reached higher and purer levels than in China; and even the Tao, a much wider Chinese philosophy, is a thing of sensibility and purity.

Mr. Bush, however, has been very reticent to go along with the kind of rhetoric with which Congress greeted the events in Tiananmen Square. His critique of Chinese stupidity—and while they are a very ancient and wise civilization, their leaders can be very stupid at times—was muted, and he made it clear that he was not going to rush to judgment nor adopt a moral position, such as that expressed by Harrison Salisbury. Practically all of the media folk, talkers and writers, expressed amazement and astonishment at this. What on earth could Mr. Bush be up to?

I bow in amazement and confusion. Not only in this incident, but on dozens of other occasions, newspaper commentators have pleaded ignorance and bewilderment when it comes to an explanation of the most obvious facts. In all the jabbering about the war in Vietnam, the media experts hewed to our duty to defend South Vietnam, our need to halt the spread of Communism, our pledges to the scruffy lot that ruled the South and, of course, our fear of the domino effect. But nobody—absolutely nobody—mentioned molybdenum, of which there is a great deal in Vietnam and which is indispensable for the manufacture of rockets, missiles and fighting planes; and of course the potentially enormous off-shore oil fields.

Whereupon, one must forgive Mr. Bush his lack of rhetoric and remember that his deepest loyalty is to the $16 billion that American banks and business have invested in China. You don't play footsie with that kind of money and you don't get cute about morality and compassion. Hell, Turkey and Iraq have slaughtered, gassed, murdered the Kurds like crazy these past 10 years but it's no use being indignant or compassionate about them because Turkey and Iraq have sewn up all the mineral rights in that corner of the world, and who gives a damn about the Kurds. We don't have a nickel invested in Kurdistan, and Turkey is a good "friend" because it gives us the rights to listening posts along the Soviet border and in return we sell it good modern weapons so that the Turks can murder Kurds in a civilized way, instead of gassing them as Iraq does.

I wish that Harrison Salisbury had balanced out his history a bit before he pronounced a moral judgment on Chinese civilization. We are a motley crew here on earth, and there's nobody without sin to cast the first stone. But if we are ever to learn to live in peace, we must come to recognize that we are all of us "homo sapiens," for better or worse, not nations but a family of man.

August 4, 1989

The Men Who Become President

Paul Nitze, in his book of memoirs that will be published in a few months, has this interesting observation on the nature of Lyndon Johnson and his state of mind during the Vietnam War: "General Krulak, a tough marine general who had fought at Guadalcanal and many other battles in World War II and killed many an enemy, came into my office one day after briefing the president. Krulak was visibly shaken. After being briefed on the difficulties the Marines were encountering in locating and engaging the Vietcong, the president had risen from his chair, his face dark with anger, and with his fist pounding the desk for emphasis, exclaimed: 'Kill the goddamn bastards, kill 'em, kill 'em, kill 'em!' "

No wonder Krulak was "visibly shaken"; he was standing before a man who, if not already clinically insane, was well on the road toward paranoia, and the same man was in the position of being the most powerful man on the face of the earth—a man who could with a brief order consign the human race to atomic destruction.

It was more or less at the time when the director Stuart Rosenberg was invited to the White House to coach Johnson on appropriate behavior before the television cameras. Returning from his task, Stuart said to us, "It was hopeless. How do you tell the President of the United States to stop picking his nose in public and stop lifting his leg to fart every time he felt a bit of gas in his belly, and how do you tell him that his favorite word, 'chickenshit,' should be reserved for more private moments?"

Of course, these are nonessential bits of behavior; one wants to think of his President as a gentleman, and even his penchant for swimming nude in the White House pool, while reporters attended him, might be put aside as a harmless bit of exhibitionism, and who is to say that the manners of other Presidents were much better?

Nevertheless we are faced with a very important question—namely, why should a country that leads the world in creativity, that produces the best physicists, the leading physicians, the most exciting artists in every discipline, inventive engineers in every aspect of modern life be unable to place in leadership men of character, compassion and wisdom? Why must a country as wonderful as ours be doomed to be led by the kind of man who wins the Presidency?

It's a question worth pondering, for something is deeply wrong in our method of choosing leadership. As a child, I remember listening to discussions about Warren G. Harding—with a child's wonder that this man could have been President of the United States. In the 1930's, I read Walter Millis's book, *The Martial Spirit*, concerning the life and times of Theodore Roosevelt, reading of this fuzzy-minded man who so often functioned in an unreal world, a kind of simple-minded adult Boy Scout—even while his head was being sculpted on Mount Rushmore along with Jefferson and Washington and Lincoln. More recently, I watched the ignoble drama of Richard

Nixon, and then, to cap it, the election of a second-rate Hollywood actor to the highest position in the land. And today, of course, we have Dan Quayle, a heartbeat away from the most powerful position on the face of the earth.

It's simply not enough to say, God help us, to pray and to believe in Mr. Bush's low blood pressure. It's time that we inquired into the machinery that puts this kind of man in office. The few examples I gave are by no means singular; more of the same winds a path back through our history.

I think of these things because we are confronted by the heartbreaking problem of the hostages. It's not that Mr. Bush is at fault; he simply inherits a White House that for decades has been home to scrambled brains. It is not only that he inherited the hostage crisis from Ronald Reagan; he also inherited an executive office long bereft of common sense. He inherited a Central Intelligence Agency that might well be called the Central Unintelligent Agency, which should have had its men in Lebanon years before and which should have been able to pluck the hostages out when they were taken. The failure of the CIA becomes a central and glaring fact in the present crisis, and of course the blame must rest in the White House. A succession of Presidents nurtured the CIA to a point where it became a government within a government, an absolutely loony organization dedicated to the preservation of Latin American dictatorships and little else.

So we have Mr. Bush with few cards to play, and that is a pity. He is the victim of Presidents who preceded him, and we are all of us victims of a system that ennobles stupidity and insensitivity and makes that a pathway to the Presidency.

August 21, 1989

The Price of Truth

The cable company Home Box Office should be congratulated for its release of a very important film, *Tailspin: Behind the Korean Airliner Tragedy*. It is a bold and daring film, which sets out to tell the truth about what happened to KAL Flight 007.

According to this film, only minutes after the airliner was known to have been destroyed by a Russian fighter, U.S. Air Force intelligence suspected that the shootdown had been a ghastly mistake on the part of the Soviets, and in the next few hours, putting together a set of brilliant deductions, the Air Force had close to absolute proof that this was the case.

Ignoring this, the (indicated) National Security Council goes into a frenzy of anti-Soviet hatred, charging this was an act of unforgivable savagery on the part of the Soviets, with one character—facsimile Zbigniew Brzezinski—ready to begin World War III, acting out a frenzy of anti-Soviet hatred. The media, picking up on a groundless, witless speech hurriedly written for President Reagan to read, parrots the Washington gang, flinging every imaginable accusation at the Russians. (Remember the control and judiciousness of the media when we shot down the Iranian passenger plane.) The Air Force chief, one of the Joint Chiefs of Staff, who has seen the evidence of the Soviet mistake, who knows Air Force intelligence is right in their conclusion that there was no way the Russian pilot could know that this was a passenger plane, nevertheless backs the false evidence of the White House. Voting together with the others of the Joint Chiefs, he condemns the Soviets for a vile atrocity and fires the intelligence officer who worked out the proof.

All this is presented with meticulous care for detail—certainly backed by good and sufficient proof. It leaves any sensible viewer cold with horror at how lightly these men play with war and peace and the fate of the human race; and my own impotence as a viewer left me in despair. However, it did bring home a fact of importance beyond the disgusting mendacity it displayed—namely, that perhaps our most dangerous enemies are not the Soviets but the neurotic and brainless men who are appointed to the executive branch of our Government and who play Russian roulette with the human race.

What an awful, unbridgeable gap exists between that strange, white tombstone-like city called Washington and the United States of America. If you include the slums with the Federal part of the city, you have the highest murder rate, the highest crime rate and the worst drug problem in the United States; and even this sickness in their own back yard does not appear to touch them or influence them. They play with the most dangerous weapons the world has ever known, and never is there even a hint that they are aware of this. The Constitution, which they are ready to chatter about at the drop of a hat, has written into it that only Congress should have the power to declare war, yet all our wars and military lunacies since 1945 have been without declaration by Congress.

The cold-blooded destruction of the career of the intelligence officer who put together the truth about 007 in the film *Tailspin* is symbolic of the action taken against almost every honest, decent American who came forward to reveal some aspect of the corruption that riddles the Federal Government, and Michael Moriarty plays the role splendidly. The film is not a projection, not a piece of What If . . . or It Could Have Happened, as was the case in *Executive Action*, the very fine film about what might have happened in the murder of John F. Kennedy. It is very much a cold, factual documentary, and it says something about the power that exists in the First Amendment to the Constitution. If that ever goes, if the power of the First Amendment to the Constitution is ever subverted, if a condition arises in America that makes the production of a film like *Tailspin* impossible, then we will cease to be even the shadow of a democracy that we are.

September 18, 1989

A Flight of Fancy, Grounded

Some things can be explained, and other things defy explanation—not miracles as such, but quirks and twists in that marvelous infinity that we call the universe. It was such a thing that happened on the morning of Thanksgiving Day in 1989. The people of the United States awakened to hear that the city of Washington, D.C., had disappeared.

No, it had not been bombed, and no great fire had raged through it. It simply disappeared, quietly, gently, leaving soft gray dust where once the Government buildings, so reminiscent of an oversized cemetery, had stood.

Understandably, the first reaction was a sort of panic. Every television crew in the country was dispatched to where Washington had been. But in spite of a brilliant collection of pundits, anchormen, college professors, Nobel Prize winners, and even old Walter Cronkite (pulled out of retirement on this momentous occasion), not one of them could come up with an answer or even an idea. Prof. G.I. Know of Georgia Tech found that the gray dust was closer to cement than to anything else, and he suggested that as much of it as possible should be mined and packed away before it rained and turned the whole surface into rock. Loved ones of those who had disappeared pleaded for emergency digs, convinced that everything was buried under the gray dust, but a succession of sinkholes convinced everyone that there had been no cover-up. The city was simply gone.

Seeking some explanation in the past, a leading poet recalled "The Pied Piper of Hamlin," where the magical piper, rejected by the town he had helped, had led the children into a tunnel across the earth; he suggested that Washington would certainly reappear somewhere. But theologians, having a field day, worked Sodom and Gomorrah as never before, and church attendance reached an all-time high. A few thoughtful pastors reminded their flocks that this had happened on Thanksgiving Day.

The panic that had momentarily gripped the nation wore off sooner than might have been expected. Strangely enough, life went on. Industry functioned. Children went to school. Police departments did their thing, and garbage was collected as usual. The disappearance of the central post office in Washington hardly interrupted the flow of mail. However, a number of things absent created curiosity if not regret—among them, the Treasury Department and the Pentagon. While the military men struggled to sort out and put together some way of functioning, the governors of the various states got together and decided that in the absence of the Treasury, it was obvious that the taxes, once Federal, belonged to the people who paid them and thereby to the people's government.

With the Pentagon gone and without the billions paid to keep the White House and the Congress going and the billions paid to the army of Washington bureaucrats, the states were flooded with money. Unemployment disappeared; wages increased, and the rebuilding of the infrastructure of every American city was immediately undertaken. The gigantic infusion of cash brought a prosperity never dreamed of. Free state hospitals blossomed; new schools and newly trained teachers appeared everywhere. The hazardous dump-sites were cleaned up in a matter of months. Creches for children appeared everywhere, and the drug problem receded in the face of people who worked too hard and dreamed too much to be bitten by drugs. New modern railroads were built, and as a result of the enormous urban renewal, theater and music reached heights never seen before.

With no Pentagon to nurture them, soldiers drifted back to civilian life, where good jobs were waiting. Even officers, even colonels and generals, their pensions gone with the Pentagon, discovered that it was possible to work for a living and make out. All over the planet, people came together in their houses of worship and prayed for the same miracle that had turned the United States of America into a land of wealth and sanity. A new center of government was put together, where those who served the people were provided with the necessities of life and no more, where campaign chests were limited to $100 a head and where candidates had to take intelligence tests before they could appear on the ballot.

As for Washington, it did rain, leaving a great field of concrete that was the perfect base for the new national space station. There was money for that now—there was money for everything.

And then of course, the silly man who wrote the above awakened from his daydream and turned on the booby-box to watch President Bush trying to figure out how he could invade Panama without actually invading it.

* * *

Having written the above in an afternoon flight of fancy, I opened *The New York Times Magazine* of October 15 and read Peggy Noonan's incredible tale of her experience as a speechwriter in the Reagan White House. Her descriptions of Reagan as an almost-deaf, halting fool, of Nancy as a sort of supervisory witch and pudgy Maureen Reagan as a bullying top-sergeant in the White House setup were not exactly new, but coming from the pen of a proudly conservative, pretty young woman whose knowledge of history and politics were, by her own admission, primitive at best—a young woman elected by no one, in an appointment confirmed by no part of the Government, but who nevertheless was the voice and mind of the Government—they were indeed something to think about.

Certainly, Ms. Noonan's reminiscences set me to thinking. Her proudest claim was that her words were not changed. Her voice was the President's voice. Her ideas were his. His most casual remarks came from her nimble pen. Her description of Government had Mike Deaver and a circle of yuppies as the pathfinders for the executive branch of Government, with the two Reagan women, the anorexic and the pudge, playing pilot and co-pilot.

Is it all one gigantic joke played on a couple of hundred million people who dutifully dig into their pockets every year and come up with the billions that make the Government payroll? Is there anything there on the Potomac worth more than 20 cents? Is it in all truth the biggest shakedown in human history? Will the American people someday ask what they are getting for their money? Or was Benjamin Franklin right?

Why Benjamin Franklin? Because he suggested that not the eagle but the turkey become our national symbol.

October 30, 1989

The Comic, the Tragic, and the Compassionate

It's not easy to squeeze a bit of humor out of the clowns who perform from day to day in what some call "politics." They are all the stand-up comics and the straight men rolled into one, with their stage on the uneasy edge of a volcano. A writer cannot invent such things, because who would believe said inventions? A government invests more than a billion dollars to build a goofy black airplane that is supposed to be radarproof. Then the Australians come up with a radar development that does away with the Stealth bomber's cloak of invisibility, but voices around the Pentagon answer that it doesn't make much difference, since they never expected the damn thing would fly; but Congress remains unmoved because to do away with the Stealth bomber at half a billion dollars a throw would put several thousand people out of work.

Come on! Who can invent such things?

And President Bush gives the CIA the license to kill—just like James Bond. Not everyone, you must understand; you can't just go around killing anyone who gets in your way—that's war, and you work war differently—but on a selective basis, singling out such characters as Manuel Noriega and his ilk.

And what—oh, what—has happened to the compassionate Mr. Bush? You know, it was the astonishing Peggy Noonan, speech writer for both Mr. Reagan and Mr. Bush who invented the "compassionate" Mr. Bush.

As Ms. Noonan put it, she had to get rid of the "wimp effect," which she did brilliantly, yet maintain the image of a man who "cared." Enter the "compassionate." It is interesting to note that in the annals of human history, the man whose name is linked to compassion, as an absolute definition, is the Buddha, the Compassionate Buddha, who preached love and life for all living things. What a position to put Mr. Bush into!

But there you are. The power of a woman is always underestimated, and since Mr. Bush danced to the tune, creating a thousand points of light to keep him company, he must perforce pay the piper. It never occurred to him that the Congress, which is mostly out to lunch, would come up with a bill that obligated the Federal Government to pay for abortions in the case of rape and incest. It had simply never occurred to Mr. Bush—I don't imagine too many things occur to him—that a child of 13, raped by her own father, might be too poor to pay for an abortion and would have to compound the initial tragedy by carrying to term and extending the agony into years to come. Nor could it have occurred to him that a woman raped by a man with AIDS might be doomed to deliver a child with AIDS, a child also doomed. Whereupon, Mr. Bush announced he would veto the bill.

To quote *The New York Times*: "Mr. Bush has been criticized for a disparity in his position because he supports abortions in the case of rape and incest for women who can afford them but not in cases of rape and incest for poor women who need Federal funds."

Well, what else is new? Of course, one must have *compassion* for the rich. How could Mr. Bush ever have become President of the United States without the rich? Can there be people so benighted and uninformed that they do not know that TV commercials cost money, lots of money, lots and lots of money? How does a writer invent this kind of thing? He'd be hooted out of every publishing house on Park Avenue South. Maureen Dowd, who wrote the *New York Times* dispatch that I quoted above, gets away with it because she is writing the truth, and I do admire the calm matter-of-fact manner in which she narrates the doings on the Potomac, conveying the wonderful sense of a loony bin that is costly but rarely functional.

But I began this piece bewailing the difficulties in burlesquing the doings of a clown show. How far is humor from tragedy? The clown takes a pratfall and we laugh, but the resulting back injury could torture him the rest of his life. The games played in the White House are not only comical, but tragic too, and they bring pain and misery to all too many citizens.

But in the deepest sense, they are the capers of a clown, who, like Pagliacci, begs for tears and laughter at the same time. When one contemplates this scene, one finds less of evil than a murky lack of comprehension, an absence of even minimal common sense. Have many of them thought through the crazy consequences of the law to make burning the flag a crime? Is the postage stamp with the flag on it included? When is a flag not a flag? How about a T-shirt with the flag on it? And the paper flags that abound? Can one shred them? And if a woman has a scarf designed as a flag—and millions of them are around—can she burn it, sit on it, cut it?

Dostoevsky said, "Compassion is the chief law of human existence." And we have Mr. Bush, the "compassionate President."

Could any writer invent this kind of thing?

November 6, 1989

One Loony Week

The trouble with doing a weekly column is that one is forced to omit or skip too lightly over the day-to-day looniness. For example, no sooner had President Bush declared that he was eminently satisfied with the performance of Vice President Quayle, up popped young Dan with the following: "It's too early for me to think of my own Presidential ambitions."

Now this deserves at least a column, if only to ponder Dan Quayle's claim to mentation. But then up came the latest caper of that strange organization that calls itself the Congress of the United States, and it made me wonder whether, considering the normal flow of intelligence in Washington, I had not done Mr. Quayle an injustice. You see, this past April, Dick Cheney, Secretary of Defense, canceled Grumman Corporation's contract for the production of the F–14D Tomcat Fighter. This meant the loss of 5,650 jobs at the big Long Island defense plant.

Now our sensitive and compassionate Congress leaped into the gap. Here were 5,650 men about to be fired. Did they offer these workers compensation, the creation of new ecological jobs, training with ample pay, training that would lead to the building of a new hospital; new schools; other construction; housing; railroad overpasses needed so desperately on Long Island; air-cushion trains, so long on the drawing boards, these or a hundred other necessities? Oh, no—no indeed.

Instead, these worthies whom we elect each year decided to save the jobs by giving Grumman a contract for 18 Navy planes that were not needed and would never be used, which would cost the taxpayers a cool billion dollars. And we are told that this was not only a noteworthy triumph for the Long Island contingent of Congressmen, but that they worked their fingers to the bone for six months to get it through.

(Blessed are the peacemakers, for theirs is the Kingdom of Heaven), but sometimes the pie is not only in the sky, but right down here on earth.

Consider the following. It comes from a magazine called the *Washington Monthly*, one of the handful of great magazines published in this country, and from the pen of its editor, Charles Peters:

> The District of Columbia has one of the largest police forces in the country. We also have the National Park Police, the Uniformed Branch of the Secret Service and the Capital Police. Since they do not seem to be preventing the daily round of murders to which we have become accustomed, what do these fellows do all day? We can't speak for all of them but we can tell you how 40 members of the Capital Police recently spent three days. They traveled to the Greenbrier Hotel in White Sulphur Springs, West Virginia, to serve as "a protective detail" for House Democrats who were holding a conference at the resort.

This beauty deserves a couple of columns. I'd have to dig around a bit. I have been to the Greenbrier, a very beautiful place that calls for a lot of hard-earned bucks from anyone who cares to sample its delights. We were there in the years before inflation; what their prices are today I can only imagine. And did the 40 cops stay at the Greenbrier? And who picked up their tab? Tell me that the Congressmen did, and I'll jump through 20 hoops. Also, as anyone who has ever been there will tell you, the Greenbrier is the last place in the world where a guest might be in any sort of danger, and anyway, no one shoots Congressmen. Why should they?

About the conference referred to, I have no information. Possibly the Democratic National Committee picked up the tab, possibly—all things are possible—the Congressmen paid their own tabs. Such things have happened, or have they? If the taxpayer paid—oh, no—I may be an old cynic, but even I wouldn't go that far.

Let me try to be serious, not an easy thing when contemplating politics today. The old saw that we grew up with was an easy "Every politician is a crook." Easy but not true; we have had great politicians, selfless politicians. I often think of old John Quincy Adams, who as President fought the Southern slavers tooth and nail, and who, after being President, was elected to Congress by his Massachusetts neighbors, not as a Senator but as a member of the House, and who carried on the struggle and died, there in the House of Representatives, challenging the slave-state Congressmen. There have been great ones in American politics, and there are a handful of great ones now. There are also all too many who fit no polite description.

November 20, 1989

A Champion of Ignorance

"A penny for your thoughts," I said to D'emas, who, as I've mentioned before in this space, is a poor, unlettered primitive from a faraway land.

"Well," he said uneasily, "I begin to feel that I am getting a handle on the American way of life, and then it eludes me entirely."

"How's that?"

"This man Quayle—well, he was elected by the same people who elected George Bush, who is President, and who thinks what is happening in Russia is a great thing for the human race, but Mr. Quayle thinks just the opposite."

"Oh, no, D'emas," I explained gently. "Mr. Quayle doesn't think."

"Oh, come on now, can a man get up in the morning and shower and dress himself and go to his office without thinking?"

"Millions do, but I was being facetious. The fact of the matter is that Mr. Quayle helps to reassure the nuttier elements in Mr. Bush's constituency that an atomic holocaust with the Soviet Union is not entirely out of the question."

"Good heavens," D'emas exclaimed, "do they actually want an atomic holocaust? Don't they understand that everyone would die, themselves included?"

"There's no way of telling, because, like Mr. Quayle, they don't think."

"I'm so eager to learn the American way of life," D'emas said unhappily, "and I'm never sure whether you're telling me the truth about things or not."

"I try, D'emas—I do try."

"What can you think of me when you offer me a penny for my thoughts?"

"Oh, no. I was not putting you down. It's simply an expression. You could say it to your best friend."

"But a penny is such a poor, worthless thing. Do you know, I have never found a single item that you can buy for a penny. Everyone I ask hates them."

"Clutter up our pockets," I agreed. "I have the damn things. But when the expression 'a penny for your thoughts' originated, many years ago, a penny was worth something. Not today."

"They why don't they stop minting them?" D'emas asked.

"Oh, no. That would be a disaster. You see, D'emas, at least 20 million families in America save pennies. No one wants to carry them around, so they throw them into jars and piggy banks. Say each collection averages five pounds. That comes to 100 million pounds of pennies, or about 50 thousand tons of copper. The Government would stop buying copper to replace the millions of pounds of copper used to make those pennies that pour into the piggy banks, and the copper companies would go bankrupt and thousands of men and women would be thrown out of work."

"That's absolutely amazing," D'emas admitted. "I never realized how marvelously complex your society is. I am trying not to be upset, but I'm sure you would ask Mr. Quayle the same question."

"Oh?" He had me confused at this point.

"What I meant," D'emas explained, "is that if you were a good friend of Mr. Dan Quayle, as I liked to think you were of me, you would say to him, 'Danny boy, a penny for your thoughts?' "

I thought about that for a while before I admitted that it was possible that I would use the same idiom. "But I wouldn't be putting a price on his thoughts—any more than I might put a price on yours."

"But you said he had no thoughts," D'emas protested.

"Yes, yes, I did, but it's a different way of defining a thought. I certainly did not mean to suggest that faced with stomach cramps, Mr. Quayle could not find his way to a bathroom. John Ford, the director, once said of another famous director that said director could not direct a diarrhea victim to a toilet—only Mr. Quayle was not meant to convey any comparison with the above. We know that President Reagan could read because he did read the speeches that Peggy Noonan wrote for him, but he had apparently never read a book all the way through, and, after all, nothing in the Constitution requires a President to be literate, so we can hardly put down the old thespian for ignorance. With Mr. Quayle, it's somewhat different. It is certainly not unfair to expect that a Vice President should know that the people in Latin America do not speak Latin. It's not simply that Mr. Quayle displays ignorance; it's his devoted and dedicated belief in ignorance that makes one wonder whether he ever engaged in the process of thought. And my remark, D'emas, has absolutely nothing to do with the idiom."

"Still and all," D'emas said, accepting my apology gracefully, "I would be happier if you did not offer me a penny for my thoughts in the future."

December 15, 1989–January 1, 1990

The Mind of George Bush

Some writers walk; others sit and brood; I'm a novelist who walks. You get a notion and then it swims around in your mind. A character is joined by others, they move, they relate, and sometimes it plays out before a mile or two of walking is over, and then you shove it into the background of your memory and look around for something else.

I did this with "The Mind of George Bush." The title fascinated me because I had to believe that somewhere, beyond the words of Peggy Noonan, there was a mind, a man, a beating heart, ductless glands and all the rest of the complex that makes up a human body. But then the key question became an endless enigma. *Where was the mind?* Where was the man? What was he, good, evil, incidental, absent on cloud 28, curious, compassionate—or simply missing? Out to lunch? Is it conceivable that a man can spend a lifetime, have an entire political career, be a part of executive administrations, head of the CIA and Vice President of the United States and be out to lunch for his entire career?

Take for example the case of New York City and the stray bullets. Now New York City is not simply the urban center of the United

States; it is the urban center of the entire world, and more than that, it is the factor that defines the art, literature and music of America. It is also a city where a significant section of the population is addicted to cocaine and where the sale of drugs resulted during 1989 in the deaths of 51 innocent bystanders, killed by stray bullets, many of them fired from rapid-fire assault weapons. Measure this against the fact that almost no similar deaths took place in any of the great European cities.

Enter the mind of George Bush and the reaction inexplicable and beyond explanation either in the words of Peggy Noonan or any other speechwriter:

1. He must know what is happening in New York. Even if he never reads a newspaper—as some rumors have it—he must occasionally watch TV. He could begin by banning the sale and manufacture of assault weapons in the United States. There is no conceivable reason why he does not do this. He could campaign for the national law for the registration of all firearms, with severe penalties for failure to do so. He could consult with the major police chiefs of the nation—all of whom have declared for the ban on assault weapons, all of whom oppose the unlicensed sale of handguns.
2. He could help New York bring the metropolitan police force up to par by returning to New York funds withheld by a nasty Reagan Administration that thought only of punishing the city it hated.
3. He could shrink the Pentagon and double the size of the Coast Guard and the Drug Enforcement Agency.

There are three very simple and easy actions George Bush could take. They are the merest beginning. He could ask Congress to stop sending millions to the medieval nuts who run El Salvador and to give the money to the Washington police who face a drug problem even worse than New York. He could also demand that Congress stop pouring money into the Contras, who murder nuns and do their own bit of drug running. He could build a job program for the inner cities that would give some incentive to life to kids who turn to drugs.

Now none of this is new or original or difficult in terms of the Administration. Cocaine does not choose between Democrats and Republicans, between black and white, or for that matter between rich and poor. So the mystery is less what to do than where these things reflect in the mind of George Bush. The media talk less and less of his "thousand points of light" with good reason; it was an invention so totally nutty and removed from reality that it is best forgotten. But what replaces it? I can't imagine that the death of a black child in the inner city, struck down by a stray bullet from an assault weapon, means any more to Mr. Bush than the deaths of the Panamanian children who died from American bullets in our glowing attack on Noriega and Panama, but surely he must understand that no Senator or Congressman or member of his Administration can walk the streets of the inner city where he lives and works without fear, without a danger to his or her life from stray bullets.

He must know this. It is simply impossible to believe that a man who once headed the Central Intelligence Agency does not know what goes on in his own backyard. It would be cute to say that he does not, and it is even possible that his predecessor did not know, but George Bush? Come on now!

So we return to the problem of an old novelist, who puts together his tales as he wanders the streets, and who is entranced by a title: "The Mind of George Bush." There has to be more to it than the simple excuse that he's out to lunch.

January 29, 1990

The Mother of Parliaments

In 1731, an English sea captain, name of Robert Jenkins, had too much to drink in a Spanish saloon and picked a fight with a Spanish customs guard. They both drew knives, and before their respective pals could pull them apart, Jenkins suffered a bad cut to his ear. The local surgeon could offer no remedy except to cut the ear off, and Jenkins, a man of vigor but little taste, refused to part with the severed member. He dried it in the sun and stowed it carefully in his sea chest.

Eight years later, with commercial rivalry between Spain and England at a fever pitch, a member of Parliament remembered hearing about the ear, found Jenkins, borrowed the sun-dried ear—somewhat disgusting at this point—rose up in the House of Commons, waved the ear and demanded to know whether captains in His Majesty's service were to undergo such pain and insult without recourse or punishment to the half-civilized offender. As one man, the House of Commons rose to cheer him—and so began the War of Jenkins's Ear in the year 1739.

I mention this odd bit of history because it became famous as a war contrived from the most frivolous of reasons or incidents. Perhaps future historians will find Mr. Reagan's war with Grenada and Mr. Bush's with Panama even more frivolous, and so take Jenkins off the hook.

However, I mention this case of Jenkins's ear less for the mockery of cause for a war than for the reaction from the benches of that great body that calls itself the mother of parliaments. Wars are fun, and if you don't believe that ask any of the hundreds of members of our Congress who rose to cheer Mr. Bush's unspeakable and rather brainless action in Panama.

Our Congress is a curious thing, indeed. Mark Twain asked, "Did you ever meet a small boy who said he wanted to grow up to be a Congressman?" This goes to the sensibility of small boys but explains nothing about that oafish, mindless, self-serving body that calls itself the Congress of the United States. The response of the British Parliament to the sight of Jenkins's ear might suggest that greed, self-service and stupidity are the inborn qualities of any "legislative" body, and the response of the previous Supreme Soviet to Mr. Gorbachev's first attempts at reform tend to bear this out. However, our Congress has its own unique code of behavior. When a bill came out guaranteeing the right of Chinese students to refuge in America, Congressmen rose as one to support it in a display of rhetorical enthusiasm not seen since they debated flag-burning. When Mr. Bush pleaded with his Republican troops to let him do the same thing by executive order, the Republican Congressmen found themselves trapped. If they chickened out now, at election time their Democrat opponents could accuse them of voting to send the youth of China back to the hangman's rope of a malignant Communist dictator, and since the only honest and incorruptible purpose of a Congressman is to be re-elected, the Republicans were trapped.

Of course Congress's concern for youth is a very curious, sometime thing. There was hardly a whisper of concern for the youths who were slaughtered uselessly in Vietnam, nor were members visibly upset by slaughter of youthful Marines in Lebanon. No cries of rage arose for the youths who died in the ultra-nutty attack on Grenada, and when the Government raided the churches in Arizona and arrested the youths who had fled the murder squads of El Salvador, there was hardly a whisper of annoyance from Congress, any more than there was ever a real cry of regret for the thousands and thousands of young men and women, a good many of them Americans, and some of them nuns and priests, murdered in El Salvador by death squads trained and armed by the United States.

But this "legislative" concern for youth and justice is most noticeable and most heartbreaking for its absence among those of us who elect Congressmen. Here in New York City, generations of boys and girls are being destroyed by dope, but Congressional action on the drug scene is so indifferent that it's hardly worthy of notice. The money dumped into the bottomless maw of the Pentagon will be larger in 1990 than it was in 1989, despite the disintegration of power in Eastern Europe, and even that increase in military spending—the increase alone—is more than what is allocated for the fight against drugs.

Ah, well, it's rather sad to recall that the rallying cry at the time of the birth of this nation was, "No taxation without representation!" It is also worth noting that the men who gathered together to form the Second Constitutional Congress, October 13, 1774, constituted, to quote Emerson, ". . . the most brilliant, gifted and wise community of men ever gathered together on this continent."

February 12, 1990

Who Destroys Our Home . . .

Sir Walter Scott's line "Breathes there the man with soul so dead who never to himself hath said, this is my own, my native land?" comes along in this year of 1990 as a sort of Victorian cliché, yet anyone who has traveled in Scotland can recognize the emotion. Or I might add, anyone who has traveled in America. Scotland is small and very beautiful. America is wide and wonderful and very beautiful, and when you come to know the forests, the snow-capped mountains, the endless prairie, the lagoons, the rivers, you become a part of it—if you have even a shred of emotion, even an ounce of sensitivity—you become a part of it, and if you are religious, you will thank God that this place was given to us.

On the other hand, if you were a politician who neither ploughed nor stitched but fattened his belly from the public trough, you might be utterly indifferent and put down what I have written above as errant nonsense. Do you remember when George Bush pledged himself to us as the environmental President—or perhaps was pledged thus by Peggy Noonan, since it's not easy to separate the early George Bush from Ms. Noonan's busy typewriter? Now Ms. Noonan has been replaced by one John H. Sununu, who politically is slightly to the right of Genghis Khan and who is neither as young nor as pretty as Ms. Noonan. As his record indicates, even for the short time he has been in the White House he appears to be not at all sure of who is President or what Presidential powers and duties are spelled out by the Constitution of the United States.

Practically all environmental scientists have come to agree that the earth is warming and that the pollutants largely responsible for this warming—which will have disastrous consequences for mankind—come in good measure from the United States. The conclusions were passed on to President Bush, and his speechwriters went to work on a speech that would spell out actions by America to help alter the process of earth warming. But Mr. Sununu, sensitive to the duty of government never to erode the profits of the rich, persuaded Mr. Bush to have the speech rewritten and to promise, instead of action, further study. Further study is an important part of the magic fuel that keeps Washington, D.C., vital and busy. Countless millions of the taxpayers' money is spent on further study. No laws to lessen pollution—until we choose a panel of worthies for further study. No help for this or that. Everything needs further study, and the endless parade of experts, professors, sundry mavens from the battalion of think tanks grows fat and prosperous out of further study.

But to return to Mr. Sununu. Let's consider his interests in wetlands. Wetlands are tidal areas, marshes, the unique combination of fish, fowl and water—such as the Everglades—that are priceless as well as beautiful. They act as giant filters against pollution; they give us food without end; they prevent floods, and if they are to be kept alive and vital, industry must stop polluting and destroying them in one way or another. But that will cost industry money, and if big business pays out money to preserve the wetlands, it will cut into profits, and any cut in profits, apparently, cuts deep into Mr. Sununu's heart.

So when William K. Reilly, Administrator of the Environmental

Protection Agency, put his stamp of approval on a Federal agreement to protect the nation's wetlands, our Mr. Sununu, White House Chief of Staff, leaped to the defense of the rich, and altered the agreement, cutting away at the parts that protected the wetlands from further development.

As with Mr. Bush, Ronald Reagan surrounded himself with people who put words in his mouth, who manipulated him, who were enraged when he attempted to take action that he believed would help the world and free us of the terror of atomic weapons—as in Iceland—but we were led to believe better of George Bush. His campaign promises were charged with such emotion that one was tempted to believe that they were sincerely his and not the bright sparks of Peggy Noonan.

However, Mr. Sununu has spoken, and I'm sure will speak again and again, so let us return to the beginning of this piece, the question of love for one's native land. I am sure we could find no more boastful or outspoken "patriots" than Mr. Bush and Mr. Sununu. Mr. Bush's jingoistic pronouncements have become so frequent and so shameless that he can't even face the possibility of peace and an end to the Cold War, and Mr. Sununu runs eagerly alongside him.

But do patriots destroy the land they claim to love? Do patriots foul the fields and streams and poison the atmosphere, all for the sake of a few extra bucks? This is our home, and who destroys our home is a criminal.

"Patriotism is the last refuge of a scoundrel," Samuel Johnson once wrote. Well said by a man who knew a thing or two.

February 20, 1990

Murderers and Liars Also Have Rights

Charles Peters, who edits a remarkable magazine called the *Washington Monthly*, wrote in his March issue:

> ... I might as well give you this cheery news about the "reform" regime we have installed in Panama. The new attorney general, Rogello Cruz, has been a director of a bank owned by one of the bosses of the Cali drug gang in Colombia. Guillermo Ford, the second vice president,

> is part owner of the Dadeland Bank of Florida, which according to The New York Times, "was named in a court case two years ago as a central financial institution for one of the biggest Medellin launderers." Guillermo Endara, the new president (of Panama), has for years been a director of a Panamanian bank frequently used by the Medellin gang.

For this happy result, we paid more than 20 American lives and innumerable injuries on our side and uncounted lives and injuries on the Panamanian side—as well as a bill presented to our taxpayers, a bill that will in time run to more than $1 billion.

Ah, well, no one looking at the scene ever argued that there was intelligence in Washington, but they do a large pitch about morality, ticking off this country and that country about neglect of human rights. Washington is very big on human rights. That's why they gave Panama the right to have a Government of ex–drug dealers, and that is why they continue to deal with and paste their blessing on the Government of China. After all, even Jeane Kirkpatrick approves of the Government of China.

Suppose we bypass the White House's CIA, an organization that knows everything about nothing, and look at the record of China in its dealing with a gentle, civilized Buddhist country called Tibet. In 1950, the Chinese invaded Tibet. They promised religious and personal freedom and for the next nine years they turned an ancient and happy society into a hell on earth. The Tibetan people then rebelled, and the rebellion was brutally crushed.

The Dalai Lama escaped to exile in India, but more than 80,000 Tibetans were put to death during the next few months by the democracy-loving Chinese. For the next 40 years, the killing of Tibetans by their Chinese "liberators" went on, a million and a half murdered of that relatively small population, until there was no family in Tibet that did not have a member murdered by the Chinese Communists. This heartless killing, not only in Tibet but in China proper, reached such horrifying proportions that it propelled Nikita Khrushchev to deliver his memorable speech to the Supreme Soviet, a speech that destroyed Stalinism once and forever and that gave warning to the Chinese Communists—a part of what led to the break between China and Russia.

But Presidents Nixon or Reagan or Bush never mentioned this horror. They were much too busy pushing investment in China and their own murderous policies in Central America. And while the horrors of Tiananmen Square produced pictures they could not evade, they doffed their lip service very quickly in deference to $16 billion invested in China.

I doubt whether Mr. Reagan or Mr. Bush has even the vaguest notion of what Buddhism is or what goes on in Tibet. Hugh Richardson, onetime British Trade Consul in Tibet, wrote: "I have never seen less evidence of hatred, envy, malice and uncharitableness [than in Tibet]. The Tibetan system produced a people who in upper levels were self-controlled, intelligent, often deeply learned, capable, unpretentious, dignified, humane and friendly. The majority of people made efforts to live as much as possible with nature, not against it."

But there is no oil in Tibet! And how can we teach them "democracy" when China and India control all roads leading there? And anyway, China beat us to the punch, and it doesn't interfere with our teaching in Panama, Nicaragua and El Salvador, so why should we be perturbed by the lessons it teaches in Tibet? After all, China is a friend, in spite of the unpleasantness at Tiananmen Square, just as the peace-loving West Germans are our friends, in spite of the thousands of tons of chemicals they sell to Libya for the production of mustard gas—so that they may solve the "Jewish problem" that they left unfinished.

Ah, well, friends, enemies, murderers, bastards and swine—you live and let live. China is there, and it was no less than Richard (*your President is not a crook*) Nixon who opened it up for proper investment. This worthy gentleman, the only President in American history to be forced to resign for various lies, small crimes and large deceptions, returned to the scene of his crimes, prompting this from *The New York Times*:

> Nixon Treated as Hero in Halls of His Disgrace . . . Congressional aides with only distant childhood memories of Watergate applauded, cheered and jostled one another to shake his hand. Newt Gingrich, the House Republican whip, positively glowed.

March 26, 1990

The White House Astrologer

Phil Donahue interviews Joan Quigley, the astrologer, and she tells him, simpering like a silly adolescent, that she was responsible for many of the major decisions during the Reagan Administration. She accomplished this, as she informs him, through her influence over Nancy Reagan, who is not only a fervent believer in astrology, but a dedicated believer in Joan Quigley. Ms. Quigley apparently was in daily telephone communication with Nancy at the White House, and Nancy, as one must infer from Ms. Quigley's remarks, was the strong rudder that steered her husband through the eight years of his Presidency.

It is no longer news to any informed American that, for the most part, Ronnie was a stand-in for Nancy, but the information that major decisions during the Reagan years were made by a foolish aging lady, based upon her belief in a ridiculous superstition, should send a cold shiver down the spine of anyone with half a brain. I used to think that we had seen everything during the changing occupancy of the White House, but this beats them all.

But Ms. Quigley is no longer news, and the reviewers have put a proper seal on the ridiculous, mindless book she published, and we have drawn our deep breaths of relief that this foolish, superstitious couple that governed us for eight years had not blown up the world and had passed safely into history. What troubled me about the Donahue broadcast was that no one in a studio audience made up of what appeared to be educated, middle-class people spoke to the marrow of the thing—namely, that astrology is superstitious nonsense without even a shred of validity, a contrivance of ancient times before the scientific method came into existence, and that every so-called "astrologer" is a con artist selling lies, inventions and sometimes slick guesses, and to call it a science is to blaspheme every advance that science has made through the years.

Yet I don't for a moment believe that this audience is unique. With a few notable exceptions, every newspaper in America carries a daily horoscope, for which they pay in the coin of the realm. Books and pamphlets on astrology sell by the millions and, whether lightly or seriously, millions of people ask each other what their signs might be. Of course, most people use it as a conversation break without investing it with even a shred of belief, but millions of others believe this nonsense as firmly as a religious person believes in his religion.

There has been endless talk over the past several years about the deficiencies in our educational system, with most of the emphasis on literacy and on the sad fact that at least one-third of this bastion of liberty and free thought is illiterate. Of course, literacy is where all education begins, and without the ability to read and write, any talk of education is meaningless. As the slave-owners of the Old South knew only too well, to read and write is to take the first step toward freedom—which is why they punished savagely any slave who attempted to learn to read or write.

But granting all this, education does not stop with the ability to read and write. That is only the beginning, and even as we have failed to educate the illiterate, so have we failed to really educate the literate. To have millions of citizens who accept astrology as a science, believe in it and accept without anger and disgust the news that for years their Government was subject to it, is to underline the fact that American education is a failure.

Where that failure will lead us, God only knows. In the same manner that so many accept astrology, we have accepted the lies that the Pentagon and its flaks fed us and still feed us. We have allowed them to infest our land with thousands of atomic weapons, concealing the fact that an atomic exchange—as they call it—would make the world uninhabitable. We have allowed them to absorb endless billions of dollars created by our work and creativity, wasting it decade after decade on their lunatic military dreams, while the infrastructure of our country disintegrated and our educational process collapsed. I believe that it is precisely this process of educational disintegration in primary, middle and college institutions that masked our ability to see and understand what was happening.

We have become a very accommodating people. We set in type the silly blatherings of a Joan Quigley and call it a book and give it a dignity that it in no way deserves. Isn't it harmless? Harmless—this silly, superstitious woman having so enormous an influence on that community of clowns in Washington who call themselves our Government? Harmless indeed—it is monstrous, and it would be beyond belief if it were not that most of what happens down there on the shores of the Potomac is beyond belief.

But then, in her defense, Ms. Quigley might say, "If Peggy Noonan can invent George Bush, why fault me for inventing Nancy?" Why indeed?

April 9, 1990

The Definition of Obscene

It was that ever-watchful, zealous guardian of American morality Senator Jesse Helms who fingered the Contemporary Arts Center of Cincinnati for its exhibition of the photographs of the late Robert Mapplethorpe; but I don't want you to think that Mr. Helms is just some uncultured redneck, even though he is a hero of the American Rifle Association, awarded its medal of distinction in 1978, or to imagine that he is some sort of besotted Ku Kluxer and racist.

No, sir! No indeed! Absolutely not! That kind of thinking would give you a very wrong impression of a man who is a United States Senator and a college graduate. And if you folks up North are narrow enough to look down on old Jesse, why you're just as wrong as could be.

For example, Jesse's alma mater, Wingate College, down there in North Carolina, has decided to raise up on their campus an amazing and very remarkable tribute to old Jesse—a museum and a library, both of them housed in a great, splendid building that will cost $5 million to put together. Now just in case you think this is a small matter, I want you to know that it has no precedent in American history, a museum dedicated to a living U.S. Senator and a library to harbor the jewels of his thinking for all generations to come. No, sir. Until Jesse came around, no such thing had ever been considered, much less built. Of course, libraries have been built to contain the papers and thinking of Presidents, even such folks as Ronnie, who never wrote very much and who avoided thinking whenever he could; but never for a living U.S. Senator.

And you might just get nosy and nasty, the way folks up North do, and demand to know where a politician like Jesse could turn up $5 million to build himself a museum. Then let me put a stop on that kind of thinking, because, according to Jesse, he never asked for any such honor, but had it forced on him by a group of good old boys who had obligations to Jesse that could never properly be repaid, no matter how hard they tried.

What kind of obligations? Come on now, you mean to tell me that you never heard tell of something called tobacco? Well, if that's the case, it's time you got some facts and figures: According to the Surgeon General, 1,000 Americans die every day from cigarette-related causes. That is a figure larger than the total of all Americans killed in action in World War I and World War II. If you crashed a jumbo jet every morning and every evening all year long, you wouldn't get that many deaths.

We were talking about old Jesse's museum and where the money came from. Well, $200,000 was dropped into the hat immediately by Philip Morris, the same sterling corporation that paid the producers of

License to Kill, the recent James Bond movie, $350,000 to have Lark cigarettes featured in the film.

The Carolina banks that did business in tobacco country chipped in with their thousands and, not to be outpaced, Brown & Williamson Tobacco Corporation dropped $40,000 into the kitty. As a matter of fact, the money was rolling in so smooth and easy that old Jesse was just about overwhelmed with the kindness of his buddies.

Would you call Jesse a merchant of death? But that would be hardly fair and hardly true, and don't forget that Jesse is just about the most outspoken defender of morality in these here United States. He fights the good fight for those who produce tobacco and cigarettes and, as he would be the first to tell you, where would they find a livelihood if not for him?

For myself, I simply don't know what to call Jesse. If you think of a person's hard work defending tobacco leading to three or four deaths, well the mind can handle that, but here's this Surgeon General of the United States talking about 1,000 deaths every single day of the year, and that just boggles the mind of any normal person. But let's be realistic; you can't call old Jesse to account for all that horror because for years and years his voice has been raised in the defense of the tobacco industry. Hell, no! He was elected, and he just did his job.

But I'm still puzzled about this combination of museum and library. I can think of all kinds of stuff to fill that museum with—racks, thumbscrews, whips, carbines, grenades, assault weapons, no end of stuff—and perhaps as a centerpiece a reproduction of the stake and kindling that they used in old Salem to burn the witches.

But in the library? Darned if I know what they could put there to celebrate a man of Jesse's culture and taste. Maybe they could begin with a dictionary, a great big fat one, like my old Webster's, which defines "obscene" as "foul, loathsome, disgusting."

Obscene is a word Jesse is inordinately fond of.

April 30, 1990

Strange Creatures

The President of the United States spoke in Washington on May 11. According to *The New York Times*, the following immortal words fell from his lips: "Tomorrow there'll be another tidal wave, so keep your snorkel above the water level and do what you think is right. That's exactly what my mom told me when I was about 6. Do your best. Do your best. I'm trying hard. Stay calm."

This was in denial of a statement by the curious John Sununu to the effect of Mr. Bush being a sneaky manipulator who is only playing to the crowd and who has no intentions of engaging in a serious debate about taxes. Why Mr. Sununu ticks off his boss so much is hard to guess; chiefs of staff made a habit of this during the Reagan years, although in those years it did not matter very much, since nobody was quite sure who was President—the Chief of Staff, or Ronald Reagan, or Nancy, or the cute Joan Quigley; but in this Administration Mr. Bush has made such a point of reading his lips that one begins to believe that he actually is President.

Yet one has to wonder who wrote the words quoted above. Peggy Noonan, who is a kind of godmother to Mr. Bush's rhetoric, would never have stooped to such banalities nor is it conceivable that so witless a speech writer could have got a job at the White House. The only conclusion one can come to is that Mr. Bush went out on a limb and fashioned words and thoughts himself and spoke off the cuff.

This is doubly interesting because on the same day the Mayor of New York City, the honorable David Dinkins, spoke to the people of New York on the subject of racism and the city. His talk was broadcast on the three major networks' local affiliates and, among other things, he said:

> The future of this city belongs to the children of this city—all the children of this city. . . . New York is again as it always has been a city of immigrants. They come in droves from Ireland and India, from Jamaica and Japan, from Ecuador and El Salvador, and up from the red clay hills of Georgia, the Mississippi Delta and the streets of Memphis and Mobile. We came to escape czars and dictators, hunger and deprivation. Our people—all of our people—share a common ancestry of oppression and a common aspiration to leave that history behind and to embrace the full promise of America.

This paragraph came toward the end of as warm and intelligent a public address as I have heard since Governor Cuomo's notable speech to the 1984 Democratic Convention. Mr. Dinkins's talk had substance, ideas, anger and hope; and I cannot help but compare it to the shameful drivel that comes out of Washington, both from the clowns who pretend to be Congressmen and who brood over nothing but their re-election, and from the covey of speech writers who crouch in the White House and try to decide what should come out of those lips that we are told to read ad nauseam.

One cannot avoid the comparison, nor does the answer lie in the fact that so many in our national Government are dolts. While that is probably the case, it does not explain the astonishing lack of compassion and simple human sensitivity that pervades the Republican Party and so much of the national Democratic Party as well. More and more, I feel that the great cities of America have nothing to do with the Government in Washington, D.C. Washington is the Government of millions of acres of golf clubs, of the sleek suburban lawns, of the sprawling shopping centers, of the great new factories, built out and away from the cities. They are a Government of yuppies turned middle-aged who never knew the city or tasted it or roamed its streets as kids, or knew the blessed entity of the block, the street, the public school, the wonderful on-foot exploration of strange streets and avenues.

They have no knowledge of history, these people in Washington. They don't realize that in all the history of mankind, there has never been such a thing as New York City or such a hope as New York holds for the world. Our city has taken in whole nations and turned them into a citizen brotherhood. In Europe, they scream about a handful of foreigners coming into one of their cities and making it impure. For 200 years, we have gloried in the racial "impurity" of our wonderful city, and out of this came a foundation of creativity unequaled elsewhere on earth. We have reared our towers to the sky, and if we have been unable to house and feed our old and poor as they should be fed, it is because those strange creatures in Washington bleed us dry, taking the wealth we create and turning it into guns and a mammoth Army and Navy, and wasting our sustenance by feeding with unslaked greed from the trough of our taxes.

May 28, 1990

Have They No Shame?

There it was, on every media box and in every newspaper, the four of them, for all the world like a police lineup. That, indeed, was my initial reaction, the people of America sitting behind the one-way glass, asked to point the finger.

Oh, it was a proper lineup; no question about that, and beginning with Richard Milhous (Your President Is Not a Crook) Nixon, followed by that sterling thespian, Ronald (Police Spy on the Membership of His Own Union) Reagan, and then Gerald R. (Can't Chew Gum and Think at the Same Time) Ford, and finally the current jewel of the constellation, George (Read My Lips) Bush, courtesy of Peggy Noonan and the curious John Sununu.

(It must be said to the credit of the fifth living President, Jimmy Carter, that his sense of decency and honor led him to excuse himself from joining the four men, who gathered at Yorba Linda, California, one to be praised and the three others to lavish praise upon him.)

The native and hallowed son of Yorba Linda was the given object of ennoblement. No matter that he was the first President of the United States to resign in the face of impeachment, that he had made an international disgrace of his office, that he had allegedly lied and conspired, that he had dragged out the war in Vietnam for endless agonizing months, that he had allowed thousands of American servicemen to die needlessly, that he had caused the Government of Cambodia to be overthrown, resulting in the loss of millions of lives—no matter that his background training school was the House Un-American Committee, where he was a companion in tyranny to the infamous Joseph McCarthy, his Senatorial equivalent, where he had fought to turn America into a land of fear and terror—no matter that he had been all of this and done all of this, he was being honored.

They had built him a library. A group of private citizens had put up $21 million to build a Richard Milhous Nixon library, and two ex-Presidents and one sitting President had come to California to take part in the dedication of that library and to shower Mr. Nixon with praise.

What is one to make of all this, and how does it define, not the United States, but the Government and the establishment of the United States? To begin, the whole business is so utterly preposterous that the tendency is to record it and let it go. That's what most of the media did, treating it as straightforwardly and objectively as one treats earthquakes, floods and other natural disasters. This, together with the fact that Americans have small historical memory or indeed in most cases none at all, may explain some of the media attitude. On the other hand, it also must serve as an indication that in today's America, honor, decency, a sense of dignity and a sense of what is or is not appropriate have ceased to have any meaning whatsoever, and we must ask and wonder what fate awaits a nation that has given up every standard of human behavior except money.

To poke fun at this grotesque happening in Yorba Linda is easy enough; and so much of Federal Governmental proceedings these days resemble clown shows that one discovers that to burlesque what is already burlesque requires only accurate description. But at a time like this, it should not and must not be laughed out of existence. When a man like Richard Nixon, who has not even the grace of Pete Rose who was sentenced to prison and on the same day, said that he was sorry and recognized the wrong he had done—something Mr. Nixon has never said—when such a man is honored by a sitting President and two ex-Presidents, then there is a deep and grave sickness at the core of this nation.

It connects with the announcement a few weeks ago of the library and museum being built to celebrate that prince of hypocrisy, Jesse Helms, rewarding him for the work he has done for the tobacco interests and paid for by Philip Morris and other tobacco interests.

Jesse Helms and Richard Nixon, what an unholy pair and what a testimony to what is judged to be right and wrong and good and bad in these United States. Legally, the criminal who is judged to be pathological is unable to separate right from wrong or good from bad—and the fate of Germany, when it succumbed to the pathological madness of Nazism, reminds one that a nation as well as a person can lose its conscience.

Almost 40 years ago, a man sitting in judgment on Senator Joseph McCarthy, asked him: "Have you no shame, sir?"

I think it might also be asked of the three worthy gentlemen who came to Yorba Linda to honor Richard Nixon.

August 13–20, 1990

Those Whom the Gods Would Destroy . . .

We are so used to embracing, supporting, feeding and arming the most loathsome species of tyrants, murderers, dictators and butchers, that when one bites the hand that fed him, we profess indignation and astonishment. That morality begins at the oil rig surprises no one, but that sheer stupidity should blazon the road that finally ends at the oil rig is somewhat terrifying—as terrifying as the loud war cry emerging from the field of clowns, commonly known as the Congress of the United States. It underlines the fact that they share a collective memory that extends back at least 20 minutes.

When the butcher Saddam Hussein murdered in cold blood more than 15,000 Iraqis, not a whisper of anger or horror emerged from that august body, nor do I recall any move in Congress to halt the flow of supplies to this demented killer.

When Mr. Hussein launched an unprovoked attack against Iran, we cheered him on and supplied a wide variety of weapons, condoning precisely the same kind of attack on a neighbor that we now condemn.

When Mr. Hussein's planes bombed an American warship, leaving dead American sailors to underwrite his calling card, Congress grinned sheepishly and wrote it off as a mistake.

When Mr. Hussein developed the means to manufacture the most deadly gas known to science, a pinhead of which can kill a man, Congress shrugged—a response in which they are quite skilled. And when Mr. Hussein used that same hideous gas not only to kill thousands of Iranians, with whom he was at war, but to murder at least eight and one-half thousand Kurds, with whom he was not at war but who were an irritation to his maniacal plans, President Bush and our Congress closed their eyes, and as for their lips—there was just nothing to read.

And according to an Associated Press dispatch dated August 10, the following material was confiscated by Customs—on its way to Iraq from their good friends and suppliers in the United States—three days after the United Nations sanctions vote:

> 960 barrels of jet fuel, 23 crates of military aircraft parts, 3 crates of radar equipment, 26 air conditioning units, 21 boxes of personal computers, a number of radios, spare parts for F–18 aircraft, and a wide variety of spare parts for Hawk missiles, Sidewinder missiles and heavy artillery.

Well, war is war, and business is business, yet this small bit of history must not be concluded without a notation on the subject of what happened 17 years ago. At that time, the Arab oil-supplying states, Saudi Arabia included, cut off oil shipments to the United States. We emerged from that crisis with the price of gas hiked $1, more or less, and ever since then the American people have been paying the Arab oil states a dollar, more or less, for every gallon we use. Result: The enormous amount of military equipment these countries now possess.

At that time, everyone in the Government who could be heard through the media, from the President down, swore to the American people that such a crisis would never again occur, that they would take measures to prevent it (another of countless large white lies).

The Government boasts today of having stored a vast reserve of oil. It could have put away far more, for the cost of a Stealth bomber or two. At that time, 17 years ago, Washington began serious studies of solar power, natural gas as auto fuel, and fuel produced from agricultural products and coal. All of these projects were ultimately washed out.

And now, instead of being independent, relaxed and prosperous, we face a war in the Arabian desert—which at this time of the year is as close to hell as anyplace on earth. I know. I have been there.

A sorry little epitaph now, concerning the lumber workers of the Northwest. Since lumbering is an accident-prone industry, and since the lumberjack who doesn't have his wits about him is not long for this world, there arose among the lumber workers a mythic figure whom they call Jesse Pyme, the fool-killer.

Jesse has his eye on all and every kind of fool, and when he finds one of a particularly egregious nature, he strikes; and often enough the damn fool dies. I have long been convinced that Jesse changed his habitat from the State of Washington to the City of Washington, where Jesse can just settle down with a never-ending abundance of fools within easy striking distance. But of course the bitter fruit of this is eaten by kids in uniform, whom the fools dispatch to make good their brainlessness.

It has been said that those whom the gods would destroy they first make mad. Without dropping the thought, let me amend it a bit: Those whom the gods would destroy, they first make stupid.

August 27, 1990

Another Flight of Fancy

On January 20, 1989, George Bush took office as President of the United States.

His first act in office was to instruct his budget team to cut the budget of the Pentagon by 50 percent. In an address to the American people, he said, in part:

"Warfare today can no longer distinguish between the civilian and military population. Since I have always felt, as any civilized or religious man must, that war is legalized murder, it is the intention of the government to defend the territory of the United States, but to take no military action on foreign soil."

On February 10, 1989, only a few weeks after he had taken office, President Bush called together the CEOs of all oil and energy companies in the private sector and informed them in no uncertain terms that he intended the United States to be energy self-sufficient in 12 months. He announced that the Federal Government would immediately undertake a program of alternate energy sources, agricultural, solar, and a variety of others. Unless the private sector joined in this effort, the Government product would undersell them at the pump. However, he assured them that he was confident that the private sector would give all its dedication to the project.

"Possibly," Mr. Bush said, "we will continue to buy from certain foreign markets. But we will cut off purchases from any country that violates the injunctions of the United Nations."

President Bush, in 1989, cut off all support money to dictatorships, such as El Salvador, as well as certain countries in South America and Central America that resisted any effort of their populations to establish democratic governments.

For the next three months, together with state and local government, President Bush and his advisors put together a vast, overall plan for ridding America of pollution and of repairing and rebuilding the entire infrastructure of the United States. While $300 billion had to be allocated to this effort, it was calculated that with the money saved by going from a war economy to a peace economy, there would be ample funds for the project, and that its employment—in due time—of better than 2 million men and women now either unemployed or reduced to petty service jobs, would so increase the national income that the national debt might well be decreased.

Mr. Bush linked this project with the problem of the homeless. In a speech on national television, President Bush said, "When I finish my first four-year term of office, I make a sacred pledge to you that no American shall be homeless. If homeless people are sick, we shall build hospitals to treat them. If they are well, we will build houses to house them."

By his ninth month in office, President Bush was able to announce to the American people that the United States was energy self-sufficient. The stock market touched 3,500, driven by the profits of the companies in the pollution and energy fields.

The prize the Federal Government had offered to any man, group, hospital or institution that discovered a cure for AIDS, and the research facilities they had set up to this end spurred the search for a cure to the point where serious scientists stated the disease would be conquered in 1990.

Mr. Bush received the Nobel Peace Prize. The United Nations created a World Prize for actions taken for the good of humanity. Mr. Bush received the first World Prize. Worldwide, better than twelve thousand streets, plazas, buildings, lakes and bridges were named for George Bush. Sixty-three colleges and universities were renamed in his honor.

Since, in one of his speeches, Mr. Bush mentioned rather lightly that he felt that any government official who used the word *basically* more than once a week should be fined $20, Oxford University gave him an honorary degree in English letters.

Perhaps his most remarkable feat in the second year of his term was to bring every member of the United Nations together in a vote and resolution to do away with all atom bombs worldwide in the period of the next five years. Together with this, under his leadership, the members of the United Nations agreed to create a world food bank, to do away with famine once and forever.

An interesting but not very remarkable incident occurred toward the end of President Bush's second year in office. A dictator in Iraq, Saddam Hussein by name, threatened to invade Kuwait. President Bush immediately announced that the United States, now self-sufficient in energy, would cut off all purchases of oil from Iraq for the foreseeable future if such an invasion took place. The United Nations stood with George Bush, and Iraq pledged that it had no intentions of ever invading Kuwait. A few days later, Mr. Bush convened an extraordinary world congress to consider peaceful solutions for the Middle East.

It was decided in 1991 to make Mr. Bush's birthday the first world holiday.

And then this silly dream finished and I awoke.

February 4, 1991

Who Represents the People?

I have, during my lifetime, been witness to many scurrilous and indecent acts by those who call themselves conservatives, but nothing so unseemly and distasteful as the full-page ad in a recent issue of *The New York Times*, denouncing Senator Pat Moynihan. "Where was Pat Moynihan when America needed him?" the ad asked, the Senator's crime being that he had voted for a continuation of sanctions and against the move to war.

Such was the Conservative Party's judgment on a man who voted his conscience in perhaps his finest hour in the United States Senate. Indeed, in the terms of a Congress that made new records of cowardice and indifference to the people's needs, the vote on sanctions was perhaps its only fearless and honorable hour. Yet instead of cherishing this moment and saluting it as an effort to save American lives and the lives of others as well, the men of the Republican Party are turning on Democrats who voted for sanctions and charging them with betrayal of their country. And sadly, instead of standing tall and proudly asserting that they had done the right thing, the intelligent thing, the humane thing, said Senators and Representatives are already running for cover, whimpering that they didn't really mean the decent and honest stand they had taken.

So it is in what we call a democracy. But when you have two parties who engage almost equally in ravaging the people of the country, with the majority party unwilling to challenge or oppose the minority party, and with each cheering the other on in new indecencies against the people, it is an illusion to imagine that this is anything other than a one-party system. And it has been my understanding that a one-party system is a dictatorship, benign or otherwise.

We have been told by the polls that 80 percent of the American people supported Mr. Bush's rush to slaughter. Knowing how polls are usually slanted and contrived by the construction of the questions asked, I hesitate to accept any poll at face value; but even if one were to do so, this still leaves almost 50 million Americans opposed to the war and policies of Mr. Bush and the very curious Mr. Sununu. (And if there is any question as to why I call him the *curious* Mr. Sununu, my answer is that two hundred years after the Constitution was written, we have a man who, to all effects and purposes, is running the country, whom no one voted into this office, whose opinions, beliefs and background have never been explained to the country at large, who is as mysterious and as little known as the average Postmaster General was in the old days—and if that isn't curious, I don't know what is.)

So we have, even by the self-serving polls of the establishment, some 50 million Americans whose will is ignored in the most critical moments of our history, who are represented by neither party, and whose voice is properly silenced by the whooping, hooting mass media that has the insolence to call itself a "free press."

But I also believe that the same polls, taken a few months from now will bring forth the same results they did before the war began, that is, at least half the people opposed to war and favoring sanctions.

But this percentile division took place on a question of foreign policy, which can be worked up by any government, a jingo cantata of yellow ribbon and American flags; but neither yellow ribbon nor American flags will support the unemployed, or heal the fouling of our atmosphere, or halt the disintegration of our cities. And as the cities decay and the bridges collapse, and the roads and streets develop more potholes than day and night bombing would provide, citizens will begin to reflect on the billion dollars a day we spent on Mr. Bush's ego trip.

The American Revolution was fought on many issues, but the issue that most inflamed the colonists was taxation without representation; and this question of proper representation became the core of the Constitution. But today, who represents the people? Who cares for the people or fights for them? Who gives a damn about the poor, about drug infestation, about crime?

Not the so-called "Democratic Party," which votes the billions for the Pentagon and war, and nickels and dimes for the people. I vote because I believe in voting, and I vote Democrat because I would be even more disgusted if I voted Republican, and because if I voted Republican, my daddy, a proud New York City Tammany County Committee-man, whose icon was Al Smith, would turn over in his grave; but my vote is only a hapless gesture. There is no party in Washington that represents the people, and now the last decent remnants of the Democrats are fleeing for cover. Of course they will lose the next election to the Republicans. Why should anyone vote for them? Forty percent of the population don't vote at all. All that the Democratic party stood for in its best moments is gone. Witless they have been, and even more witless today, they believe that by aping the Republicans they can crawl back into power.

But the Republicans don't need them. They have their party, and they proudly represent their constituency, the rich and the powerful. They give honest and consistent representation to the millionaires and the billionaires. They don't need the running dogs who call themselves Democrats.

Postscript. From *The New York Times*, March 10, 1991, a doctor in Basra: "Your great American soldiers can go home to their families now. They can tell them that they devastated our lives and the lives of our children. Our country is no more."

March 25, 1991

Bush Is Sickened

By this writing, practically every person on earth who owns a television set has witnessed the cruel beating of a black man by the Los Angeles police. I am sure that the response has been varied but hardly ever astonished. I can see the Turkish cops asking what the fuss is all about.

"Small potatoes. We do it every day."

The Special Branch at Scotland Yard might point out that they do worse to the Irish, who aren't even black, and I'm sure that the South African police watched the L.A. incident with hoots of laughter that such amateur stuff deserved. As for those units of the CIA that taught the art of police reprisal and torture to Central and South American police forces, I'm sure they sneered at the primitive methods prevailing in Los Angeles.

But of all the various responses, I found nothing quite comparable to that of the President of the United States. Mr. Bush said that *it sickened him.*

There it is, and he's gone public: George Bush has stated, for all the world to hear, that the sight of a black man, beaten cruelly by the nightsticks of cops, sickened him. The thousands of dead torn to pieces on the sands of Kuwait did not sicken Mr. Bush; the women and children who died in the bombing of Baghdad did not sicken him; the four thousand Panama civilians, massacred in his ego-prompted war did not sicken him. But lo and behold, one poor black man, beaten by cops on a Los Angeles street did sicken him.

What is one to make of this strange pronouncement by the President of the United States? Does it mean that somewhere in that unsmiling, desiccated body there resides a soul—a seat of feeling or compassion or decency, so well hidden until now but blossoming forth in this Easter season of renewal and rebirth?

Forget it! Forget it! Just think about the black vote. Dead Arabs were not voters, even live Arabs don't vote, so don't for a moment be beguiled into imagining that Mr. Bush had gone soft or that he had remembered that he had pledged us a "kinder, gentler" America. He had simply given the appropriate nod to black voters.

A man is measured by his deeds and his words, and the actions of Mr. Bush in destroying most cruelly, most heartlessly a country and a people thousands of miles from our shores, spells out one measure of a man—a man so cold, so removed from human emotions, so unimaginative and without empathy that he can engage in slaughter that would have shocked Attila the Hun, and not even be perturbed by the results.

Such is one measure of a man. Another is the fact that people must be judged by the words they speak or write; but the words that Mr. Bush speaks have been written by others, by a staff of White House speechwriters, and the ideas and notions and pronouncements that they write do not reflect the mind of Mr. Bush—whatsoever that mind may be—but the thinking of a shadow group in the White House that actually directs the affairs of this country.

Of course the enormous national and international press force that covers the White House knows this; but they also know that if any one of them should even hint that the voice they listen to is not the voice of the President, they would be given short shrift—and off and away from the honored press corps of the White House.

So we come back to the man who says that what happened in Los Angeles "sickened me."

But what happened in Los Angeles was a shedding of what we call—in terms of police action—restraints. And only the day before, Mr. Bush had informed the nation that one of the things he intended in his so-called "war against crime" was the release of the police from the bondage of "restraints." Well, which is it? You can't have your cake and eat it too, and you can't give the same bloody freedom to kill to the police that was given to General Schwarzkopf, and still plead that the sight of one man being beaten turned your stomach.

But if this is a prime example of rhetorical confusion, it is also an example of a man who cannot think clearly and whose understanding of everything but his own enormous yet childish ego is truncated and tragically limited. Great problems face this nation, and Mr. Bush's response to them will have far-reaching effects; but in the light of the above, what can his response be? Lewis H. Lapham, writing in *Harper's*, has this to say of Mr. Bush's recent homily for some of the problems in America:

> His attempt at genuine emotion proved as unctuous and vacant as the sentiment sent to an unknown nephew on a Hallmark card. . . . His failure was one of the imagination. . . . His words were empty because he couldn't see through the veil of abstraction to the scenes of human suffering implicit in the numbers. He didn't know, quite literally, what he was talking about.

April 8, 1991

How Could He Know?

Kurdistan. Let me tell you a little about Kurdistan. In size it is an area of 74,000 square miles, almost twice the size of the state of Pennsylvania—a vast area of mountains and valleys. The Kurds have inhabited this land for almost two thousand years. There are almost 8 million Kurds. They speak a language related to Persian, and their land is held in the main by three countries, Iran, Turkey and, in terms of the largest section of their population, Iraq. They are a poor people, mainly because they have been in subjugation for hundreds of years, denied free trade and denied any opportunity for education or prosperity. They have fought for their freedom bravely and uncompromisingly for hundreds of years.

In the course of these struggles, they have been the victims of attempted genocide, brutality beyond description, mass slaughter, and unceasing torture and oppression—mainly by Turkey and Iraq. At the end of World War I, when many subject nations were liberated, the Kurds were forgotten and left to the tender mercies of the Turks. At the end of World War II, England, backed by her allies, specified the shape of the Middle East by enforcing the boundaries we have today. The land of Kurdistan was divided among Turkey, Iraq and Iran.

Since then, the Kurds have struggled unremittingly for their independence and self-determination. Crushed by the military machine of Saddam Hussein, they took new hope from the American attack on Iraq; but with President Bush's unwillingness to support them, or to finish what remained of Mr. Hussein's military machine, they were defeated and fled from Iraq and from the death squads of Mr. Hussein.

In spite of constant pleas, Mr. Bush said stoutly that he would not come to the aid of the Kurds and that he had no real interest in their struggle. He would feed them—as a response to the cries of anger all over the world—but no more than that. They had no legal right to the land they had lived on for over a thousand years.

Occupied Palestine. As with Kurdistan, the Palestinians have an ancient right to their land. Their land, consisting of the West Bank and the Gaza Strip, is less than one-tenth the size of Kurdistan, and in population they number less than 2 million. In the course of the *intifada*, they have suffered grievously, but no genocide was ever practiced against them, no mass murder, no mindless murder of children, and in spite of the support and affection for Mr. Hussein while Israel was being bombed by Scud missiles, no reprisal was taken against them.

None of this is an argument against the Palestine will for independence, but simply a statement of the two conditions, that of the Kurds and that of the Palestinians—and along with that a small inquiry as to why what's good for the goose is not equally good for the gander. If the Palestinians deserve a land of their own, then surely the Kurds deserve a land of their own. If the Palestinians deserve freedom in the land they occupy which was the land of their fathers, then surely the Kurds deserve freedom in the land they occupy which was the land of their fathers.

But even as he dispatches Mr. Baker to Jerusalem to press the cause of the Palestinians with the Israelis, Mr. Bush snorts with anger if a reporter mentions Kurdistan and the Kurds.

The Palestinians are Arabs and Muslims, and with a large cry that they are brothers before God, Saudi Arabia, Iraq, Syria and Iran have poured millions and millions of oil dollars into the cause of the PLO, and for the PLO, they have launched terror against innocents, murdered, pillaged—all in the cause, as they put it, of Palestine Freedom.

But for the cause of the Kurds—who are also Muslims but not Arabs—not a penny, not a weapon, not a decent word or helping hand. (An exception must be spoken of Iran today, for they are feeding and helping the Kurds who have fled to them for refuge.)

So what is to be said? Of course, the lonely mountains of Kurdistan are less visible to the West than the Holy Land, but the Europeans, the Americans, and the Arabs are all aware of what goes on in both places; and if the intention is to stand up for what is right, let's play no favorites.

Consistency has never been a quality of Mr. Bush—unless one is to give him points for being consistently muddle-headed. Forty thousand Syrian troops, backed by a dictator who makes Mr. Hussein look like a boy scout, have invaded and taken over law and order in Lebanon. PLO troops hold much of southern Lebanon, but there's no oil in those places. No oil in Kurdistan. No oil on the West Bank. But in Kuwait 500 oil wells are on fire, burning millions of gallons of oil each and every day and adding up to one of the worst ecological tragedies in the history of the planet Earth.

Mr. Bush pleads a lack of anticipation. He had no crystal ball to reveal the future, he cries, his old whimper back in place. How could he know? How could he anticipate the burning of the oil, the pollution, the giant puddle of oil in the Gulf?

We are all so damned polite in American government. Every boob in Washington calls every other boob "my dear friend," "my good colleague." With all the billions we pour into the CIA, it appears to be incapable of the most primitive information, namely that oil will burn. As for Presidents, we wait until the term is over to buy the books that tell us what we elected. I suppose it's better than never knowing.

May 5, 1991

Where Is the Public Outrage?

Bit by bit, implications mount in what would be the most notorious and incredible criminal conspiracy in the history of the Presidency, if the allegations are true. The people investigating this conspiracy tread very slowly and carefully, as indeed they must, but each day brings additional facts to light.

It began with an article on the Op-Ed page of *The New York Times* by Gary Sick, a former National Security Council official and presently a university professor. Mr. Sick writes that there is strong reason to believe that shortly before the 1980 Presidential election, the 52 hostages held in Teheran by the Iranian government were scheduled for release. If they had been released, as scheduled, before Election Day 1980, there is little doubt that Jimmy Carter would have been the major recipient of the joy and relief of the American people and almost beyond question would have been re-elected for a second term.

Now what Professor Sick implies, backed up by his personal research, is that Ronald Reagan and the men around him made a deal with the Iranian Government wherein the Iranians promised, in return for arms and money, to delay the release until after the election, thereby crippling the Carter campaign and practically ensuring the election of Ronald Reagan.

Now, in case one suspects that Professor Sick's charges are without real substance, *The New York Times* of May 1, 1991, printed the following: "Several senior members of the House of Representatives, encouraged by Speaker Thomas S. Foley, are beginning to explore informally charges that the 1980 Reagan-Bush campaign staff dealt with Iran to make sure 52 American hostages were not released until after the election."

For the moment, these are merely suspicions, but the enormity of the crime, if true, is so great that even the charges must be taken very seriously. Thomas S. Foley, Speaker of the House, is by no means a man of distinguished fortitude, nor has he a reputation for walking where angels fear to tread, whereby his open interest in the above charges must be taken very seriously indeed.

Along with these charges come the resurrection of a rumor that has been all over the place since the death of William J. Casey, onetime campaign director for Ronald Reagan and subsequently head of the CIA, namely that Mr. Casey's death had been hastened somewhat because, as they say in Hollywood, "he knew too much."

Is it possible we do such things in this clean-cut, constitutional democracy which will lead the new world of peace and decency? Heavens forbid! Yet what are we to do with specific facts put forth by Professor Sick: that in July of 1980, a series of meetings took place between William J. Casey—Mr. Reagan's campaign director but not a member of the government then—and a top Iranian cleric, and that later meetings in Paris, from October 15 to 20, consummated the deal. These charges and suspicions were printed not once but several times in *The New York Times*.

So a question must arise and cannot be ignored or sloughed over: where was George Herbert Bush when all this was taking place, and what role did he play? We cannot believe that Ronald Reagan was capable of designing this kind of caper. It has the earmarks of CIA all over it, and part of the team, namely Mr. Bush, was an ex-chief of the CIA.

I recognize that the charges put forward by Professor Sick are incredible; they spell out a plot and a crime that not only has no precedent in the history of the United States, but as a piece of infamy rates number one in all the dirty tales of rigged elections. Yet where is the public outrage? Where are the burning editorials? Where is the press that Thomas Jefferson said would make us free and keep us free?

And what on God's earth has happened to us? During the terms of three Republican candidates, Richard Nixon, Ronald Reagan, and now George Bush, we have been treated to a parade of cheap and expensive crooks, liars and bunco artists of every kind and persuasion—and yet we accept this without even a murmur of anger or protest. And now we face a crime both disgusting and unprecedented, and we appear to be ready to let it slide out of our memories with no more than a cough of embarrassment.

According to the Constitution of the United States, a President of this country is subject to impeachment for having engaged in "high crimes or misdemeanors," and under those words, we forced the resignation of Richard Milhous Nixon. Yet Mr. Nixon's dirty little cover-up pales into insignificance when measured against the international plot spelled out by Professor Sick.

May 13, 1991

Choosing the Vice President

According to *New York Newsday*, in a speech delivered in the Middle West, Vice President Quayle referred to our *aggression* in the Gulf war. A psychiatrist might interpret this as the stirring in his unconscious of some shreds of comprehension and compassion. An educated layman might prefer to see use of the word as an evidence of ignorance concerning the language spoken by Mr. Quayle's constituents. That Mr. Quayle has a tin ear where language is concerned cannot be doubted, but one may also presume that Mr. Quayle possesses only a minimal amount of both education and intelligence, since absolutely nothing in his behavior or speech tends to contradict such a conclusion.

This is not intended as a criticism of Mr. Quayle. Every human being has the right to be stupid, but the practice of taking stupid, and often viciously stupid people—see Vice President Spiro Agnew—and placing such people only a heartbeat away from the Presidency, is a terrifying habit indeed.

When Mr. Bush first chose Mr. Quayle as his running mate, a gasp of disbelief came from the politicos, both Republican and Democrat. The choice, on the surface, considering the amount of political talent available to the Republicans, literate and educated men of intelligence, seasoned politicians, made no sense whatsoever. Then, in due time, light began to dawn. When one eliminated every other possibility—as Sherlock Holmes always pointed out—the single remaining possibility, no matter how bizarre, had to be the truth. Mr. Bush chose Mr. Quayle to be his Vice President because, for reasons unknown to the general public, Mr. Bush faced the possibility that he might be in danger of being recalled, or as it is called in the Constitution, impeached.

In light of this, Mr. Quayle was his insurance, for who would dare to raise charges of "high crimes" against Mr. Bush with Mr. Quayle lurking in the background, waiting to take over the leadership of the United States. If this appears to be too harsh an interpretation of the situation, then think back to the past 10 years of Republican stewardship of the executive branch and you will recall a parade of common and uncommon criminals, wrongdoers and bunco artists that compares favorably with the cluster of White House jailbirds that were the gift of the Nixon Administration to the people.

But the whole question of Mr. Bush's foresight is less important than the whole issue of the Vice Presidency. Two years ago, Mr. Bush seemed to be in a state of ebullient health, or at least that was the impression he gave the public; and a man in such a state of health cannot easily accept the notion that he is mortal; and I would like to think that if it were today that Mr. Bush had to pick a running mate, his choice would consider the public weal, in spite of his protestations that he will cherish Mr. Quayle and maintain him as his choice. This does not change the fact that it is inconceivable that in a democracy, one man by will or fancy or anger can choose the President of the United States.

I have been poring over the Constitution of the United States, trying to find some indication or hint that the framers intended such a hapless process for the choice of a President. There is no hint, no such suggestion.

Nevertheless, the fact is that the present manner of choice is undemocratic, and beyond the political definition, it is utterly preposterous. Certainly, sooner or later, there must be a new amendment to the Constitution that makes the choice of the Vice President more sensible. It is true that in a parliamentary form of government, the prime minister would have great powers in terms of his successor, but still not a matter of simple choice; and beyond that, we are not a parliamentary democracy.

I have no bias against Mr. Quayle, and the only thing I know of Mr. Quayle through my own observations is that he appears to have little sensitivity and less education, and perhaps only a glimmering of what this country is—if indeed that. The people in Washington who know him and watch him in action have no better an opinion of him; and while the man we elected to the Presidency is callous and muttonheaded, to put it without malice, he was at least elected. To have a President even more muddled in his thinking process is something this country does not deserve.

June 10, 1991

Chutzpah

The Yiddish word *chutzpah* cries out for a new definition. In its introduction into the English language, it was defined—or better said, explained—as the plea for clemency by a young man who has just murdered his father and mother. He bases his plea for mercy on the fact that he is now an orphan.

Outdated. I would replace it with a single phrase: the Senate of the United States. These strange (what does one call them: creatures, con artists, colleagues of Mr. Quayle, green-goods men, pols, quick-change artists?) gentlemen—why not, since the word is used in a variety of ways—these strange gentlemen have voted themselves a wage increase of $23,000.00 a year. This will now bring their yearly take to $124,000.00, but only as wages. The perks that go with it amount to far more than their pitiful paycheck, and like the young man above who murdered his father and mother, they plead for sympathy. As Senator

Timothy E. Wirth, a Democrat from Colorado, put it, quoted in *The New York Times*, "This is becoming an institution that people who do not have money cannot afford to come here."

Never mind the syntax. Literacy was never a condition for becoming United States Senator.

Ralph Nader—bless his heart—holds that the American people have "been stiffed" in "a pre-midnight raid on taxpayers." The money these worthies vote themselves comes out of our pockets, my pocket, your pocket, the pockets of those who bring home five or six or seven dollars for an hour of work, the pockets of the women you see in any supermarket, desperately trying to figure out how to afford tomatoes at $2.00 a pound, potatoes at 40 cents a pound, a box of dry cereal at $2.59, and so forth and so on. *In New York City*, on the very same day that the wage raise was announced, the Chemical and Manufacturers Hanover banks decided on a merger that will put thousands of people out of work—to add to the millions who are already unemployed. By my own count, during the past two weeks before this writing, there have been only two business days when some announcement of mass layoffs did not appear in the press.

Now I am well aware that some citizen interested in fairness might argue that Senators do not go into supermarkets, and that the need or ability to read either *The New York Times* or the *Washington Post* is not a requirement for election, and that it's not fair to accuse lawmakers of inappropriateness or a lack of a sense of decency or shame or conscience, since they were not elected for their humane gifts but only on the basis of how much money they could spend on TV commercials.

On the other hand, since they pretend to be public servants and to uphold the Constitution, and since their pay comes out of our pockets, and since they are sworn to protect this country and its institutions, it is only proper to list some of the things they did and did not do for the money they take home:

1. They did nothing to prevent the mindless slaughter of a quarter of a million Iraqi people or to impose any prior restraint on Saddam Hussein, or to exercise the right of only Congress to declare war.
2. They made no effort to interfere with or prevent Mr. Bush's decision to go to war against Panama and destroy four thousand civilians in the process.

3. They sat by and allowed all the work done to find a native substitute for gasoline to go to waste, even as they allowed all the laws for gasoline economy to be set aside.
4. They have done nothing concrete to broaden the struggle against AIDS, and they sit on their hands as the national health system crumbles.
5. They sit and watch the infrastructure of the cities crumble, the housing disintegrate, the poor increase and civic bankruptcy approach, and they do nothing.
6. They watch our great and boundless country become sodden with pollution and atomic waste, and they make no real move to halt it.
7. They watch us turn into a nation of murder and violence never equaled in the past, and yet they refuse to pass an adequate gun control law.
8. They watch our forests die of acid rain, and they whimper that they can do nothing about it.
9. They watch our national debt grow beyond the power to compute it, and they do nothing to quell the appetite of the Pentagon.
10. And they give free rein to the CIA, an outfit John Kenneth Galbraith calls "the most inefficient, stupid and worthless intelligence system of any Western nation."

For all of which we, the people, pay each and every one of this fine body called the U.S. Senate $124,000.00 and perks. Churchill said that democracy is a terrible system of government, but that all the other systems are worse. I suppose so. But there is no need for the United States Senate to labor so diligently to prove the point.

August 5–12, 1991

A Short Jaunt Down Memory Lane

Mencken once observed that no one ever went broke underestimating the intelligence of the American public. My own paraphrase is that no one ever went broke underestimating the memory of the American public; and in honor of this miasma and mist, I propose a few reminders out of the past:

In 1981, in his first inaugural address, Ronald Reagan said: "For decades, we have piled deficit upon deficit, mortgaging our future and our children's future. . . . To continue is to guarantee tremendous social, cultural, political and economic upheaval." The public debt was then under a trillion dollars. Now it is over $3 trillion.

In 1980, talking to her husband on an amplified telephone, Nancy Reagan said that she wished he could be there to "see all these beautiful white people."

In 1984, in one of his rare non-anecdotal moments, Mr. Reagan said: "They tell me I'm the most powerful man in the world. I don't believe that. Over there in the White House someplace there's a fellow that puts a piece of paper on my desk every day that tells me what I'm going to be doing every 15 minutes. He's the most powerful man in the world."

In 1985, at a news conference, Mr. Reagan said: "I've found that the Bible contains an answer to just about everything and every problem that confronts us, and I wonder sometimes why we don't recognize that one book could solve a lot of problems for us."

In 1983, Mr. Reagan addressed the Congressional Medal of Honor Society in New York. He told them his favorite Medal of Honor story. A B–17 coming back from a raid over Germany during World War II is badly damaged. A young ball-turret gunner, badly wounded, can't get out of the plane. Quoting Mr. Reagan: "The last man to leave the plane saw the commander sit down on the floor. He took the boy's hand and said, 'Never mind, son, we'll ride it down together.' Congressional Medal of Honor posthumously awarded." A *New York Daily News* reporter dug into the records and found that not one of the 434 medals of honor in World War II matched Mr. Reagan's story. Finally, after more research, it was discovered that the pilot's actual line was, "We'll take this ride together," and the speaker was Dana Andrews in the 1944 war movie, *A Wing and a Prayer*.

In 1985, Mr. Reagan refused to visit a Nazi death camp but decided to honor a Nazi SS cemetery with a visit. His explanation opened new fields in syntax: "Since the German people have very few alive that remember even the war, and certainly none of them were adults and participating in any way, and they have a feeling of guilt and a guilt feeling that's been imposed upon them. And I just think it's unnecessary."

In 1984, Mr. Reagan had his neat little war. Some 7,000 U.S. soldiers landed in Grenada, which was defended by a few hundred armed

Cuban laborers. Nineteen American soldiers were killed. Mr. Reagan ordered the award of 8,612 medals, a good many of them to soldiers who had never left the mainland.

In 1987, the Navy frigate U.S.S. Stark was hit by Iraqi missiles, and 37 U.S. sailors died a horrible death. Mr. Reagan gracefully accepted Saddam Hussein's apology. An accident.

In 1987, it was suggested that if a wealthy American were to give $300,000 toward the support of the Contras, a mercenary army we maintained in Nicaragua to fight the legal Government, the President would welcome the contributor to the Oval Office and spend as much as 15 minutes with him.

In 1987, as the summer was just beginning, the Secretary of the Interior, Donald Hodel, suggested that increased regulation of the spray-can industry was not necessary at the moment. Though the ozone layer was dissipating, he said, the effects of that dissipation could be safely endured with hats, sunglasses and skin ointment.

In 1985, Attorney General Edwin Meese III was awarded $427,190 in Federal funds toward the costs he incurred in mounting a defense at his confirmation hearings—a defense against charges of misdeeds.

Ah, well, it's a little from here and a little from there for a sentimental journey down the halls of time. Mr. Reagan is taking a well-earned rest in California, where what is is not necessarily so, and Mr. Bush is in there doing bigger wars than his predecessor ever dreamed of. No reason to howl about it. We elect the Presidents, don't we?

September 16, 1991

Clowns and Fools

The story around is that George Bush, greatly perplexed, turned to Margaret Thatcher for help. The problem was a question of intelligence, as he put it to Mrs. Thatcher: "How does one know? Where is the measure of intelligence?"

"I found a simple way out of that difficulty when I looked about me for a prime minister," Mrs. Thatcher replied. "I asked John Major a riddle that went directly to the point. If he answered correctly, it was an indication of a mature intelligence."

"Indeed. Wonderful. Tell me the riddle. I can certainly use it."

"Very well," Mrs. Thatcher agreed. "Who is the son of your father who is not your brother?"

"Oh?" Mr. Bush moved carefully. "And what did Mr. Major say?"

"Me. I mean his answer was himself."

"And that was the correct answer?"

"Absolutely."

Mrs. Thatcher departed, and alone in his office in the American Embassy in London, Mr. Bush called the White House and asked to talk to Dan Quayle. "Danny," Mr. Bush said, "I have a riddle for you, and it's very important for me to have an answer—particularly in terms of the coming election and yourself as my running mate."

"Absolutely, Mr. President," Dan Quayle said. "Absolutely. Right on."

"Who is the son of your father who is not your brother?

"Oh?"

"Exactly, who is the son of your father who is not your brother?"

"Can you give me a few minutes on that?" Quayle asked. "I'll get back to you, sir."

"Certainly," Bush agreed.

Dan Quayle put down the telephone, and then called Henry Kissinger.

"Henry," he said, "I need your help. I have something in the top order of importance, and I want an answer from you."

"If I can, certainly, Dan. Shoot."

"It's a riddle. Who is the son of your father who is not your brother?"

"That's it? That's all?"

"Right."

"OK," Kissinger said. "The answer is me. Myself. Henry Kissinger. Got it?"

"You're sure?"

"Of course I'm sure."

"Thank God," Quayle said, and called London immediately. When they finally put him through to Mr. Bush, he said, "Mr. President, I have the answer."

"Good. I'm listening."

"Henry Kissinger."

Bush sighed. "Danny, you've done it again."

"You mean I'm wrong?"

"You couldn't be more wrong. The answer is John Major."

It's a funny story, but I take no pleasure in it. If it has any point at all, it's a sort of public barometer, a reflection on how low and contemptible the office of the President of the greatest country on the face of the earth has fallen. After eight years of a semiliterate and bad actor, who slept away his years in office, while his martinet wife ruled with the guidance of an astrologer, we are promised another eight years under the guidance of a man who threw this nation into two bloody and brainless wars, who is bent on turning the Supreme Court into an imperial star chamber, and who responds with indifference to the most desperate needs of this nation.

He has become a sort of seer–prognosticator on the future of the Soviet Union, while indulging an incredible pretense that his own country is without problems. While he chants the virtues of a market economy for the Soviet Union, he ignores the 20 million unemployed here at home, the disintegration of the cities, the crime and the terror and the avalanche of drugs eating away at the vitals of our nation.

As for the majority of the people of this country, they have accepted the fact that no one—certainly not the corrupt and cowardly Democratic Party—offers them a political alternative. There is nothing the Democrats offer that is any different from the Republicans. They want a piece of the pie, but not a different pie; and to all effects, like the people of the old Soviet Union, we have a one-party government, so solidly in power that they elevate, most shamelessly, clowns and fools to do the work of the military-industrial complex and the great oil companies.

And we, the people, comfort ourselves with cute stories, a whisper of anger and contempt that means little indeed. So it has always been, from the sardonic wits of ancient Rome to the stories passed from person to person in the Soviet Union.

September 23, 1991

Uncommon Thieves

Words are interesting: *Politic* comes from the Greek, meaning "belonging to the citizens." *Politician*, according to my fine old Webster's, rates as its primary definition, "a politic person, a schemer, an intriguer." Webster's further explains, "In modern usage, politician commonly implies activity in party politics, especially with a suggestion of artifice or intrigue"—no mention of Robin Hood or Jesse James, no implication that these worthies take from the rich and give to the poor. Of course not. The reality is that they take from the poor, the middle class and the rich too, that theirs is a glorious and bottomless honey pot. Any assertion that they are common thieves would be hotly contested. Indeed, they are very uncommon thieves, and in the process of their work and play, they suck the blood from this nation.

I am not dwelling today on high crimes. High crimes are so mind-boggling that the ordinary citizen cannot deal with them. For example, when Congress votes a billion dollars for a bomber that is not needed and that will probably never get off the ground, the price numbs us into inaction. The average blue-collar worker knows that if he were given 10 lifetimes of perpetual employment, he still could not put a dent in $1,000,000,000. The sum becomes meaningless. On the other hand, the practice of cheap chicanery, of dirty little cons, swindles and petty thievery, is something that at one time or another touches every one of us and is well understood.

Thus, when your citizen reads in *The New York Times*: "Washington, Sept. 21—Lawmakers bounced hundreds of thousands of dollars in personal checks written on the accounts of their Capitol Hill bank and paid none of the penalties a normal citizen would face," he sees a familiar and bitter condition. A returned check is something that will happen occasionally in our uncertain society to hard-working people who try desperately to meet their bills, to pay for a child's sickness or a grocery bill when jobless; but it doesn't just happen to people (our elected legislators) who are paid $124,000 a year, command a small army of paid assistants and enjoy perks galore. Yes, precisely, these are the gentlemen members of Congress who have bounced hundreds of thousands of dollars of bad checks in a sweetheart bank that doesn't penalize them a penny.

An aberration? Hardly. But low, cheap, mean? Well, let's step down a rung or two to the ethical subcellar. That's a place called The House Restaurant. It's not enough that we overpay these characters who compose our Congress, not enough that we grant them staff and perks out of mind, not enough that we do all this, but we also give them their own restaurant and run it at a loss so that these characters pay less than what other citizens pay for their meals. Only, they don't pay. They sign chits.

Bless their hearts! From *The New York Times*: "Two veteran members of Congress today charged that many of their colleagues owed thousands of dollars in long overdue bills in the House restaurant, and said that if they do not pay up the debts should go to a collection agency."

How much?—$667,416, as of this past June. The amount, along with 8,331 bad checks, moved one of the members to remark: "That adds to the feeling of people that we're all a bunch of thieves."

Really? How mistrustful people are getting to be! The thievery—cheap as well as major—is not limited to Congress. Thousands of our own city employees daily rip off New York with perks that are unnecessary, incredible and shocking, driving to work in city-owned cars and collecting paychecks of $100,000 or more for jobs that could either be dispensed with or done for half the price—in a city where millions are wasted on the unwritten deals awarded to one branch or another of the mob.

It all comes out of our pockets. I go to the supermarket with my wife, and we watch the desperation of women stunned by inflation as they try to feed their families, agonizing over the cost of a bag of groceries—their lives sucked dry by the worthless and contemptible men chosen to represent them in what is called a democratic society. When the hell was the last time you were in a supermarket, Mr. Bush?

October 21, 1991

Democracy Explains It All

It is some time since my friend D'emas turned up here in New York. D'emas, you will recall, is a dark-skinned native of one of those tiny Pacific islands where they have no army and only a single policeman. Thus his frequent visits to the United States to study freedom and democracy—visits, I may say, that deepen his understanding of those two precious things.

This time he was fascinated by the Clarence Thomas affair. "You see," he said to me, "what is so remarkable is that now, after he has been sworn in and made a Justice of your Supreme Court, everyone admits that Professor Anita Hill has been telling the truth."

"Of course. No one ever doubted her."

"Then why did they reject her testimony?"

That kind of thing is typical of D'emas.

"For heaven's sake," I told him, "Professor Hill is a woman. She complained of sexual harassment. If every member of Congress who practiced sexual harassment had to resign, who would be left to govern us?"

"I see," D'emas said slowly. "I never thought of it that way. From reading papers like *The New York Times* I had begun to believe that the big problems of democracy today were things like unemployment and drugs. But I guess women are more of a problem."

"Of course," I assured him. "In Washington, things like drug addiction and unemployment do not matter. Mr. Bush tells the nation that the drug problem is being solved."

"And that does it?"

"Absolutely. Ever since George Washington confessed that he had chopped down his daddy's favorite cherry tree with his little hatchet, Americans have believed that their Presidents do not lie. Even when President Nixon hinted to them that their President was a liar, they rejected the suspicion."

"But now Colonel North says that your President Reagan knew all about Mr. North's deal with Iran. President Reagan swore that he did not know."

"Of course. Everyone knows that Mr. Reagan was lying, but that doesn't mean they believe it."

"But if they know it," poor D'emas pleaded, "don't they have to believe it?"

"Not at all. Colonel North says that Mr. Bush must have known about the Iran affair. If he did, it might very well be grounds for impeachment. The same as Professor Hill. You just can't go around doubting people like Mr. Bush. After all, Mr. Bush says that unemployment is not a problem. If we called him a liar, everyone would become very disturbed. It's not the American way."

"But there is enormous unemployment, isn't there?"

"Yes, but it doesn't matter because Mr. Bush says it doesn't matter. You want everything in a democracy to be simple and forthright, D'emas. It doesn't work that way. For instance, consider the question of ozone."

"Oh, yes—yes indeed," D'emas said. "I was going to ask you about that. Even back on our little island, we're dreadfully worried about the ozone, and we are given to understand that most of the damage is done by American industry."

"There you are," I told him. "Mr. Bush says we have nothing to worry about."

"But how can he say that when all the scientists disagree with him?"

Poor ignorant savage—it's so hard to explain democracy to him. "D'emas," I said gently, "Mr. Bush used to have Peggy Noonan to teach him how not to be a wimp and about the thousand points of light, but now he doesn't have Peggy Noonan anymore, because Miss Noonan discovered that it was more profitable to write books and magazine articles than to teach candidates how to talk and how not to be wimps. Instead, Mr. Bush has someone called the curious Mr. Sununu, who is not nearly as pretty as Miss Noonan, and he tells Mr. Bush how to deal with such matters as Saddam Hussein and the depletion of the ozone layer. The scientists say the depletion of the ozone layer will amount to thousands of cancer deaths in the coming years, but Mr. Sununu says there's nothing to worry about and it's all a left-wing plot."

"Is it really a left-wing plot?"

"Doesn't matter. For the past 50 years, anything that Washington wanted to destroy or disprove was named a left-wing plot. That's the way our country functions, and every good citizen believes it. Except, of course, subversives. Subversives are the enemies of freedom and democracy."

"But you said before that the real enemy is women. Are all women in a democracy subversive?" D'emas asked.

"Oh, no—no indeed. Only those women who want the same rights as men and the right—which all men have—to do what they wish with their own bodies. They're the subversives."

"But there must be millions of such women."

"Absolutely. And can you imagine what would have happened if the Senators admitted that they believed Anita Hill was telling the truth? All those millions of subversive women would have been impossible to handle. They might even want a real share in the government, and then what would happen to democracy?"

November 11, 1991

The President Tells How to Save America

Bob Krantz, who had been out all day looking for a job, arrived home before his wife Ethel. She had a job at the checkout counter at the neighborhood Grand Union, and when Bob opened the door for her, she staggered in, loaded with as many packages and shopping bags as a healthy young woman could carry.

"What on earth have you been doing?" Bob demanded, helping her with the bags. "You're pregnant. You shouldn't be carrying this kind of load."

"That's nothing—nothing," Ethel replied stoutly. "What is my being pregnant compared to the sacrifice of the soldiers in the Gulf War? They fought for their country. Now I'm fighting for mine."

"This—what's this?" Bob asked, unwrapping one of her packages.

"The newest coffee maker."

"We have a coffee maker. Seventy-five dollars. We don't have $75."

"I put it on MasterCharge. Look at this. Isn't it darling?"

"A stuffed bear! Honey, you're only in your fourth month. Twelve dollars. We don't have $12."

"You don't understand," Ethel said patiently. "Today, at the store, they broadcast a speech by President Bush. Do you know what he said? Bob, look at me and listen to me. Do you know what he said?"

"We don't need a new toaster!" Bob cried. "We have a perfectly good toaster that we bought for $10. This is $37. We don't have $37. I haven't worked in 14 months. My unemployment insurance has run out. We're living on what you make at the checkout at the Grand Union."

"Bob, you're not listening to me."

"Caviar!"

"It's not real. It's made in America."

"Ten dollars for this little jar!"

"Doesn't duty mean anything to you? Doesn't your country mean anything to you?"

"Four ounces! That's $2.50 an ounce!"

"Will you listen to me, please, Bob? Will you let me tell you what President Bush said? If you do, you'll understand."

"This sweater!"

"It's for you."

"It's $60!" he shouted. "Sixty dollars! We don't have $60! We don't have 60 cents!"

"I bought it because I love you."

"I don't need a new sweater! I have three good sweaters! Why are you crying?"

"Because you hate me."

"I love you. I just don't understand why you've gone out of your mind."

"I haven't gone out of my mind. All I'm asking is that you let me tell you—that you listen to me, so I can tell you what our wonderful President said."

"Asparagus! Asparagus is $3.50 a pound!"

"Not at the Grand Union. It was only $2.90 a pound. You don't love your country. You hate me and you hate your country."

"I love you. At least I loved you before you went crazy."

"All right!" Ethel shouted through her tears. "Now you will listen to me! President Bush gave this long speech on the radio, and he said that all the bad things that are happening here in the United States are the fault of the consumers. That's why we have a recession and that's why you can't find a job, that's why there is so much crime and unemployment and why the cities are going to pieces—because the consumers are not consuming, because we have suffered a loss of faith and a loss of confidence. That's what the President said, and Presidents don't lie."

"He said that?"

"That's what he said, Bob. That's exactly what he said, and he said that unless consumers start to consume like crazy, there's no hope for our country—our country, Bob, our wonderful country. He even quoted President Kennedy, who said, ask not what your country can do for you, but what you can do for your country."

"He said that?"

"Yes, he did. And we are consumers. You can't deny that. We are consumers."

"Yes, sure, but all we're able to consume is three meals a day, mostly pasta, and we're behind in the rent."

"That's just it. Men die for their country. He's asking us to save America. He says there's no other way."

"I didn't understand," Bob said ruefully. "Please forgive me. I shouldn't have doubted you. You're a wonderful woman."

"Thank you, Bob."

"I love my country. Let's buy a car—an American car."

"But we don't have the downpayment. You can't buy a car on MasterCharge."

"We'll sell the furniture. God Almighty, Ethel, you've inspired me. No one is going to say I don't love my country. We'll sell the furniture and make a downpayment on the car. The President calls, and I will not refuse him."

"Bob, I love you and I salute you!"

December 2, 1991

Labels Can Be Accurate

Some weeks ago, a correspondent to the letters column of *The New York Observer* took umbrage at my use of labels. In referring to parts of our Government, I used such words as "stupidity" and "unspeakable gang." I also referred to the media as an "electronic voice that harangues the people night and day," and I described the invasion of Panama and the Gulf War as "bloody, unjust and unnecessary." Finally, to cap my sins, I made reference to "the so-called free press."

The correspondent, one Seymour Durst by name, concluded his letter by stating that "fewer labels and more thought can maintain international peace among nations of the world."

Bless his heart. It was *labels* that caused Germany to invade Belgium and, of course, it was nasty rhetoric such as I use from time to time, when discussing such worthies as George Bush and the curious Mr. Sununu, that was responsible for Panama and the Gulf War. What an engrossing view of history Mr. Durst puts forward! He has probably never attended a session of Britain's House of Commons. The language used there, labels being the least of it, would, by Mr. Durst's definition, plunge the world into war at least two or three times each week.

I am not trying to put down Mr. Durst's affection for good manners. We are a nation so addicted to every aspect of vulgarity that any improvement in common politeness or good taste should be welcomed. However, the good manners and courtesy that members of Congress display toward each other is a *sickening* cover-up for their *duplicity*, *dishonesty* and *cowardice*; there's a fine gaggle of labels for Mr. Durst to brood over. Let me underline my point by quoting Lewis Lapham, writing in *Harper's* magazine on the Clarence Thomas affair:

> With respect to the testimony of Anita Hill, none of the members of the committee (Democrat or Republican) understood what it was that she was talking about, or why anything she said was important to anybody other than themselves. . . . Uneasy with the testimony for reasons of their own, the Democratic Senators made no attempt to shape her observations into a coherent narrative. The Republicans carried out the White House brief to do whatever was necessary to discredit the woman's statement. They did so with a mean-spirited singleness of purpose that was as effective as it was dishonorable. Senator Orrin Hatch (R., Utah) distinguished himself by virtue of his smirking hypocrisy; Senator Alan Simpson (R., Wyoming) by his ignorance; and Senator Arlen Specter (R., Pennsylvania) by his talents as a sophist and a bully.

Of Judge Clarence Thomas, Mr. Lapham wrote: "His manner was that of an outraged British duke during the reign of George III, and his response to even the smallest whisper of seditious libel about the moral beauty of his soul could have been expressed in the phrase, 'How dare they?' "

A label can be either a noun or an adjective. Both usages appear above, and since Mr. Lapham is not only a gifted essayist, but a truthful one as well, it is difficult to imagine how he might write the above without the use of pejorative phrases. The disgusting and disgraceful behavior of the men on the panel that judged Anita Hill was a scene calculated to shock the sensibilities of any thoughtful person. On the committee were scoundrels who behaved like scoundrels but, in all the media, how many were there who dared to say what Lewis Lapham did, not by inference, but forthrightly and flatly?

Labels only hurt when they are false. If we are to survive as a democracy, we must begin to state facts as facts. In his action to prevent physicians from discussing abortion with their patients, George Bush violated our Constitution as blatantly as ever it was violated. In this act, he proved himself an enemy of American democracy. What does one call him? The invasion of Panama and the Gulf War, which the President (or his alter ego, the departing Mr. Sununu) organized and manipulated into being, resulted in the deaths of thousands—without need or justification. What does one call a man who put two such slaughters into action? The great George Bush? Symbol of democracy? Prince of decency? He has turned the Supreme Court of the United States into a Star Chamber, a black-robed set of obedient lackeys, studiously chipping away at every hard-won freedom of the past 50 years. He has crippled affirmative action and he has exhibited a malignant indifference to the suffering of the poor and the homeless and the unemployed.

In an adroit and unconscionable use of racism, he used the example of Willie Horton, a criminal who happened to be black and who violated his early release, to manipulate voters. George Bush ran on a program of fear and hatred. How does one label him?

Turn on C-SPAN. You will see Senator Jesse Helms, lord of tobacco and intolerance, or another of his mind-set being addressed by a so-called liberal as "my good friend" or "my estimable colleague." This kind of thing, which goes on constantly in Congress and which went on in the most sickening manner among the committee that sat in judgment on Anita Hill, is neither politeness nor evidence of manners. Quite to the contrary, it is a further muddying of mental processes that were neither very clear nor very honest to begin with. I am all for honest labeling on food and medicine—and on the men we pay to make our laws.

December 16, 1991

Chapter 11

The United States and Latin America

Silly Questions

D'emas, who is just a silly, uneducated savage from across the seas, keeps mumbling about the Noriega case.

"I don't understand why you keep dumping on him," D'emas said.

"I told you that he rigged the elections. We don't approve of rigged elections. We are a democratic country. We want everyone else to be just like us."

"That's a very nice thought," D'emas said. "But just a few months ago, your CIA rigged the election in El Salvador."

"Nonsense!"

"Well, if you'll look in *The New York Times*—"

"OK, OK," I agreed. "The trouble with trying to explain anything to you, D'emas, is that you miss the subtleties."

"I'm sorry."

"You see, D'emas, in El Salvador we support a bloody dictatorship that is our ally."

"But all of the media call Noriega a bloody dictator," D'emas said.

"But he's not our bloody dictator. He used to be when we approved of him running cocaine into our country, but then we changed our minds."

"You mean he became too bloody?" D'emas asked eagerly.

"Oh, no, no, no. He became too unruly. We do not like bloody dictators that are too unruly."

"But years ago, when the CIA and the Nobel Peace Prize winner, the good Dr. Kissinger, rigged the election in Chile and overthrew Salvador Allende and put the bloody dictator, Pinochet, in power—"

"Oh, no, D'emas, you have it all wrong, which is not surprising, considering your education. They did not rig the election in Chile. They engineered a military coup, which is quite another thing."

"Yes, of course."

"It wasn't until later that we had to rig elections in Chile, to keep Mr. Pinochet in power."

"But wasn't he a bloody dictator?" D'emas asked with some exasperation.

"Our bloody dictator, D'emas, and he faced a Marxist opposition. Can't you understand anything?"

"I try, but it's all terribly confusing. Now in the 50s—I remember reading that the great Mexican painter Diego Rivera painted his door black and against the black, the map of Guatemala, protesting the rigging of an election by the CIA—" he paused when he saw the look on my face. "Wrong again?"

"Absolutely wrong again. We did not rig an election. The CIA engineered a military coup because the legally elected Government of Arbenz Guzman—"

"Was Marxist?" D'emas asked eagerly.

"No. That was a long time ago, and we used different code words. The Arbenz Government had *socialist tendencies*."

"I thought you trained the death squads only when there was a Marxist threat?"

"You poor silly savage, it's the same thing. And we had to establish death squads in Guatemala. The Arbenz Government had such a large majority that there was no other way to keep it from returning to power."

"And in Honduras—"

"Oh, come on, D'emas, you can't be so ignorant as not to know about Honduras. It's our military base, our training ground. We keep thousands of troops in Honduras, and we just can't let any soft-headed reform government get in there and tell us what to do and what not to do and start messing with such things as legal trials and habeas corpus and the rights of an individual. It's also our base for running the Contras, and training and supplying them and providing backup for the war against Nicaragua. Do you think the Contras would last 10 minutes if we didn't have that huge, expensive base there in Honduras? My goodness, D'emas, do you realize how many millions it takes to hold on to Honduras? If we didn't rig elections and train their death squads, we'd have nothing but trouble."

Subdued, D'emas nodded. "I'm beginning to understand," he said, "but about Nicaragua—when you had your own bloody dictator, Mr. Somoza, right in your pocket, ready to do anything you wanted him to do, rigging every election just as his father did before him, just as obedient and sycophantic as your average Congressman—when you had him right there in the palm of your hand, why did you let the people throw him out?"

"We made a mistake," I admitted. "Every government makes mistakes, D'emas. We're not infallible."

May 22, 1989

What Brave Fellows

Suppose that Polish Communists had tortured and murdered six Jesuit priests, then cleaved open their skulls so that the brains poured out: Can you imagine the outrage that would have shaken the whole Western world, the screams from our anchormen, the roar of rage in Congress, the editorials, the denunciations? It's not hard to imagine, is it?

But it didn't happen in Poland. It happened in El Salvador, in a tiny country in Central America, a country the size of Massachusetts with a population of fewer than 6 million of the poorest people in the Western Hemisphere. And the Jesuit priests were murdered by death squads trained in their art by the CIA, wearing uniforms made in America, carrying American weapons that our Government gave them, and driven by a hatred for the Catholic Church unmatched in any country on earth. In pursuit of this hatred, these death squads have in the past murdered Catholic lay workers and nuns, raping the nuns in the process. They also murdered, at the altar of his church, the Catholic archbishop of El Salvador.

In all of this, there was no question of where the guilt lay. The murderers of the nuns were arrested and put on trial and convicted. Then they were released. All of the murders were a part of the process by which a tiny minority of rich planters and merchants held the entire country as their medieval fief.

Now, all of this, every step of it, was known to Washington, to both the Administration and the Congress. More than a billion dollars of taxpayers' money has been funneled to this tiny minority in El Salvador, and this money has paid for the slaughter of 70,000 citizens of this poor, damned land. So our hands, your hands and mine, are stained with the blood of saintly people who lived only to work among the poor and help them.

The excuse for this is that the few thousand armed guerrillas who resist the death squads and their masters pose a threat to the United States because they are "Marxists," and that this tiny country, a thousand miles south of our border, must be taught *democracy*, as we know it. The teaching of democracy, USA–CIA style, is in progress as I write these words. American helicopters are machine-gunning the civilian population. American bombers are reducing the towns and neighborhoods of the resistance to rubble, and our well-trained local death squads are killing anyone who speaks a word in protest.

Now if this were an act of insane brutality on the part of our Government, part of a plan with a purpose, it would be another matter entirely. But there is no plan or purpose. As in Vietnam, the totally brainless club in the White House have worked themselves into an act of endless horror, and none of them know why they are there or how they got there, and even those who have a suspicion that they have been taken in and hornswoggled dare not speak up. This is the terrible tragedy that we face, not that the people in the White House are wicked, but rather that they are incapable of anticipating the consequences of their actions. In a criminal trial, such inability would be specified as psychopathic. But our media are so pathetically weak and craven that they would not dare to frame such an indictment. Instead, they buy the garbage about Marxists and whisper that no one really knows who commits these abominations.

As for the Congress that systematically votes these millions for the death squads and the people who run them, what is one to say? They have just voted themselves a pay raise—something they have planned and plotted for months, stiffening their backs to meet the first public wave of anger and indignation, retreating with the promise that when the public disgust abated, they would try again. And they did, brave souls! They quietly put together a bill granting them a pay raise, and then, when the world exploded with the news that the Berlin Wall was no more, they moved their bill and passed it. What a brave and ingenious lot they are, these guardians of the Republic!

Their last moment of passion came when they were able to spring to their collective feet and denounce the burning of the flag. What brave fellows they were, each following the next with spicy and eloquent tirades against flag-burning! But the question of traducing the flag, shaming it, putting it in the service of murderers and torturers, wetting it with the blood of martyrs—this question never arose.

Ah, well, we are told that this is the era of greed and shamelessness, and perhaps we would be disappointed if our fine Congress did not lead the way and give the whole world lessons in greed, shamelessness and buoyant cowardice. How proud they must be!

December 4, 1989

A Letter to the President

President George Bush
The White House
Washington, D.C.

Dear George:

Wow! Do you realize that you did it? Absolutely, and nobody but nobody will ever call you a wimp again. Wimp indeed! Do you realize that this is the first time in 3,000 years—the first time since the fall of Troy—that a great leader declared war and destroyed a city to avenge the honor of a woman. And people should remember this—that when Paris, the Trojan, lifted Helen out of Agamemnon's bed, he not only insulted her; he raped her and took her off to Troy, and no wonder Agamemnon and his brother Menelaus and Achilles and Odysseus and the rest of them decided that there was nothing else to it but to pull together maybe 60,000 Greeks, maybe 70,000, and teach the Trojans that you don't go around raping and kidnapping women.

I say that was small stuff. You leaped to the defense and honor of womanhood before that gross Panamanian thug (Panamanians who backed Noriega are all thugs, as opposed to the Salvadoran freedom fighters who murder priests only when they have to) could even have a go at raping a clean, decent, virginal American woman. You stopped it right in its tracks, and you told the whole world that nobody, but nobody could kick an American Marine in the groin or insult American womanhood. You didn't wait until some Panamanian thug raped this clean, decent American woman, as Agamemnon did, sitting back on his kiester while some Trojan thug raped his gal and walked off with her.

Wimp? No way. It's true that 25 American boys are dead, and people might take that amiss and be prone to criticize you. But it seems to me that you have spelled out your dislike for General Noriega so vehemently that any American with a tittle of sense should realize that he had to go, no matter what the cost. Why, if we didn't rouse out 25,000 soldiers, and warplanes and tanks and choppers and even a warship or two, you would have been frustrated, and wouldn't that be a hell of a note, a President who was frustrated! A man doesn't break his back and work his ass off and raise millions of dollars and travel the country back and forth a dozen times and spend sleepless hours memorizing every word Peggy Noonan writes for him to end up being frustrated. No, sir. A frustrated man is a wimp, and George Bush is no wimp. Let the world get that through its skull.

Of course, the mothers and fathers of those 25 kids who died might not see the whole picture, but that's to be expected. People do get upset when their children are killed, and the first question they ask is why. "Why did my son die?" And you can't just tell them that their kids died to get General Noriega and bring him to justice, as you're so fond of saying.

And then those 200-plus American kids who were wounded, they might not see the whole picture either; but that's their own lack of patriotism. You know, we all watch "M*A*S*H" and we know that when a kid's wounded, there's Hawkeye to sew him up, and before the end of the half-hour of television, he's good as new. But on the other hand, the fact is—and the media rarely mention this—that modern weapons inflict terrible wounds that shatter bones and limbs and minds, and that wounded men carry this honor for a lifetime, with no Hawkeye to mend it or stop the awful and endless pain. And it's just your bad luck that right now a new film called *Born on the Fourth of July* has opened, and the foolish people who see it are going to ask a lot of questions about whether it was worth so many dead and wounded American boys to try to get General Noriega

Well, no one ever said that being President is like tending a rose garden, and you just stick to your guns, the way Ronnie did when we lost a battalion of Marines in Beirut, and hell, if a President can't take a few losses in carrying out his policies, what's the use of being President?

I think, Mr. President, that we can all be grateful that nobody in the media is making much fuss about the innocent Panama civilians who died in this war. They may number in the hundreds or in the thousands, but nobody's going to know because we don't count them, and when you come down to it, they're not even white. What I find real annoying is that so many pictures of Panama City almost totally destroyed are being shown, and what do people think—that you can make an omelet without breaking eggs? People go around muttering that you didn't have to destroy the whole city, and what else can you expect from people who don't know the first think about national defense.

We all feel for your disappointment in not catching Noriega at first, and people who don't understand frustration are saying that the whole war was for no reason that anyone can figure out, but don't let that get to you. The wimp factor is gone. You sure as hell showed them, and you did it without a word from Peggy Noonan.

January 15, 1990

What Every Nicaraguan Understands

In all the reporting, both print and electronic, of the election in Nicaragua, there has been an almost sublime unwillingness to think or illuminate. It is very easy for any thoughtful person to tick off the media as willing tools of the Administration, but that kind of conspiracy-response has little validity. What the media lack are imagination and, most frequently, common sense.

Take for example the position of a very average woman in Nicaragua. First of all, she understands what every citizen of Nicaragua understands, summed up best in the Mexican expression of agony: "Too far from God and too close to the United States." For 10 years she has witnessed her children's hunger. She has seen days when not a bean nor a grain of rice was available. She has lived in constant fear that Contras would come out of the night and murder her children. She has seen her husband unemployed with no hope of a job in the future. She has watched her children's clothes disintegrate. With all her heart, she may support the Sandinistas, but she knows that all her agony comes from the United States and she knows that the agony will not end so long as the Sandinistas are in power.

She knows that the Government in Washington has organized an army of mercenaries and pays and supports that army in Honduras, a land that the United States owns, body and soul, and that this army, armed and paid by Washington, will continue to war against her country for as long as Washington desires. She also knows that the Sandinistas cannot destroy this army, since should the Sandinistas even venture onto Honduran soil, where the Contras base themselves, it will elicit an immediate armed response from the United States. And she knows that since the Contra soldiers are illiterate—at least 90 percent of them—there is no way of reaching them or changing their minds.

She knows all this because everyone in Nicaragua knows this, and I, a long way from Nicaragua, also know it. There is no mysterious source for my knowledge. It all comes from that very excellent paper *The New York Times*. But what does not come from *The Times* is any real explanation of what its reporting means. For example, take a story by Lindsey Gruson on March 5:

> They [the Contras] harbor a deep hatred for the Sandinistas. But lacking political experience they fall back on the confrontational language that sustained the largely illiterate army during its years of combat. As a result, there is little uniform opinion or discipline among the rebels.

This is the third time I have seen in the pages of *The Times* a suggestion that the Contras were illiterate and confused. In the rest of the media, nothing. But in *The Times*, ample evidence of everything I have attributed to the knowledge of the Nicaraguan woman. I put it together from the newspaper; she lives it and, living it, she votes for Mrs. Chamorro. It does not matter how much she loves the Sandinistas, how much she may admire Daniel Ortega, how much she may despise the Contras, she has seen enough of horror and misery and hunger and she knows that the only way to end it is to give in to the United States and the way to do that is to vote for Mrs. Chamorro.

To know this, to be able to put two and two together and arrive at four is simply basic common sense. Every woman with a family and children will accept what I have written here. I have been through enough of war and associated horrors in my own lifetime to know that people are not, by and large, heroic. When they do perform heroic acts and endure great suffering, then they are driven by an extraordinary necessity. In the light of this, it is not Mrs. Chamorro's victorious vote that defines the situation in Nicaragua, but the amazing fact that Mr. Ortega got more than 40 percent of the votes. Any reporter, print or otherwise, should know enough political history to understand that voters do not, by and large, vote ideologically. They vote against higher taxes, for social security, for security as they see it, for the right of choice, against abortion and so forth and so on. And when the husband is unemployed and when the kids are hungry, they vote for what will ease the hunger.

With this in mind, the situation in Nicaragua after the election should be looked at in a different way; but that would be too much to expect from the media. The slavish acquiescence to the frequently idiotic and childish releases from the Government in Washington does not define a free press. We see this quite clearly when we observe the change in the Soviet Union from a Government-controlled press to the beginnings of a free press. It is time that we saw some beginnings in our own country as well.

March 19, 1990

Why Our Great Democracy Goes To War

My friend, D'emas, who comes from one of those tiny South Sea Islands so primitive that they have neither an army nor a proper prison, is in New York studying American democracy. I try to help him when I can and clear up some of his more obvious confusions. This time, it was the trial of Gen. Manual Antonio Noriega that bewildered him.

"It would seem," D'emas said, "that according to what I read in *The New York Times*, the Government's case against Mr. Noriega is so slight and so brittle that they may have to drop the charges against him."

I agreed that such was a possibility.

"I have never understood this Noriega business," D'emas said. "Even if he was a criminal, still he was the head man in Panama."

"He was indeed."

"I've been studying that wonderful document, the Constitution of the United States, and I can't find any mention in it of the right of the United States to go into another country and arrest the president or prime minister or whatever of that country."

"Of course," I agreed. "That's the remarkable thing about the Constitution. It could not possibly anticipate every contingency that might arise. How could the framers possibly anticipate that there would be a Drug Enforcement Agency in 1991, and that this agency would make a deal with Mr. Noriega for him to give them information about other drug dealers?"

"Is that why they arrested him?" D'emas asked incredulously.

"Oh, no. They claim to have arrested him because he dealt in drugs."

"But even if he did," D'emas argued, "he was the head of another country."

"Well, not really. You see, we're somewhat uncertain about whether Panama is a sovereign nation or whether we own it."

"But I recall," D'emas argued, "that you yourself wrote that Mr. Bush went to war in Panama because one of Mr. Noriega's soldiers had insulted an American woman."

"Oh, yes—of course. Mr. Bush is a gentleman, with prep school and college and all sorts of old family money behind him, so it just infuriates him to see an American woman insulted by some wretched Hispanic."

"And that's why you attacked Panama?"

"D'emas, D'emas," I said soothingly, seeing that the poor primitive was beginning to work himself into a state, "we are a responsible nation. It wasn't only the case of a woman being mistreated. The Panamanian soldiers killed an American soldier."

"But that was in Panama—in their country."

"D'emas, I tried to explain to you that Panama is not really an independent country."

"You mean, it's a part of the United States?"

"Sort of."

"But then you went on and killed almost 3,000 Panamanian civilians. Would you do a thing like that if Panama was your own country?"

"We had to. To get Noriega. Mr. Bush hates Mr. Noriega."

"But Charles Peters," D'emas said, "who is editor of the *Washington Monthly*, wrote that the Noriega government was replaced by a new set of drug dealers."

"That's the trouble with people like Charles Peters," I explained patiently. "He has no faith in what the White House says, so whenever there's an announcement from the White House, he sets out to prove that what the Government said is a lie."

"Is it always a lie?"

"Almost always, but that doesn't change anything. If everyone was to disbelieve everything the White House puts out, how would the Government function?"

"By telling the truth?" D'emas asked very tentatively.

"No government can function by telling the truth, D'emas. Do you think anyone would ever support a war if the Government told the truth? Here we won a glorious victory over Iraq, and we killed at least 105,000 of them and had no losses ourselves except one building struck by a missile and a handful of troops killed by friendly fire, and we draped practically the whole country in yellow ribbon, which was wonderful for the ribbon makers and salesmen—"

"But right here in *The New York Times*," D'emas said, interrupting me, "it says that the Kuwaitis treat their working people like dogs. They say of one maid, 'She was refused permission to leave [her workplace] for even a few minutes . . . her work began before dawn and ended long after midnight . . . [I]f she failed to respond fast enough, she was beaten . . . she was raped.' And there are dozens of similar examples."

"Exactly," I agreed. "And do you think that if we told the truth about what kind of tyrannical swine the Kuwaitis are, we could have had all that yellow ribbon and all the parades?"

"But perhaps you could have avoided the war?"

"D'emas, D'emas, we can't avoid wars. We're a great democracy, and the only way you can teach other benighted nations about democracy is to go to war and kill enough of them to make them understand that the Pentagon is the fountainhead of democracy, and if we stop making guns and killing people, our democracy will collapse."

"Then I certainly hope you will convict Mr. Noriega," D'emas said. "Otherwise you've killed all those people for nothing."

"Not for nothing," I countered gently. "After all, they did insult an American woman."

February 3, 1992

Chapter 12

The Collapse of Communism

A Prison and a Church

Thousands of men and women of good will have had a lifelong dream shattered as they witnessed the apparent disintegration of the Soviet Union. With the Soviet Union's failure, as they saw it, went man's hope for socialism and brotherhood; but for myself, I simply do not accept as any blueprint for socialism a system that did away with democracy, competition and any sort of viable market-system. But if not socialism, what was it? What happened after Lenin, speaking to the Russian masses in 1917, said, "Comrades, let us begin the building of socialism"?

Did a socialist structure collapse, or was it the Leninist structure that imposed this awful burden on the Soviet people? Stalin, a murderous madman, is too easily blamed. Better to think of Lenin, mummified at the Kremlin, the living-dead god of a new religion.

In 1914, Lenin and his comrades, revolutionaries exiled from Czarist Russia, watched as the socialist parties of Europe voted to support the great war that was then beginning. Party after party, pledged to peace, betrayed their membership and the socialist ideal. This was most tragically apparent in Germany, where the largest socialist party in Europe supported the Kaiser in his aggressive attack on France and the Low Countries.

Lenin, heartsick at this, decided that a new kind of socialist party must be created, a party where decisions once made would be the result of discussions at the bottom—the mass level of the party. By imposing upon such a party an absolute discipline, the leadership would always be responsible to the membership and, in turn, decisions of the leadership would travel down to the membership, there to be discussed and ratified or rejected.

He called this new pattern of organization "Democratic Centralism," and to separate it from the prewar socialist movement, he called it the Communist Party—communism being the final stage of socialist development. Democratic Centralism was intended as a means to give power to the rank and file party units—"All power to the soviets (councils) of workers and peasants," as the slogan went. At the bottom, the party units, at the next level, regional and factory groups, at the next level, state groups—in all, a pyramid leading up to the central committee and the general secretary of the party. And as this structure went, so would the power go, from the basic groups to the next level to the next level and to the top. Whereby, the power of the members—all members—would control the party and its decisions.

This was Democratic Centralism. The only trouble was that as centralism, it worked, as a democratic function, it did not work. Instead of decisions going from the members upward, the decisions went from the leaders downward. In his theoretical democratic structure, Lenin created the perfect vehicle for dictatorship.

Now it is important to remember that in every governmental structure, most of the power flows down, not up. Anyone who reads the newspapers knows that what Washington does is not the will of the people or to the benefit of most of the people. The difference is in dissent, and the Leninist structure was used by the Soviet leadership to stifle dissent. Without the power to dissent, the *democratic* part of the structure was totally castrated.

With a vision of brotherhood slowly disintegrating—for no brotherhood or decency is possible where great power is used without checks—the Leninist structure became a prison and a church. As a church, it paraded Marxism as a religion, a new earthly religion given as new knowledge, and as a prison it sealed the minds of its believers. He who questioned or doubted was cast out of the church, or imprisoned or executed. The hammer and sickle became as sacred as the cross or the scimitar or the six-pointed star, and while the leaders could not call upon God, they could call upon the mystery of Lenin and Marx. I recall a Russian scientist telling me that he had to give lip service to the party's denunciation of Einstein as a capitalist fraud, while he used Einstein's calculations as a basis for his work on the atom bomb.

What happened in Russia between 1917 and 1990 was not socialism. It was a new form of dictatorship that Lenin had all unwittingly invented, and the great accomplishments of Russia, the defeat of Hitler, the scientific achievements— these were of the Russian people, in spite of the dictatorship.

Nor was it socialism that failed. Like Christianity, socialism has never really been given a fair try. It still remains the best hope of man; and the destruction of the Russian farm, the execution of intellectuals, the gathering of the power of an immense country into the hands of one lunatic, the prostituting of art and literature to the control of incompetents, the increasing paranoia of its rulers before the time of Mikhail Gorbachev—all of these had nothing to do with socialism.

At the very beginning the men who took power in Russia forgot that dissent, disbelief, questioning and doubt are the only roads to the stars. The devil has two names—orthodoxy and righteousness.

June 25, 1990

Let Anti-Communism Be Laid to Rest

In August 1954, my wife and I were guests of the great Mexican painter Diego Rivera. On the door to his house, there was a freshly painted replica of the flag of Guatemala, and when we asked him about it, he reminded us that only weeks before, the legally elected Government of Guatemala, the first such freely elected and democratic Government in Guatemala's history, had been overthrown by the Central Intelligence Agency of the United States. Together with a company of hired killers under the leadership of Colonel Carlos Castillo Armas, the CIA overthrew the elected President, Jacobo Arbenz, and installed one of the world's cruelest and bloodiest dictatorships—a system of government that continues to this day.

The current dictator of Guatemala, General Hector Alejandro Gramajo, cheerfully explains the techniques of controlling a society with the following (as quoted by the Center for Constitutional Rights): "As a professional soldier I just did my duty, and I'm very proud of it. You needn't kill everyone to complete the job [of control]. If you kill only 30 percent of the people, it is enough."

Bless his heart! And this protector of the people, still kept in power by the CIA and millions of American dollars, current master of the continuing bloodbath that we established 37 years go, was granted, only a few months ago, a special master's degree in public administration by Harvard University's John F. Kennedy School of Government. Blessed be those who move through the stately halls of Harvard!

As Diego Rivera said to us at the time: "How else does a painter cry out in anger? Like Mexico, Guatemala is too far from God and too close to the United States."

In regard to that current ruler, General Gramajo, upon whom our Government casts not only a warm avuncular eye but also millions of dollars and sundry military and police advisors, the Center for Constitutional Rights lists certain abuses. One that is more or less typical is the case of an American nun of the Ursuline Order, Sister Dianna Ortiz, OSU, as follows: "Sister Dianna was kidnapped, tortured, raped, burned and otherwise brutally abused in Guatemala by military and security personnel under the direction and control of General Gramajo. Then the general had the unspeakable gall to defame Sister Dianna by repeatedly asserting that her abduction and torture were the result of a love affair."

The abuse and murder of Catholic nuns, priests and at least once a bishop is a continuing affair in Central America that Washington and our Congress conveniently ignore and the Pope in Rome sees fit to mention hardly at all. It is one of the curious imbalances of George Bush's foreign policy. Had any of those obscenities taken place in Poland or Lithuania, the rage in Washington and the screaming anger of the media would have shaken the globe, but murder and torture in a client state, such as Guatemala or Honduras or El Salvador, is quite another kettle of fish, something to be whispered about approvingly and never, never to appear in the press.

The easy word to cover and explain those obscenities was "communism," the various nuns and priests deserving of death since they were working in support of communist resistance. Once the State Department labeled a government Marxist or Communist, then no practice against the people of said government, no matter how vile and indecent and brutal, would be condemned.

The cheap and bloody deceit upon which such practice is founded must be re-examined seriously in the light of recent events in the Soviet Union. The so-called "Marxist" resistance must be recognized for what it actually is, a movement against tyranny, with no relationship to the bugaboo of communism. Communism as practiced in the Soviet Union has moved off the world stage of history—and the only place where it was ever practiced as a mode of government was the Soviet Union. Repression here in the United States reached its ugliest and most damnable form with the excuse of opposing communism, and it is unhappily remembered as "McCarthyism." Oppression as exercised abroad in the foreign policy of the United States also took its justification as being central to the struggle against communism. The whole unspeakable race of cold-warriors arose as the "sacred" enemies of communism, and, money-wise, they did very well for themselves. A clownish footnote was created when the coup against Mikhail Gorbachev appeared to have some measure of success, and in those few hours, the almost forgotten cold-warriors emerged from under their various rocks and out of their various crevices to crowd the television screens, to put themselves back in business and once again to scream of the evil Communist menace that confronts us. Fortunately, they crawled back to rest as soon as the coup failed.

It is time that all of us recognized that the evil we do is done out of greed and the lust for power. Let communism as the enemy be laid to rest, once and for all.

September 9, 1991

Why Soviet Communism Failed

There is an extraordinary list of "experts" of various persuasions ready and willing to tell us why communism failed in the Soviet Union, and since very few of them make much sense, I thought I might try my own hand at the game. At least, I have lived through most of it, and can thereby exercise my own hindsight, and perhaps I can clarify a point or two.

Firstly, we must understand that communism in Russia was an attempt to impose socialism on Russia and the other parts of the old Czarist empire by force and violence, namely what Lenin called the dictatorship of the proletariat. Karl Marx had never dreamed of socialism in Russia, which, in his time and in Lenin's time, was an agrarian society of latifundia and small peasant holdings. Ninety percent of its population were engaged in agriculture, as opposed to 5 percent in the United States today, and its so-called "proletariat" was tiny in terms of the overall population. Marx conceived of socialism as a stage of society after capitalism, and he spoke of its possibility in Germany, France or England—never in Czarist Russia.

Nevertheless, Lenin, followed by Stalin, went ahead in a desperate effort to turn the vast agrarian masses into industrial workers in a single generation. It failed for the following reasons:

1. Most importantly, because Stalin launched a malignant campaign against the small farmer, the *kulak*, a ferocious and bloody cam-

paign which destroyed not only the middle-sized farmer, but millions of peasant holdings as well. (China avoided this error.) They were to be replaced by factory farms, but the factory farms were so badly and indifferently managed that it took five acres to equal the output of a single acre in a family holding. The result was endless food shortage. A society that cannot feed its population cannot survive.

2. In its creation of industrial units, the Soviet's rejection of syndicalism as being anti-Marxist resulted in the virtual elimination of industrial competition. Most simply, syndicalism is the ownership and operation of factories by the workers in that particular factory. As a result, workers had no interest in production other than holding their jobs—as guaranteed by the society—and as many as 40 years ago, goldbricking became a national disease.
3. The virtual destruction—death and exile—of Russia's small middle class in the course of the revolution narrowed its pool of educated planners and managers and scientists to the point where the men in power had to substitute a mystical set of facts and values (which they called Marxism and which dishonored the name) for reality.
4. The creation of a national master-plan of production for the entire and vast Soviet empire succeeded in robbing member states of initiative and inventiveness, and was so unrelated to local need and reality that it turned into chaos.
5. The intervention of British and American troops briefly in Siberia in the 1920s, combined with a very Russian fear of the outside world, produced manifold levels of paranoia not only in the view of the world outside the Soviet Union, but its enemies (real and imagined) inside the Soviet Union. So convinced were the Soviets that they had created a house of cards, that they saw every word of dissent and disagreement as part of the gigantic capitalist plot to overthrow them. The initial rigidity built into the Communist Party by Lenin to make certain that it could not be betrayed, turned into a priestly mania, rivaling the Spanish Inquisition in its war against heresy. This led to an institutional terror that served to stamp out not only imagination and scientific inquiry, but art itself. All government seeks thought control; here in America we have constitutional as well as traditional protections; in Russia, there was no such constitutional protection, nor was there any

> tradition of free thought. It is interesting, that in the land of the icon, iconoclasm should have been so savagely punished.

The enormous arms program of the Soviet Union was in good part a response to their fears and in good part a response to the military threat of the Western democracies. A military program such as we have witnessed on the part of the Western nations over the past forty years served to bleed the strength from all the great powers; but its effect on the Soviet Union was catastrophic. Starting without a comparable industrial base and work force, the Soviet military program literally pauperized the country. Thus, history, its internal errors, the isolation forced upon it by the western powers, the destruction by the invading Nazis, combined with hunger to cause the disintegration of the Soviet Union.

Now, of course, a hundred books would be required to tell this story properly and in detail, but the American people are entitled to see and understand the major forces at work. At its best, the Soviet Union was a dream of equality and brotherhood; at its worst, the Soviet Union became a monster, a prison house of nations and people, and of their minds. But let us not forget that the Red Army of the Soviet Union was the major force in destroying the Nazis and Hitlerism and, thus, making it possible for democracy to survive and flourish. The age of communism is over, but socialism has not failed, and without some trust in the possibility of democratic socialism, the future will be bleak indeed.

September 30, 1991

Chapter 13

The Failures of the Media

Front-Page Criminals

It is time we took a long, hard look at ourselves and at what we so blithely call our civilized society. A sick, drug-ridden sociopath, who has been brutalizing his live-in girlfriend for years, indifferently beats a lovely little 6-year-old girl to death. In a literary sense, Joel B. Steinberg is a monster, and Mayor Koch, whose brain always functions at least a block and a half to the rear of his tongue, declares that Mr. Steinberg should be boiled in oil.

Boiling in oil has never been a judicial solution for a crime, not even in Saudi Arabia; and as shocked as he might have been by the horror of the incident, Mr. Koch could have pointed out that in Joel Steinberg and Hedda Nussbaum, we have two very sick people. That does not make their crime—she to observe while he performed—less horrible, but it at least begins to make it understandable in a clinical sense. This city has thousands of mentally ill people.

But what I find as shocking as the crime itself, and much more indicative of the nature of our society, is the response of the public and the media. Joel Steinberg was brought to trial, his right in a society of law. He has committed the crime; Hedda Nussbaum bore witness to it, and a day or two in court would have spelled out the facts of the case and allowed the jury to make a judgment. Instead, two lawyers, well aware that the media gives a badge of celebrity to anyone whose face appears on the television a sufficient number of times, moved into the case as the defenders of Joel Steinberg; and from that point on, the Steinberg Trial became the media circus of America.

Weeks went by, yet the media treatment of the Steinberg case never slackened. Day after day, ad nauseam, the news of the world and the country and the city took a back seat to an endless repetition of the horrors of the Steinberg case. For weeks, one could not turn on a local news program without being treated—for what must have been a thousand times—to another sight of Hedda Nussbaum's bruised, broken body, as well as the injuries of the murdered child. Again and again, the television cameras moved in for closeups of Hedda Nussbaum's savagely mutilated legs, her broken face, her dulled catatonic eyes. There was never enough of it, and the cumulative horror of this evidence of insane cruelty reached a point in our household where we would look at no local news program until the first 10 minutes—the Steinberg section—was over. The newspapers, not to be undone, kept pace with television, and even the exalted *The New York Times*, on January 31, the day after the verdict, devoted not one but two large front-page stories to the Steinberg case, as well as a front-page story the following day.

Why? During this same period, events of earth-shaking importance occurred. Why was the country's—not simply the city's—attention fixed on the Steinberg case? Why did the public never tire of this display of horror? Why did no one cry, enough? Why have horror and violence become our mother's milk? If it seems that I overstate the case, then how does one explain the almost sadistic delight with which the TV newspeople brought us each new tidbit of this sorry affair?

Am I imagining things when I speak of sadistic delight? Perhaps I am, but even an exaggeration has a source.

And of course, the fact that Joel Steinberg and Hedda Nussbaum were Jewish—no mention of that anywhere, not even a whisper. I counted 11 brutal murders of children during what we might call "the Steinberg period." All of these victims were black or Hispanic, but they were just as alive, just as beautiful in that wonderful aspect of beauty that all children possess, and all they received in the way of notice was a few lines on page 12. They did run a couple of stories about the gentleman in Florida who admitted killing some 36 people before he went to his reward, and he had engaged in such innovations as chopping off the arms and legs of the teenagers he raped, but he was a white Christian, and apparently that makes a newsworthy difference. Some will hold that I must admit that such crimes are by no means common among Jews, and I agree; but at the same time, history forces me to recall that Jew-bashing is an integral part of "civilized" society.

I have been around for a long time, and perhaps that adds to my sensitivity, but I feel in my bones that it was that "fortunate" combination of horror and anti-Semitism that the media could not resist.

February 13, 1989

The Truth Is There If You Look for It

Some 1,800 church and synagogue people, priests, ministers, rabbis and other clerically connected paid for a full-page advertisement in the

Sunday, January 7, Connecticut edition of *The New York Times*. The advertisement said, simply:

> It is time. Truly it is past time. Past time for those of us from the religious community of Connecticut to acknowledge and to confess, as citizens of the United States and as people of God, our complicity in the violence and death in war-torn El Salvador. Let us acknowledge that we have allowed the resources of those great nations to supply bullets and bombs which have torn through the bodies of thousands of innocent children, women and men. We confess that $4 billion in United States aid over the last ten years has contributed to the deaths of over 70,000 persons, making miserable the lives of impoverished Salvadorans while the needs of our own poor go unmet.

Then this passionate and humble plea addresses itself to Christopher J. Dodd, United States Senator from Connecticut and chairman of the Senate Foreign Relations Subcommittee on Western Hemisphere Affairs. It calls for an end to arms shipments to El Salvador and it pleads for our nation to become a voice for peace and justice "and not an accessory to oppression and death."

Now, of course Senator Dodd does not need the voice of these good people or their information to know what has been going on in El Salvador. He has known for years about the death squads trained and armed by the CIA. He has known about the murders, the murder of the nuns, the archbishop, and lately the Jesuit priests; and he has voted again and again for a continuation of our role there. The gentle voice of this advertisement does not speak of the corruption of Senator Dodd, of the pretense he has made, over and over, of being both a liberal and compassionate man. But a liberal and compassionate man would not require the gentle plea of 1,800 people of God for him to display a human and humane stance.

What a travesty it is that we should elect a man to the Senate and then have to plead with him to represent us and to abandon the morality of a barbarian, but this is the way of government in the United States today. The people are forced to organize and plead for every common decency, for the right of women to own their bodies, for the right of the poor to have shelter, or the right of the hungry to eat, for the right of the sick to be healed, for the right of justice to the poor and oppressed of other nations, for the right of blacks to have equal justice, for the right of minorities to be represented—yes, I could go on and on.

But there are other rights for which we need no pleading at all, which require no demonstration of the people's will, namely: the right of the Government to spend billions of our hard-earned tax dollars on a bloated, mindless, military machine, on a CIA that even Hollywood portrays as a band of infantile, morally benighted nuts.

And lest we, the people, come out of this as upright citizens, endlessly put upon, there are other questions to be asked: not simply who voted Senator Dodd into office (he made the face of a liberal), but who voted Senator D'Amato into office? When we vote for a D'Amato, how do we dare plead for compassion or humane responses? And with all good feeling, I must ask the clergymen who took that fine advertisement in *The Times* where their voices were these past 10 years? Did it take the murder of a nun by the Contras to finally convince them that what we are told about Nicaragua and the Contras as well as El Salvador is something less than the truth?

Well, God be praised, we are learning. It comes slowly and hard but we are learning, even as the people of Russia and the people of China are learning and, in our own back yard, it is not likely that we will re-elect a D'Amato—or for that matter a Christopher Dodd. And if the 40 percent of our population eligible to vote does vote, Mr. Bush may be the last of his ilk to sit in the White House.

As for the question of the truth and how does one find it in a nation where every video station and almost every newspaper sings with the same contrived, manipulated voice, I can only say that the truth is there if you look for it. It can never be covered over entirely, and as one small proof of that I recommend to you the January 8, 1990, edition of *The New Yorker*. There, as the first piece in the *Talk of the Town* section, is a brilliant and bold story about Manuel Noriega and the truth of the war unleashed on Panama. It is a story told nowhere else in the major media, an unmasking of the gross lies we digest daily under the heading of news.

And once again underlining the fact that the *New Yorker* is and has been perhaps the best magazine published in America.

January 22, 1990

News Not Fit to Print

Some months ago, directly after the publication of my book of memoirs, *Being Red*, my publishers sent me on a book-signing and speaking tour of Washington, D.C. Part of it was a half-hour interview on the CBS program "Nightwatch," which runs from 1:30 A.M. to 4:00 A.M. and then is repeated.

My interviewer was a charming and knowledgeable young woman, and after some 20 minutes of conversation, she said to me, "Tell the story about Ronald Reagan and the Communist Party."

"You're kidding," I said.

"Oh, no. I want you to tell it."

"Where on earth did you hear it?" I wanted to know.

"It's been around. Our newsroom in New York knows about it."

"Come on," I said. "The story's been around on the coast for years, and I heard it from enough places to believe it, but we're on CBS—national television. You don't want me to tell this story on national television?"

"I certainly do. Look, Mr. Fast, we're at the end of your section of the program. If the powers-that-be don't want the story, all they have to do is snip it out."

"OK," I agreed. "Be it on your head.

"It happened in the 30s, and Ronald Reagan got carried away by the stories of the Communist Party helping the dispossessed, the Okies, the unemployed and the homeless. On top of this, many of his friends, men and women he most liked and respected, were members of the party. He turned to them and informed them that he wished to become a member of the Communist Party.

"This news was brought to the local leader of the Hollywood Communists, a noted film writer, dramatist and historian, now deceased. He asked around about Reagan, and word came back that he was a flake and not to be trusted with any opinion for more than 20 minutes. Whereupon the decision was taken to keep Reagan from joining the party, but to keep him on hold as a friend of the party and a supporter of party projects. The task of talking Reagan out of joining the party was given to an important and intelligent actor, still alive, but it was by no means an easy job. The actor and his wife sat with Reagan into the small hours of the morning before they convinced him that in his case, he served better as a friend of the party. So was history changed. And if you run this on national television—well, you won't."

"We'll see," my charming interviewer said.

She told me the day and the time, and dutifully, at 4:00 A.M. on the given day, I staggered to my television, turned it on and waited. And then, sure enough, it appeared, precisely as she had demanded it and I had told it, not a word excised, not a word changed. There it was, on national television, on a program which, I was told, had 10 million viewers.

Now one would imagine that a story like this—true enough, only a piece of gossip that had been rolling around newsrooms and dinner tables for over half a century, but even so an explosive tale—would be page-one news even without proof to substantiate it. I believe the story, because I believe the people I heard it from, and once, years ago, when a news director on a national network was trying to put together a TV show on the witch hunts and I suggested the "Ronald Reagan story," he replied that they knew all about it, but no way could it go out over the air.

When it did go out, after my interview in Washington, as far as I know, not a single newspaper, not a single media person anywhere in the United States picked it up. In light of this country's decades of slander and damnation directed against the Communist Party, one would think that a one-time decision of the man who would be President to join the Communist Party would be a matter of importance, if only for the historical record; yet by common, unspoken consent the so-called "free press" of the United States ignored it.

I call it to mind now because the dam has been broken by a most extraordinary and bold woman, one Kitty Kelley, who has written and published a biography of Nancy Reagan that holds both Nancy and her husband up to such shame as to make all the previous scandals of the White House and the Presidency mere childish escapades. The crassness, the stupidity, the greed of these two people, a man and his wife, who ran this country for eight years with the aid of two bunco experts who called themselves astrologers and mystics, can only be matched by the emperors of ancient Rome. Their naked mendacity boggles the mind, and the ease with which they hoodwinked millions of Americans into believing that they were people of decency spells out a sorry future for our country.

We put uninspired, stupid and worthless men into the Presidency, and then we say, *Respect the office if not the man.* This is bullshit, and to believe and honor a slogan so witless is to bring on our own destruction.

We have just been witness to a President who without cause or reason, but simply to support his own ego, put a nation and 100,000 and more human souls to death—a killing which he began and which will go on and on. We bring such awful things into being because we are unwilling to challenge the lies we are constantly fed.

April 22, 1991

America's Lost Voice

It was the Emperor of Japan in *The Mikado*, who sang out so forcefully, "My object all sublime, I shall achieve in time, to make the punishment fit the crime, the punishment fit the crime."

There's a heady aspiration, but not so easily done, and most of those who sit on the judge's bench are neither as sensible nor as compassionate as the Emperor of Japan. Ernest Brown Pryor, a 19-year-old student at the University of Virginia, was sentenced to 13 months in prison for passing on to a Federal agent a half-ounce of pot and a bit of hallucinogenic mushroom. Whether this was a sale or a gift is difficult to determine from the information I have, but simply passing the stuff is a crime under Federal law. The sentence of 13 months was specified so that the boy would lose his right to vote and other rights of citizenship, things he would retain if the sentence were less than a year.

Judge James Michael, who pronounced the sentence in the Federal District Court, hedged on the mindless cruelty of such a sentence by pleading that he had to conform to mandated Federal guidelines. The attorneys I talked to felt that guidelines could always be altered out of sufficient cause, so Judge Michael is by no means off the hook.

And what of the boy? Not only is his life stained by a jail record, but 13 months with criminals is not calculated to teach any variety of honesty or goodness or contribute to any elevation of soul and character. What has he done? As an imaginative kid of 19 years, offered hallucinogenic mushrooms, I would have grasped the opportunity to try it, having read so much about it. And as for pot, let he who has never tried a toke, my age or any other, come forward—and I'd likely say he was a liar if he did.

But before we leave Ernest Brown Pryor to the senseless punishment meted out to him, let us cast an eye on another sinner. The name of this one is Neil Bush, and he happens to be the son of President

George Bush. In a story datelined Washington, May 29, *The New York Times* states that:

> Federal regulators agreed in principle today to a $49.5 million settlement in their $200 million lawsuit against Neil Bush and 12 other former directors of Denver's defunct Silverado Banking, Saving and Loan Association . . . . The lawsuit singled out Mr. Bush for criticism, saying he had violated his obligation to avoid conflicts of interest by his participation in approving Silverado loans to William L. Walters and Kenneth M. Good, investors with him in the JNB Exploration Company.

Anyone who protests that young Mr. Bush may have been unduly tempted by the glow of millions may be overlooking another incident reported in the same issue of *The New York Times*—where we learned that, "Neil Bush was disqualified from a tennis tournament last weekend for playing in a category below his United States Tennis Association ranking." But that was not a legal offense, and allegedly diddling with bank loans isn't going to cost Mr. Bush one damn day in jail.

So the Pryor kid will stay in jail for a year and a month and watch his life turn into ashes, and Neil Bush will go on playing tennis as he sees it. So does the punishment fit the crime. Discussing this inspirational stuff with a friend of ours, she put forth the proposition that we have reached a point in our history where nobody gives a damn about anything at all. A President of these United States addresses a great meeting of Southern Baptists and tells them, weeping as he speaks, that he prayed to God for guidance before he gave the signal to put a nation and 200,000 of its citizens to death, and a week or so ago, we held an enormous and expensive parade in New York City to celebrate the victory, even as the good Mussolini paraded his troops through Addis Ababa in the 1930s to celebrate the victory of his aircraft over the spear-carrying Ethiopians. Mussolini's son, flying one of the fascist bombers, said feelingly that when one of his bombs burst, he saw it as a beautiful rose unfolding. An American airman said that as he strafed the fleeing Iraqis, they resembled cockroaches fleeing from the light. And we hear no cry of outrage, only the silence of a nation that has ceased to give a damn.

I don't agree with that. We have not lost a sense of pity, of outrage, of compassion, of human decency. We have lost a voice that we once called a free press. We call it *the media* today, and the media say nothing the establishment does not desire us to hear. And in any 24 hours, the media can convince the public that night is day and that wrong is right. And they do, by golly, they certainly do.

June 24–July 1, 1991

Truth, War, and the Fate of Our Planet

What is the nature of news, truth, freedom of the press or freedom of the airwaves? The Federal Government assures us that the recession is over, and the media reflect that assurance—in spite of the fact that every aspect of reality states that the Government is lying.

The Government reports 6 million unemployed, when a simple addition of inner-city unemployment, teenagers who have never had their first job, unemployed who out of despair have ceased to hunt for jobs, homeless jobless people and agrarian jobless people adds up to an additional 12 million. Where is that reflected in the media?

The media have forgotten Desert Storm, and its overweight hero is quietly penning his multimillion-dollar memoirs, but *Greenpeace* magazine informs us:

> Few observers outside this country are as enamored as most Americans are with the success of the military campaign. Baghdad's electric and water infrastructure is destroyed. . . . Between 20,000 and 30,000 cubic meters of raw sewage are pouring into the Tigris River each day. A Harvard study reported in May that 55,000 Iraqi children have already died as a result of the "indirect effects" of the allied bombing and predicted that 170,000 more children will die by the end of the year.

Buried by the media, if reported at all—as compared to the millions of words hurled at us to advertise the antics of the "holy" rioters in Wichita. When is a child a child, and when is murder murder?

As to why so little is said about the most devastating ecological disaster in the history of mankind, Brent Blackwater of Friends of the Earth observes, "It is hard to get anyone to say anything publicly. People will lose their jobs. The scientists are walking on eggshells, perhaps out of fear of loss of research funding. They have begun effective self-censorship."

In terms of other things muted successfully by our so-called "free press," *Greenpeace* magazine goes on to say of the Gulf War:

> For the first time, the potential impact of war on the environment was raised in advance of the actual battle. The wisdom of Desert Storm can in part be judged by how well these factors were considered. The White House knew as early as November, three months before Desert Storm began, that Hussein had wired the wellheads with explosives. The President opted for war despite the potential impact . . . and over the objections of nearly half of the U.S. Congress and several of the President's senior advisors.

The key to the above is the fact of the wired wellheads. The President of the United States has access to any and all scientific information, as Truman once demonstrated when, after calling the country's leading physicists to give testimony before the Joint Chiefs, he decided to forgo his plans for an atomic raid on the Soviet Union. I have no admiration for Truman, but when he was assured that the atomic bombing of the Soviet cities might bring about the end of most life on earth, he put his beloved plans for destruction to rest. Mr. Bush, on the other hand, had ample opportunity to calculate the damage—not simply to Kuwait and Iraq and Iran, but also the planet and its ecosphere—and to weigh the potential damage carefully.

It is what you might expect from the leader of a nation that holds the fate of the planet in its hands and, while I do not compare the current damage to the terrifying results that might have been effected by Truman's plan, it is the most awful ecological disaster in the history of mankind. Here is a partial assessment of that damage by André Carothers, writing for *Greenpeace*:

> Roughly three to six million barrels of oil a day are going up in flames inside an area the size of the greater New York metropolitan area. The plume [of smoke and pollution] represents 10 percent of the oil the world burns in a single day, but it is burning far less cleanly, and therefore releasing a greater amount of toxic particulates. The toxic pollution released in a single day in June was ten times that released in a day by all the industries in the United States, according to the Worldwatch Institute. Between five and ten million tons of sulfur diox-

> ide will be released in a year by the fires, more than the combined output of France, Germany and the United Kingdom.

The fact that the President and his curious assistant in the White House, Mr. Sununu, anticipated no part of this result can be attributed to one of two things, a callous indifference to the fate of the planet Earth or a stupidity beyond measure of conscience. In either case, Mr. Bush has not been called to an accounting, either by the so-called Congress of the United States or by the media—the electronic voice that harangues the people night and day, the newspapers or the multitude of magazines that crowd the newsstands and fill our mailboxes.

Of course, there is nothing new in this. Some day, an honest historian will write the truth about the unspeakable gang—excepting a handful—of Presidents who have occupied the White House since this country came into being, and who have lied to the public, destroyed evidence, engaged in monstrous malfeasance and taken us into bloody, unjust and unnecessary wars, slaughtering and dispossessing a hundred Indian tribes, taking their land by conquest and occupying it. But those were local slaughters, spread out over the years, and never endangering the planet itself. Today, this has changed. We have demonstrated that we can slaughter a quarter-million human beings in days and that we can bring the planet into mortal danger. Let's think about it.

October 7, 1991

The Film *J.F.K.*

In 1976, the Chicago-based Henry Regnery Company published a book titled *Betrayal*, written by one Robert D. Morrow, a CIA contract operative. It spelled out the story of the Kennedy assassination—in very much the same way as the recently released film *JFK*. The book is more specific than the film, in that Mr. Morrow uncovers the plot in more detail and names the assassins. In his introduction, the author writes:

> Much of the information in this book has already been supplied to the U.S. Senate Committee on Intelligence. That is why I offered to reveal

in secret testimony before that committee additional information that I could not in good conscience include here.

Whether the committee ever heard that additional information I do not know, but it is not difficult to surmise what it was, and I will write about that below. Meanwhile, here was a situation where an ex-CIA operative and writer, sound enough to convince a reputable publisher to publish his manuscript, named a number of men as actively participating in the murder of an American President, and had his testimony rejected out of hand. Not one of the assassins he mentions was ever brought to trial, and the very existence of the book was shrouded in the familiar media silence. With good reason: The accusations spelled out in this book are so shattering and reach so widely into various sections of the Federal Government that they amount to the greatest and most reprehensible scandal in the history of this nation. They also add up to a terrible indictment of the CIA.

Now, almost 30 years after the assassination, the same material that appeared in *Betrayal* is presented to the world in the form of a superb and electrifying film—perhaps one of the most important films ever made. The logic of the film is almost incontrovertible. For three hours I watched spellbound—not because the contents of the film were new to me but because the courage and talent of Oliver Stone had turned the material into a heart-breaking human document.

In the film, Mr. Stone hints at the involvement of then Vice President Lyndon B. Johnson in the assassination plot. This is very delicate ground—it is possibly the material Mr. Morrow left out of his book—yet for years, in private conversations, this possibility was discussed: Johnson as the man who had most to gain, Johnson as a man without compassion or mercy, and to my mind without a shred of human decency. I have a few lines of hearsay to add to that notion. A week or so after the Kennedy assassination, my wife and I were invited to dine with two old friends, Ceil and William Field, and to meet a friend of theirs who worked for a Dallas newspaper and who very much wanted to speak to me. A bright, amiable and sensible woman, she told me the following story:

Her assignment on the day of Kennedy's death was to cover the reception at the Johnson home, scheduled for later that November 22, 1963. Thinking to do some background reporting, she went directly to the Johnson home, so that she might describe the preparations under way for the intended celebration. But, as she told us, there were no preparations. The house was locked, and when she looked through the picture window into the living room, she saw the room in a mess, newspapers scattered around, no indication of anything spelling out the anticipation of receiving an honored guest.

"In other words," she said to us, "the Vice President knew quite well that Kennedy would not arrive, not that day, not ever."

Of course we challenged her story. It was only days since the President had been murdered, and we were all still in shock, still filled with the horror of that moment, and still impressed by the calm and dignity with which Lyndon B. Johnson had taken over the reigns of government. The true nature of Johnson was still to be revealed, the thousands of young voices chanting, "Hey, hey, L.B.J., how many kids did you kill today?" still in the future, the 75,000 dead of the Vietnam War still alive, the grim statistic of 30,000 Vietnam veterans among the homeless not yet calculated. Johnson was still the Texas schoolteacher turned politician, not the obsessed, murderous leader of the war with Vietnam.

Thus, when the reporter from Dallas told her story, we were loath to credit it with any importance. Certainly, if Johnson was in a conspiracy to kill Kennedy, he would have covered his bases by making all preparations for the party. At that time, the very notion of a conspiracy was unthinkable—and yet her story remained with me.

In the years since then, one investigation after another centered its efforts on the Kennedy murder. Painstakingly, dozens of investigators put together the facts of the conspiracy that, as I said above, had been spelled out so meticulously in Robert D. Morrow's book. That such a thing could happen in an open society such as we boast of is terrifying; but to follow it with a cover-up as widespread as the original conspiracy is even more terrifying and more shameful.

Sections of the media have shouted violently that Oliver Stone has created a fiction, but anyone seeing the film realizes that this cannot be a fiction and is not a fiction. If indeed—as the film asserts—the assassination was a prelude to the Vietnam War and responsible for the subsequent death and suffering, then we are obligated to see it, assess it properly, and use it as part of a dedication to the end of the madness that marked the years of the Cold War.

January 13, 1992

Chapter 14

Praise

Bishop Paul Moore

I thought of the Ayatollah Khomeini the other night as I watched an interview with Bishop Paul Moore on Channel 13 [PBS]. It is always more difficult to write of a good person than an evil person. If I were to call Bishop Moore saintly, I think he would be irritated; yet he more than any other person in public life contradicts Mark Twain's statement that Christianity is a beautiful religion that has never been tried.

Bishop Moore practices Christianity and, together with Dean James Morton, has turned the Cathedral of Saint John the Divine into the peace and compassion center of New York. In the interview, Bishop Moore spoke of Central America and Nicaragua, asking how a person in the United States, reacting to the suffering of a child at home, could be indifferent to the murder and suffering of children in Nicaragua. A cross 20 feet high in the cathedral itemizes the villages and men and women and children who have been murdered by the Contras.

(Two days before Bishop Moore's interview, the Ayatollah Khomeini, another religious leader, put out a $5 million hit on the novelist Salman Rushdie for writing a book that the Ayatollah had not read but that displeased him. The Ayatollah called upon anyone anywhere in the world to find Mr. Rushdie and kill him.)

We evidence a woeful dislike here in America for putting two and two together, and on those rare occasions when we do, we pretend that the answer is not four. On February 21, shortly after the Ayatollah shocked the Western world with his enormous contract on Mr. Rushdie, the trial of Oliver L. North began. In case you have forgotten, Mr. North, whom some irreverently call the pink-eyed weeper, is on trial because he made a deal with the functionaries of the Ayatollah to sell them state-of-the-art American weapons, in exchange for money to send to the Contras so that they might increase the number of murdered children who are memorialized on the cross at the Cathedral of Saint John. Two and two make four, not six or eight.

Mr. North's defense is that as a loyal officer in the Marine Corps, he simply carried out the orders of his superiors in what he considered a patriotic mission. These superiors will be difficult to locate or identify since most of the evidence leading to them has been specified top secret and cannot be used.

Now I am not, in this case of the Ayatollah and Salman Rushdie, faulting Mr. Bush. It took him a little time, but finally he did come out with an appropriate if not eloquent denunciation of the Ayatollah's contract on Mr. Rushdie. But the fact remains that Mr. Bush was privy to many dealings with the Ayatollah, if not the business of Mr. North, and certainly Mr. Bush and others in the Government were aware of the thousands of men and women put to death in the course of the Ayatollah's blood lust, and of the willingness of certain people to use Iranian money to support the Contras.

All of the expressions of outrage at the Ayatollah's hit-plan that I have seen speak of freedom of speech, and of course there is a very real *right to publish and read* involved here, but there are other important matters, and pointing this toward writers, as if only they were concerned, is a mistake. If the Ayatollah has no right to put out a hit in Great Britain, do we have the right to put out our own hits in El Salvador, Nicaragua and Afghanistan? He puts up $5 million—an interesting expenditure in a country where so many are near starvation—but we put out our hits in the billion-dollar class, undercutting legal governments, supporting torture and murder, as in El Salvador for years on end, intervening where we have no business, and dealing with a good number of Ayatollah-class dictators.

In concluding his interview, Bishop Moore made the point that if we become indifferent to the suffering here at home, indifferent to the homeless people on the streets of New York, indifferent to the suffering we inflict on other nations, we will reinforce our growing cult of naked greed, harden ourselves, and become a people without compassion or charity. He reminded us that Germany, once one of the most brilliant civilizations in the Western world, turned into the horror of Nazi Germany.

"It happens," he said, "when we forget we are all of one family."

March 6, 1989

George Washington

This is about George Washington. I love and admire the man, and for me, he looms high over the tawdry lot—with a few exceptions—that followed him in the Presidency. I published a book about him in 1942, which *Time* magazine called the best book about World War II to date.

It was a book about defeat, and General Washington's greatness lay in his manner of facing defeat. I love and revere him because he adored women. You didn't know that, did you? But how much do any of us know about the man we call the father of our country?

He loved women—and they adored him—and left a string of conquests across the Colonies. He loved good wine, and he put a bottle away with dinner each evening. He loved cards; he was a careful but inveterate gambler, keeping note of his winnings and his losses, and perhaps as much as anything, he loved a good horse race and put many a guinea on his favorite. And dollars, too, in his later years.

When the British came up the Potomac and decided to burn his home in Mount Vernon, Washington's cousin, caretaker at the house, bought them off. Washington was furious enough to want to kill his cousin. "When the smoke of patriots' houses fills the sky, you dare to protect mine and buy off the swine with gold!"

Of course, it was not all nobility. He knew and admitted that the burning of his beautiful home would have filled the troops under his command with anger against the British and connected him even more deeply with their own misery. He was an aristocrat, but he adored Thomas Paine, who was the epitome of the common man. Like Jefferson, he was an agnostic who had a distinct distaste for churches. According to Rupert Hughes, whose fine three-volume biography of Washington is by far the best that has been done, he would enter a church only under duress.

When he became President, his wife, Martha, said enough of this nonsense, or words to that effect, and dragged him off to church here in the same downtown New York where they were fudging up his memory like crazy last week.

As he entered and seated himself in the last pew, the minister switched his sermon in mid-sentence to the story of the lost sheep. It was not something to throw at this handsome, six-foot, three-inch Virginian. He listened in stony silence, and then rose and stalked out of the church. We have no record of what Martha said to him afterward.

He led an army, but it was the pacifist Quakers and Mennonites who took in his wounded and sheltered them and healed them. He had never heard of the Mennonites, who had come to Pennsylvania from Holland, and who were dedicated pacifists, but when they filled their homes with his sick and wounded soldiers and cherished them as their own, Washington visited them, talked with them for hours, and wrote that under other circumstances, he might well have embraced pacifism.

He also had a reputation among his soldiers for swearing and for an uncommon use of Anglo-Saxon four-letter words. His officers were enchanted by his ability to swear, and there are dozens of notes and letters bearing witness to his skill. At the Battle of Monmouth, he came upon General Lee fleeing the battlefield. Washington, sword in hand, broadsided Lee's horse, knocked him to the ground, whipped him with the side of his sword, raging in a voice that could be heard over the sound of battle, " . . . bastard . . . swine . . . coward . . . whoremonger." The rhetoric turned the retreat, and afterward, there were a dozen different variations of what the general had said, all of them somewhat similar to the above.

In December of 1776, leading an army that had shrunk from 25,000 men in July to 6,000 who had fled across the Delaware in December, he decided to return across the river and either capture the 1,200 Hessians encamped at Trenton or die in the attempt. Had he failed, it would have meant the end of the revolution. He divided his remaining troops into three divisions, but only the 2,000 under his own command managed to cross the river.

The others lost their nerve or were turned back by the weather. It was Christmas night, and he hoped to attack the sleeping Hessians before dawn. But everything went wrong. The river was full of ice. A sleet storm turned into icy rain, and the 2,000 shivering, bearded, ragged kids left in his army, with muskets that could not be fired in the rain, stood on the west bank, beaten already, waiting to cross over.

Washington himself couldn't wait. Here is what happened, as described in a book called *The Crossing*, issued in 1984 by the New Jersey Historical Society:

"Washington stepped into the boat, picked his way among the men to where Harry Knox sat, nudged him with the toe of his boot and said vibrantly: 'Shift that fat ass, Harry—but slowly, or you'll swamp the — — boat.'

"It dissolved the spell of despondency, and it broke up the men in the boat. As the boat pushed off, the laughter could be heard out into the river, less because of what he said than the way he had said it. The men on the shore came to life, and everywhere, up and down the line of shivering soldiers: 'What did he say?' "

It saved the day, and 10 hours later, still in the pouring rain, a half-hysterical, screaming lot of bearded, half-naked kids poured into Trenton with muskets that couldn't fire, and without losing a single man, captured the Hessians and cannon and blankets and clothes and food; and in the end, there was America.

As we learned from Churchill, a bit of rhetoric can move mountains.

May 8, 1989

People of Love and Courage

I remember years ago, when *The March of Time* was a major radio news program, the deep voice of the announcer spelling out the obituary of the day, "As it must come to all men, death came today to . . . ." and then the name of the celebrity whose death was news. The first seven words were in the way of an apology and a reminder—as it must come to all men. But we put that aside, and we try to leave no place in our minds for the unavoidable, the absolute, which all men fear. You will recall in the Bible that only Moses was given knowledge of the moment of his death; God's gift was that no man should know it.

But that was many years before there was AIDS. I have a daughter, and she and her husband are analysts and people of great compassion and great sensitivity. The onset of the epidemic of AIDS, with its absolute inevitability of death, moved them deeply, and they gave a great deal of thought to what they could do to perhaps ease the suffering of people who were stricken with the disease. This was a new phenomenon in their experience as it was in the experience of so many others. There was little training to guide them, no books, some experimental methods, but mostly their own will to do what they felt must be done by people in their field.

With that, they brought together a group of homosexual men who were already stricken by the AIDS virus and already aware of what they faced. The group they started was *pro bono*, and Rachel and Avrum, my daughter and her husband, stayed with this group for something more than a year and a half. In the course of these months, most of the men in the group died.

In the ordinary course of things, my daughter does not speak about her patients. She observes the code of confidentiality that her work requires; but in this case, she spoke to me of her own pain and agony. She had to. She had worked for years at Rusk Institute, and had seen death and pain and people maimed and hurt beyond description; but this was different. Here was a group of men, well-formed, handsome for the most part, some of them seemingly full of vitality and the stuff of life, but day and night they walked and lived with death. The essence of what my daughter conveyed to me when she spoke about the sessions was the dignity, the courage and simple beauty of these men as they faced their deaths.

I had never given too much thought to homosexuals. Those I knew were gifted and gentle people, and my own disgust and distaste for the macho image, which I had seen crumble into abject cowardice so often in my life, made me feel that the homosexuals I knew were a sort of antidote to the hell that macho has brought to human life. When I wrote about them I would counterpose them to the simple mindlessness of the ultra macho. But that was not to say that I knew them very well. Like millions of other Americans, I read in the press the malicious and stupid lies and slanders printed about homosexuals.

Then my daughter began to tell me about the group she was counseling, not of intimacies or confessions, but of a kind of simple, sweet and incredible courage, and a wholly new picture began to form in my mind. We celebrate heroes who are great killers, politicos who make wars; we celebrate politicians and generals and raise statues to commemorate them, and on occasion we even celebrate a scientist or an artist. But I have not yet seen a celebration, a memory, a monument to this group of people who through no fault of their own have incurred a sentence of death, and who face death gallantly and whose lives have so often enriched our own lives and our culture. They share a fate that most of the human race is exempt from, and I think that even in death, they leave something precious for us.

There is something wonderful about the black wall in Washington that was raised as a monument to the soldiers who fought and died in Vietnam. It speaks darkly of war, and it remembers those who died bravely, and it is wonderful because it does not honor war but the dead. I want to honor the victims of AIDS for the courage they exhibit, for their affirmation of humanity, for their gentle whisper that the human mind and the human soul are unconquerable.

I want the world to see them as my daughter saw them, people of love and courage who walk bravely into that dark valley that waits for all of us.

Surely, that is not asking too much. We have erected so many sculptures to those who manufacture death for others, that it seems to me high time to erect a monument to those who die, not in an act of war or other violence, but in their youth and creative moment, quietly and bravely.

March 12, 1990

The Wonder of Books

Of all the films I saw as a kid, before the age of 12, I can remember only one. It was a weekly half-hour serial called *Buffalo Bill and Art Accord.* Who played Buffalo Bill, I don't know. Art Accord was played by an actor called Art Accord, the non sequitur unimportant in those early days of filmmaking, and the reason it remains in my mind is that the hook at the end of each piece was the death of either Buffalo Bill or Art Accord, and that gave us kids a week of discussion in which we fought the battle of the dead or the not dead. Most vivid is the ending when Art Accord lay unconscious on the floor of a cabin. A group of redskins stood around him, full of hate and shooting their arrows into his supine body. At close range, they put at least two dozen arrows into his chest, and that was followed by a week of very bitter argument among the kids. The dead party won, and we all agreed that there was no way Art Accord could survive.

But when we packed the nickel movie house the next Saturday, we were confounded yet overjoyed to see Art Accord sit up and open his shirt, and there was his Bible, pierced by all two dozen arrows, but never a scratch on his skin.

I go into this wonderful escape against odds to explain why I recall this film so well, but at the same time, I have to state that of the 300 or 400 films I saw before age 12, double and triple features, I remember practically nothing. This thought struck me as very odd indeed, and I tested it on my wife and a few other older citizens. The result was the same. They had never given it much thought, but it was true: They could not recall much of the films they had seen as preadolescents.

But books were something else entirely. I recall the first children's books I ever read, and I recall at least 200 or 300 others that I read before the age of 12. I recall them so well that I could write a passable synopsis today of at least a hundred of them—and the same is true, to one extent or another, of my wife and the friends I spoke to.

Now I am well aware that a handful of subjects do not constitute a valid test, yet nowhere in my life have I read or seen or heard of any educational inquiry that took this approach: weighing education by book against education by film. If there's any validity—even a reasonable measure of validity—in what I have discovered, then this might very well be an important path for investigation.

During the early 30s, I worked as a page in the New York Public Library. The chief librarian in that branch, in southern Harlem, was one Miss Lindsay, related in some way to Mayor Lindsay, and I recall her saying once, "Our books are not stolen because people who read books are not thieves." I have often thought of that, and I tend to believe it to a certain extent. With exceptions, I would guess that people who read books begin to have a different view of the world than people who do not read books. I would go out on a long limb and say you cannot educate people with television or film; you must give them books and find a way to make them read books.

Perhaps we should be thankful for this, since we in America, from Rambo to the muscle-bound Schwarzenegger, make the most inhuman and brutal films made in any country. The mind that could be shaped by this river of filth, violence and brutality would offer nothing but hell on earth to the future.

On the other hand, a large American firm has created a thing called Channel One. They supply free TV equipment to schools that will accept it, and they offer a news show for young students, asking only that they may insert commercials. Hundreds of schools have accepted this offer, but I would reject the supposition that the sound bites flung at students educate them in any important way. Except for the painstaking and wonderful work done by Public Television, films made for children and only for children—except for this kind of thing—television does not educate or elucidate. It puts forth ideas that a child must reject or be destroyed. It promotes the notion that certain people kill at will, and that such killing is admirable. It shows, again and again, people beaten so badly that there could be no recovery, and then it shows these same beaten and tortured people leaping up, hale and healthy. It gives the children role models that are demented killers, and total crazies, people who fling punches at people at the drop of a hat, who fight endlessly and without reason, in a world of good guys and bad guys.

So we can thank God that it does not educate or influence as much as it might. For now and for the immediate future, books remain the source of knowledge and civilization. Only with a book can a child's imagination create a wonderful world of its own, and such creativity is the basic shaping of knowledge.

July 16–23, 1990

The Congressman Who Voted His Conscience

It came as no surprise that Senator Alfonse D'Amato of New York, representing a state that is home to millions of blacks and other ethnics, voted to sustain President Bush's veto of the Civil Rights Bill. Mr. D'Amato has always worn what goes for his principles, lightly, doffing them as easily as a hat and assuming them just as thoughtlessly. His vote would have put the bill over the top, but the party put the word out and Mr. D'Amato snapped to attention when the signal was given.

All of which moves me to recall a bit of history. John Quincy Adams, the son of John Adams, and a man of great courage, dignity and honor, became the sixth president of the United States. He served only a single term, defeated because of his unwillingness to compromise with the slave owners; and then, his term of office over, he returned to his farm in Massachusetts, ready to begin a calm, contemplative life of reading and writing and working his farm. He had few guilts about this; he had a lifetime of public service behind him; he was in his sixties, and he felt that his retirement was well-deserved.

However, the farmers who were his neighbors felt otherwise, and they got together a committee that went to see Mr. Adams with the following request:

President Adams, we need a new candidate to represent us in Congress, and we've been sorting out the possibilities, and we've come to the conclusion that no one is more fit for the job than you. We know that you have been a United States Senator, a Secretary of State, and

President, but there's nothing in the Constitution that says you can't be our Congressman.

Or words to that effect. It had never happened before that a President of the United States, finished with his term of office, had entered the lists for another elective post, nor has it happened since that time, but Mr. Adams thought it was an interesting notion and agreed to think about it and talk it over with his family. He thought about it, and then in due time, he asked the committee to visit him again and told them what he had decided. This is the essence of it, although we have no verbatim record of that conversation.

He agreed to stand for the seat in the House of Representatives, but at the same time he set out certain conditions. He said that whenever there was a difference between their needs or requests and his conscience, or the party's platform, needs or requests, and his conscience, he would vote his conscience. In other words, they were electing a man whom they considered to be a person of honor and intelligence, and they must accept the right of this man to do what he felt to be best for his country—not for the narrow requests of his constituents; and if they were willing to accept those conditions, he would be happy to be their candidate.

They accepted the conditions, and John Quincy Adams, ex-president of the United States, was elected to the House of Representatives, and re-elected three more times—and for seven years he led the fight in the House against slavery and slave owners, a tireless lion of a man who never wavered in his principles and who died there in the House in the midst of a denunciation of those who bought and sold human flesh.

So we return to Mr. D'Amato, with an almost apologetic admission that he is too easy a target. He wears his coat of sleaze as easily and as mindlessly as he ran his campaign, and to talk about his voting and his "conscience" is something of a non sequitur. But the other night, William Proxmire, onetime Senator from Wisconsin, talked about his colleagues on Public Television and about their integrity, which he underlined, and that made me think about the whole meaning of integrity, which my Webster defines as "moral soundness; honesty; freedom from corrupting practice." Who votes his or her conscience in the Congress of the United States? Are we to believe that among the hundreds of Representatives and the one hundred Senators there are not at least dozens who understand that this wretched war looming on our horizon is a naked struggle to dominate the oil reserves of the Middle East? Have we put into office to govern us a circus of brainless boobs who are taken in by Mr. Bush's whimpering that he is preparing for an honorable struggle against aggression?

If this is so, if this is what the people in Congress believe, then indeed we are doomed. But we all know that this is not what they believe, that they understand very well indeed the nature of a war that will leave thousands of dead American kids on the altar of oil and the oil companies, and that they are, with very few exceptions, indulging the dishonor of silence.

I told the story here of a Congressman who voted his conscience. Apparently, we have come so far since then that the life of John Quincy Adams amounts to no more than a quaint fairy tale for our time.

November 12, 1990

The Compassion of Norman Cousins

A few weeks ago, at age 75, Norman Cousins passed away. We don't have much of a memory for anything except film stars here in America, so it is understandable that most of the population had only a vague notion of who Norman Cousins was, and a long, two-column, full-page obituary in *The New York Times* gave only a single paragraph to the core meaning of his life. Here is the paragraph:

"Over the years, as a writer and an editor, Mr. Cousins was a champion of nuclear controls, the United Nations and world government, among other causes, and was also a social critic. So strong was his interest in nuclear issues that he helped to arrange for victims of the atomic bombing of Hiroshima—the 'Hiroshima Maidens'—to come to the United States for medical treatment. He adopted one of them, a daughter."

Most of the rest of the obituary is devoted to Norman Cousins's struggles to keep the *Saturday Review* alive. The *Saturday Review* was a magazine that he edited and that reflected his beliefs. The name of one of the Hiroshima Maidens he brought to America and cherished and healed and adopted as his own daughter was Shigeko Sasamori.

The New York Times saw fit to engage in only a passing mention of her. But her story is worth far more than a mention.

When Harry Truman made his decision to wipe two Japanese cities, Hiroshima and Nagasaki and all the humanity they contained, from the face of the earth, Shigeko Sasamori was a schoolgirl in the Presbyterian School on the outskirts of Hiroshima, where, among other things, she was taught the virtues and ethics of Christianity. The school was several miles from the atomic epicenter, the point where the bomb struck, and the playground of the school was surrounded by a stone wall. It is to the existence of this wall and to the fact that a small brook ran through the play-yard that Shigeko and the other Hiroshima Maidens owe their lives. Here is how Shigeko described the experience:

"First we heard the plane pass overhead, but we went on playing because planes frequently passed over the school. Then we heard this great boom and then the air caught fire and the whole world was filled with fire and my hair and my clothes caught fire. Then I managed to get to the brook and throw myself in, and that saved my life."

Her life was saved, but Shigeko's body, from chin to groin, was covered with burns. The other children were in similar or worse condition.

Norman Cousins brought Shigeko and 24 other young women from Japan to the United States—not by himself, of course, but as the moving force behind the effort. This was some nine years after the fact. The 25 Hiroshima Maidens were no longer schoolgirls. They were grown women, terribly scarred, terribly injured. Mr. Cousins organized an effort that raised hundreds of thousands of dollars to care for and treat these women. In New York, at Mt. Sinai Hospital, two of the most gifted plastic surgeons in America, Dr. William Hitzig and Dr. Arthur Barsky (brother of Dr. Edward Barsky, who created the first M.A.S.H. unit during the Spanish Civil War) dedicated themselves to the effort of doing away with some of the terrible scars of the atomic holocaust.

These two physicians performed hundreds of operations, driven by a sense of conscience and by a deep compassion, and they gave to most of these women the courage to look at the world and live in it without being marked as deformed creatures. As far as I know, the Federal Government gave this effort not even a nod.

Norman Cousins was the constant driving force in this, publicizing, pleading, involving himself totally, to the point where he and his wife, Ellen, adopted Shigeko Sasamori—legally, as his own daughter.

When something like this happens, the shadowy bit of faith I retain in the human race is strengthened, and in a sense I feel that we are, all of us, redeemed. We all share the guilt of Hiroshima and Nagasaki, just as all of Germany must share the guilt of the Holocaust, but how very few of us exhibit a shred of compassion or give even moments of our lives to trying to change what was and is so terribly wrong; and in the modern cult of cynicism, those who do are chalked off as woolly-headed dreamers.

Norman Cousins was such a dreamer, and insofar as it was within the purview of a single individual who was neither a president nor a king, he turned at least some of his dreams into reality. His lifelong effort to produce a body of writing and thinking toward the creation of World Government was by no means wasted. The ideas he sponsored and nurtured took root in many places, and today we see the beginning of what may be a sort of world government, a *United Nations* that will possibly shed the cloak of corruption and dishonesty it has worn almost since its beginning. At no time in his life did Norman Cousins lose faith in the *United Nations*, and now, at long last, there is the very real possibility that his work and his faith may be rewarded.

I think that favorite line of Eleanor Roosevelt, out of the old song, might well be his epitaph: "It is better to light just one little candle than to sit and curse the dark."

December 24–31, 1990

Kitty Kelley and Others

If I had my way with the Medals of Freedom, I would give one to Kitty Kelley; yes, the same medal that President Reagan pinned onto Frank Sinatra, an action, by the way, as vulgar and inappropriate as his comparison of the Contra chief to George Washington. I would give it to Kitty Kelley, because in my book she performed a service to this country that far outweighs the total of Ronald Reagan's dozing days in the White House. She spelled out a lesson to the American people which might well be summarized as follows:

As citizens of the United States, again and again you give the Presidency, and all the power that goes with it, to fools, liars, thieves and scoundrels of the lowest moral persuasion. These managed candidates lie to you, hoodwink you, con you and bamboozle you, and you have neither the will nor the information to challenge them. So here is a book that details the lives, lies and chicanery of two people who ruled this country for eight years and who cut the heart out of its economy and its future, the future that belongs to your children; and in this wretched performance, they were aided and abetted by both parties in a government we elected.

There is an old saying to the effect that if you know the truth, the truth will make you free. Well, maybe—maybe sometimes. You see, this is not a past practice. This is not something that Nancy Reagan—the President we did not elect—invented, nor was it the invention of Richard Milhous Nixon. You can find the same thing in the distant past, in the administrations of such scoundrels as John Tyler and James K. Polk, to name only a couple. In a free and open democratic society, deception is a powerful weapon indeed.

Let me give some examples of what I mean. Start with a bit from Barry Commoner, a respected writer on environmental subjects: "The EPA had prepared an executive order to set up a Federal program for ecologically sound and energy-conserving purchases that was to be announced by President Bush on Earth Day 1990. It was killed by White House Chief of Staff John Sununu. Yes, the country needs an energy policy and we know what it ought to be. But we'll never get it from the present occupants of the White House."

The above is typical of the syndrome I laid out. If Peggy Noonan was the mind and voice of Mr. Bush during the election, then the very curious Mr. Sununu is presently the mind and voice of George Bush. Who the hell is John Sununu to decide our future, to turn down an energy policy that every thoughtful environmentalist in America has been pleading for? Who gave him that right? Who elected him to anything? And if George Bush hasn't the guts to stand up against Mr. Sununu for the people of the United States, when the very lives of our children and their world are at stake, he should resign the Presidency.

And why does no one in the Congress speak up? Why don't they ever speak up? For instance, examine this bit. It comes from Robert Fisk, a courageous correspondent in the Gulf War, writing in *Mother Jones* magazine:

> At one U.S. air base, a vast banner is suspended inside an aircraft hangar. It depicts Superman, holding in his arms a limp, terrified Arab

> with a hooked nose. The existence of this banner, with its racist overtones, went unreported by the pool journalists at the base. A pool television crew did record Marine Lieutenant Colonel Dick White when he described what it was like to see Iraqi troops from his plane. "It was like turning on the kitchen light late at night and the cockroaches started scurrying." This astonishing remark went unquestioned, although there was certainly one question worth asking: What is the New World Order worth when an American officer, after only three weeks of war, compares his Arab enemies to insects?

Of course, it went unquestioned, and in print, as far as I know, only in a small West Coast liberal magazine. And not one single brave soul among the Democratic majority we have elected to Congress had the courage to stand up in the House and ask, "How does this differ from Adolf Hitler's view of Jews, Poles and Russians?"

The lifeblood of democracy is anger at wrong—indeed rage at wrong, opposition to the powers that be, resistance, and a constant careful, obsessive nurturing of the people's knowledge. It is not enough to make facts available. *The New York Times* can boast of that, as for example on the 24th of April, when the front page of *The Times* printed this headline: AIR FORCE CHOOSES LOCKHEED'S DESIGN FOR FIGHTER PLANE/$95 BILLION MAY BE SPENT.

The headline is true, but it is also a throwaway of the deeper truth, that once again, in spite of the finish of the Cold War, the lifeblood of the American people is being drained to build more and still more weapons of death—and to repeat an old saw, when millions of our people live in the filth and poverty of Third World countries, when unemployment is going out of bounds, when our cities continue to disintegrate, our roads decay, and crime turns streets into battlefields, we have only one purpose, one goal, to build the murderous weapons of death for the pleasure of the brain-damaged men who rule us.

That is why Kitty Kelley deserves the Medal of Freedom. She stands against the liars, the thieves and the killers.

May 27, 1991

An Artist and Her Art

Bette Fast is a sculptor. She is also my wife of 54 years, and through November she is having a retrospective show of her work at the Art Center in Greenwich, Connecticut.

Norman Cousins wrote of her work: "What distinguishes the work of Bette Fast is its manifest sense of completeness. Viewed from any angle, her work demonstrates complete consistency, clarity of conception, clarity of line clearly revealed; integrity of approach and integrity of craftsmanship fully apparent. It is this mastery of the who that is most characteristic of her art."

Louis Untermeyer said of her work: "She endows bronze with living flesh and hot blood. Each of her sculptures is a monumental piece, celebrating humanity and waiting only for some city to raise it as a monument."

For all the decades I have lived with this remarkable woman, I have watched and marveled at her work. When we are at home, where she works, no day passes without clay in her hands or without drawing. She draws with a pen line that admits of no correction, and like her sculpture, her drawings are of living flesh, all of them a sort of testimony to life. A Japanese Rashi, looking at her work, said: "She draws like a Zen master."

We live in a strange country: the only Western country that practices such contempt for the arts that its yearly handout to all the arts together is less than its payout for a single bomber. We have no national theater, no national policy for painting or sculpture or dance, no plan to support people who give their lives to creating, no real interest in any form of art that cannot be turned into a substantial cash flow. With few exceptions, our state and municipal endowments for monumental sculpture celebrate soldiers, generals and various and sundry practitioners in the business of killing. The notion of celebrating life is alien to us.

We whimper about the quality of our civilization and the failure of our educational system, about the destruction of our national morale by dope and crime and increasing contempt for human life, but it never occurs to our leaders that the very money machine that defines all our values is also destroying us. Sixty million dollars will be put on the line for some barbaric senseless film—via free enterprise, of course, and the market—that glorifies violence or pornography, but to find a few thousand dollars for some gifted young playwright or painter or actor or sculptor is written off as impossible. Art is the measure of the quality and richness of each and every civilization since civilization began; but so long as art in America is specified as the product of indifferent gifts from the wealthy, it will wither and the society will wither as well. The two are not disconnected.

I began this piece by talking about my wife's art and her retrospective exhibition. We were both of us children of the Depression years, but in a sense every artist is a child of the Depression years. We clawed our way through our early years, and we managed to survive, not simply as people but as artists; but it was no harder for us than it is today for the young artists and actors and writers I see today, living at one-quarter of the poverty level, an uneven fringe on the edge of a society that initially has no use for them, but is willing to pour money at fame and bow and scrape to the handful that is kissed by success. We have discovered that if art and literature are so degraded as to be better identified as spiritual garbage, it can be sold profitably to millions.

When Emile Zola had his great literary success with *Nana* and moved into one of the most expensive apartment houses in Paris, his friends chided him for having deserted the common people, of whom he had written so warmly. His reply was that an art that could not offer a good bourgeois living to the artist would soon perish. He was absolutely right, and while art survives in America today, it is on a knife edge, and it survives only because people are willing to make commitments deeper than any other commitments in our society. You cannot separate this from the broad fact of education in America today, an ignorance of the classics unprecedented in modern society, an absence of history that is dangerous, so very dangerous that it could lead us to destruction, an inability to write simply and rationally even in our highest levels of education, a pathetic ignorance of geography and a relationship to entertainment more primitive than that of tribal society hundreds of years in the past.

That said, when a woman like Bette Fast can dedicate an entire lifetime to the production of beauty in sculpture, consistently and modestly, never asking for recognition or renown, it seems to me a thing that must be celebrated. Nor does it strike me as unseemly that I, her husband, should celebrate it. I have had the wonderful good fortune to live my entire adult life with a gifted artist, whose modesty and talent have always been beyond my whole understanding. She has stood by me always and asked only that she might pursue her art.

America is the richer for this.

November 18, 1991

Political Cartoonists

In the post–World War I period of the Palmer Raids and the loony persecution of the handful of Socialists who had won elective office, Art Young drew his famous cartoon poster. It was a picture of Christ with a crown of thorns, and the legend beneath read somewhat to this effect: Wanted—rabble rouser and revolutionary, proclaims un-American notions of equality and peace, has taken a stand against the Government. (By no means a quote, since I cannot lay hands on a copy, but in the manner of the piece; I quote it from memory.)

I evoke it because, it seems to me, few people think about the stand taken by political cartoonists since the beginnings of this country—and how absolutely consistent they have been in the defense of freedom and human dignity. Of course there have been conservative and reactionary cartoonists, but I can't think of the name of one of them, or one that was quoted or remembered. On the other hand, hardly a week goes by without my hearing someone whoop with delight over the most recent cartoon of Herblock or Paul Conrad, that wonder of wonders in the *Los Angeles Times*, or Pat Oliphant or R.J. Matson or any one of a dozen others.

No other group in the media has been so steadfast, so brilliantly incisive, so willing to cut through the baloney and come right to the point; no other group has seized upon the issue day in and day out—and, possibly, no other group has been as effective in holding up a mirror to the bubble-heads who inhabit our Congress. Art Buchwald punctures the silly self-importance of the politicos with rare humor and talent, but there is only one of him as against a veritable army of cartoonists.

For months President Bush and Secretary of State Baker have tossed away Mr. Gorbachev's disarmament proposals, thrown into spasms of terror lest they be forced to cease the production of armaments, and, backing them, the pundits drooled out the same arguments they have been using since the cold war began. Herblock cut to the core of it with a cartoon of Mr. Bush at the podium in Congress, saying, "After a full and careful review, we've decided that we liked Stalin and Brezhnev better."

Not earthshaking? Who else in the national media has said flatly, "Mr. Bush and Mr. Baker and the money behind them do not want peace and are terrified of what will happen if we stop making guns." Of course, the statement is implied—but that's what the cartoon does; it forces the viewer to think and create what is implied. In the famous case of Boss Tweed and Thomas Nast, one could say not only that the picture was worth a thousand words but that it was worth a hundred thousand votes. Tammany Hall was a name; Tweed was a name. Nast drew it into a picture still famous, the evil, slavering, fat-bellied villain that still stands in our memories, so that when one says, "Tweed," one recalls not the details of the swindle but the cartoon of Boss Tweed the man.

It is the innocence of the cartoon that gives its maker the unique freedom he possesses. The great antecedents, Daumier and Goya, walked and worked freely among the ruling classes they despised and mocked. During those dreadful years between 1945 and 1955, when the unspeakable J. Edgar Hoover was the shadow dictator of America and McCarthyism ran amuck, no cartoonist was called before a Congressional committee, not even the brilliant William Gropper of the *New York Daily Worker*. Yet, through those tired years, the cartoonists stood almost alone in their defiance of the police state that loomed upon the horizon.

It is the magic of innocence. Like the little child in the marvelous Hans Christian Andersen story who blurts out the fact that the king has no clothes on, the political cartoonist symbolically strips his subjects naked and allows the confused and misled reader to draw his own conclusions. The cartoonist also relies on wit; he brings his wit to the subject and challenges us to laugh at evil and horror and, since for the most part those who aspire to high office are without wit or humor, it may be that they never get the point.

I often think that an evocation can be more successful than an explanation. Charles Addams was not a political cartoonist, but what book, essay or poem has better evoked the inner spirit of New York than his famous cartoon of the manhole. If you recall it, an octopus is half out of an open manhole in the street, and a typical New Yorker type, middle-aged and bespectacled, is in the coils of the octopus, struggling and striking at it with his umbrella. Half a dozen people stand on the sidewalk, watching, but neither alarmed nor involved. One of two Wall Street types, passing by, says to the other, "Doesn't take anything to draw a crowd in this city."

June 26, 1992

Chapter 15

Notes from the Asylum

A Matter of Use

When Mrs. Brown buys a Widget dishwasher and it turns out to be a dud, the word gets around, and either Widget cleans up their dishwasher act, or they go out of business. The same goes for washing machines, mixers, and any other gadgets that are subject to use. But when the Pentagon blows a quarter of a billion dollars on a so-called "Stealth" plane that may not work any better than the B–1, but may work when they whip it into shape, no one goes out of business and no one besides you and me picks up the tab.

The difference is very simple. The washing machine is built for use, the bomber is built for lunacy. The washing machine will be tested with dirty clothes; the bomber will never actually be put to use or tested with anything more than a trial run. Think back to the tanks that exploded when hit by a shell, the guns that couldn't fire, the decoy planes that ran into the hundreds of millions—well none of it really mattered because nothing was built for use and practically everything was built for profit and to keep people working.

This lunatic junk bill is paid, as they say, to defend this country against the Soviets. Come on! Can anyone who has been reading the dispatches from Russia these past weeks believe that Russia is waiting to attack us? Atomic weapons? Ask any scientist, and he will tell you that atomic weapons don't have to be delivered. Explode a few hundred either here or in Russia and the earth will be uninhabitable. Hitler, who built the greatest war machine of our time, was unable to cross the few miles of water between the continent and England—and the Russians are going to invade us? As always, the first victim of the military is common sense.

But, the voice of reason will counsel us, we are protecting the continent. Oh? With the Stealth bomber. You know, a moment arrives when even the accepted insanities that we have been living with for decades fail to comfort us. The Russians cannot feed their people without buying millions of pounds of grain, their railroad system is in desperate need of repair, their metropolitan infrastructure is almost as bad as ours, and now they are trying to cope with one internal tragedy after another—yet for 40 years the American people have been euchred into throwing countless billions of their hard-earned dollars into the bottomless pit of the Pentagon. We have fed and pensioned—royally—generations of admirals and generals who have never contributed a day of creative work to our society, and by admirals and generals, I mean the whole uniformed-officer lot who earn their daily well-buttered bread by conning us out of our common senses.

And now the Stealth! A quarter of a billion dollars for a piece of technological junk that has no real use and will never be used. Since the Air Force figures that any new-model plane has to expect a dozen mishaps, we face $3 billion worth of crashes before the contraption becomes airworthy. Then to build a fleet of 40 will cost another $10 billion. Total: thirteen thousand million dollars. Remember how the late Senator Dirksen put it, "A billion here and a billion there, and soon you're talking about real money."

Very real money. Thousands of men and women sleep on the streets of New York, and thousands more sleep on the streets of Boston, Philadelphia, Los Angeles and many other American cities, and there is no money to build them homes. Thousands are dying of AIDS, and there is no money to build them hospices. Our roads are disintegrating, our bridges are ready to crumble, our railroads are beyond disgust—and there is no money to repair them. Our educational system is in shambles, and there is no money to hire first-rate teachers, and our entire society is ridden with the crime and sickness of drugs—and there is no money to stop it. But for that eternal piece of insanity we call the Pentagon, there is money without end.

Recently, the General Accounting Office has come up with a figure that practically doubles the cost of a Stealth bomber, from a quarter of a billion dollars to half a billion dollars, enough money to build 10 major hospitals and pay all patient and operating expenses for a decade. The cost of one plane. It has been well said that those whom the gods wish to destroy they first make mad.

January 16, 1989

The Going Price of Human Life

What is anything worth? What is price? King James I, as the story goes, was called the *wisest fool in Christendom*. They say he conned people into unanswerable questions and then whipped them when they failed. One question: "What am I worth?" A wiser fool answered, "Our

Lord was sold for 30 pieces of silver. I value you at one less." Sneaky, and hardly anything to offend even a king. A bit of shining stone goes for a million plus, and the Ayatollah pegged a hit on Salman Rushdie at $5 million. Price is a variant factor. Karl Marx said that the value of anything equals its price. That may be scientifically correct, but it strikes me as an odd notion.

Some years ago, Bert Stern, the very important photographer at that time, was commissioned to photograph Franz Klein, the nonobjective painter. Bert decided to show Klein at work. He took a piece of window glass, 5 by 7, propped it up and put Klein behind it. He bought a can of black paint, a five-inch brush, and he told Klein to make three brush strokes, two horizontal and one vertical. Klein dutifully made the three brush strokes and Bert photographed him.

Watching this procedure was an old friend of mine, Irvin Shapiro by name. When Bert finished, Irv said to him, "May I have that piece of glass?" Bert said that he had no use for it, and that Irv was welcome to it. Irv took the sheet of glass, framed it, and subsequently was offered $175,000 for it, the going price for a large Klein at that moment.

I offer no artistic opinion. I simply talk about price. According to the definition put forth by Marx, the glass under the three brush strokes has assumed a value of $175,000. Jimmy Breslin, who is as much an authority on Brooklyn as anyone, says that in parts of Brooklyn, a human life is worth about 20 cents.

But then that's more of a literary expression than a going price. In El Salvador, our death squads—I call them ours because, while they consist of locals, they have been organized, trained, armed and protected by us—have done away with 60,000 lives, if you count women and children and newly born infants, and I calculate that over the years of the Reagan Administration, the cost to us was about $300,000 per body, again if one prices the infants at the same going rate. (That was before we became a kinder and gentler nation.) In Nicaragua, the price is vastly higher—since the Government forces are better able to fight the death squads, called the Contras—perhaps as high as $1 million a body.

In my childish wonder at how three brush strokes increased the value of a piece of glass to $175,000, I have come to look newly upon the men and women we see on our streets, wrapped in newspapers, pieces of plastic and shreds of ancient blankets. I try to calculate their value based on price, and not to think of the fact, as a scientific friend once put it to me, that the chemicals and other measurable compounds that compose their bodies are worth about 65 cents.

There are about 80,000 of them, 80,000 people here in this city who have no homes, no warmth, no place to lay their heads. If they stood holding hands, the line would stretch from Battery Park to 225th Street and Spuyten Duyvil. Do you know what it would cost to take one of those ruined areas of the Bronx and build decent houses that would provide single room occupancy for each one of these homeless people? Just about what it cost to kill each man, woman, child and infant in El Salvador and Nicaragua. And if you doubt me, talk to architects and builders yourself.

On the other hand, there is the alternative proposed facetiously by Jonathan Swift as a solution to Britain's "Irish problem." "Since there is no money to feed them," Swift suggested, "why not butcher them, salt them down and use them to feed others?"

Does it shock you? Is it any more shocking than the fact that in this wealthiest of all cities in this wealthiest of all lands, the situation exists? If we calculate the value of a product by its price, as Marx suggested, then the price of those 80,000 lives is a good deal less than the price Jimmy Breslin puts on a life in Brooklyn.

March 27, 1989

German History I

There are debts that have to be remembered, and there are debts that have to be paid, and the media, turning handsprings over the fall of the Berlin Wall, have given less than the requisite minute of silence. Before we run the word *freedom* into utter absurdity—a practice not uncommon here in the United States—suppose we recall that 50 million human lives was the price exacted from the human race by a united Germany.

We remember the Holocaust, six million Jews murdered by Germans in an act of such malignant and brutal dimensions as to have no counterpart in all the history of mankind; but we fail to remember that the full price exacted from the human race by the "freedom-loving Germans" was 50 million human lives, French, Russian, American,

Czech, Polish—and on and on to include every nation, every ethnic group in Europe in a bloodbath so enormous that the mind can never truly comprehend it.

So as I watch the dance of "freedom" on the wall and listen to the well-paid trumpets of the media having verbal orgasms over the joy of the poor "suffering" Germans—so well-fed and so very well-dressed, I am a little less than enthralled. I listen to the 60- and 70-year-olds, speaking the broken English they learned in the Allied prison camps, and I recall that when my wife and I toured Western Germany, border to border, after the war, we discovered not one Nazi—only anti-Nazis who were forced to operate in an underground that never existed.

The Germans who loved honor and cherished freedom were dead—put to death very early in the game, not by Adolf Hitler alone, but by the millions and millions of Germans who carried out his orders, and who put so many millions of others who were not Germans to death. I watch the joyful avuncular and matronly faces exploding with happiness and tributes to liberation, translated by our network newsmen, and I do my own bow to the marvels of forgetfulness. Robert MacNeil of the MacNeil/Lehrer show interviewed Willy Brandt, a postwar leader of Germany and a dedicated anti-Nazi, but even Mr. Brandt was loath to recall the past, much less fear it. When Mr. MacNeil asked him whether the Israelis and the Dutch and others might be right in expressing their fear of a united Germany, Mr. Brandt brushed that aside. He felt that new generations of Germans were nonviolent.

Nonviolent? Of course. Let's take just a moment to observe the practice of nonviolence by the East Germans, those who claim that they observe the brotherhood of socialism. Let's look back to the 1972 Olympics. You will recall that then, in Munich where the games took place, Arab terrorists attacked and murdered the Jewish (Israeli) contingent of athletes. The Jewish athletes and the East German athletes were housed in buildings facing on a narrow court. The Israelis were on the second floor, facing the court. The East Germans were on the ground floor, with doors and windows opening directly onto the courtyard. The East German athletes had their own armed guards, and these guards stood by the doors and windows, watching the Jewish athletes fight barehanded for their lives a few feet from the East Germans. Not only did the East Germans make no move to intervene—as any normal men would have—but, endorsing their stand of nonviolence, they forbade their own athletes to call the police.

Ah, well—East Germans. The West Germans are different, aren't they? The Palestinian terrorists had locked themselves in the Israeli quarters. A top Israeli terrorist-expert told the Munich police that there was only one possible way that the Israeli athletes might be saved without bloodshed. The building they were in had a hot air system; he proposed that the Munich police blow anesthetic gas into the building. It was without any lasting effect, and it would put the terrorists and the athletes to sleep.

This the Munich police refused to do. Their excuse was that if anything went wrong and the athletes died, the world would point a finger at them for revising the Nazi practice of gassing Jews as a quick and convenient way of killing them. Of course, before the Arab terrorist attack finished, every single Jewish athlete held hostage had died.

As I have said before in these columns, I do not believe in punishment and I do not believe in revenge; but I do believe in *memory*. If we forget the past, if we misshape it, distort it, misspeak it or just flatly reconstruct it as a lie, we will pay a price, and today when such prices are paid, they are very high indeed. The wall is gone. East Germans can go to West Germany and vice versa, and that is certainly a large step in the right direction. But "freedom-loving Germans?" Let's be a trifle less hysterical and wait and see. They are still Germans, and the 50 million dead are still warm in their graves.

November 27, 1989

German History II

I have just finished reading Barbara W. Tuchman's brilliant *The Guns of August*, a book that was highly praised when it was published almost 30 years ago. I read it because my memory of the details of World War I was rather hazy, and with all the talk about a united Germany, I felt it might make sense to review the near past of that strange people.

Tuchman's book covers the month of August 1914 and a few days of September, and tells in great detail the events of the Battle for France, the opening battle of World War I, fought before trench warfare set in, and the largest and most awful battle in the history of the human race. On all fronts, more than three million soldiers were engaged and half a million were casualties—all in a bit more than 30 days. The German attack was without cause, driven by the lunatic need of the German Kaiser to conquer France and rule Europe. An estimated 98 percent of the German people backed his ambitions.

The main attack was through Belgium, where the brutalities practiced against the civilian population, the thousands of civilians murdered, villages burned to the ground, horrors perpetrated that are almost beyond description—were as monstrous as the works of Hitler and the Nazis. A long, carefully contrived whitewashing of these atrocities in subsequent years charged them off as propaganda. They were not propaganda, and Tuchman documents them carefully. One reads in horror, unable to believe that these atrocities were the work of human beings. Let me quote just a paragraph:

> On August 19 after the Germans had crossed the Gette and found the Belgian army withdrawn during the night, they vented their fury on Aerschot, a small town between the Gette and Brussels, the first to suffer a mass execution. In Aerschot 150 civilians were shot. The numbers were to grow larger as the process was repeated, by von Bulow's army at Ardennes and Tamines, by von Hausen's in the culminating massacre of 664 at Dinant. The method was to assemble all the inhabitants in the main square, women usually on one side and men on the other, select every tenth man or every second man or all on one side, according to the whim of the individual officer, march them to a nearby field or empty lot behind the railroad station and shoot them.

And the penetrating horror of it was that these acts were not hidden from the German civilian population, but were printed in German newspapers and approved by the people of Germany. Multiply the instance above by thousands and you will have a feeling of what it means to be attacked and invaded by Germans.

The cost of this war, of this demented German obsession to rule France, was 25 million human lives; and 21 years after this carnage, the German people decided to do it all over again. They will argue, "No, no, not the German people but the Nazis and Adolf Hitler," but the Germans who opposed Hitler were only a handful, while the great mass of the German people backed him. The atrocities of 1914 were only a prelude to the killings of 1941, as if the Germans were obsessed by the need to murder, and during the next four years the Germans put to death, not soldiers, but the following civilians: six million Jews, one and a half million Poles, 500,000 gypsies, three million Russians,

60,000 French—and the list goes on and on. In all of the history of the human race, there has been no such slaughter as the German people imposed on mankind, and the end result of World War II was 50 million dead.

And now we listen to the mindless bleating of the media about a united Germany. Have we no memories? I watched and listened to Jack Kennedy telling a screaming crowd of Germans that he was a Berliner and proud of it. I wonder what the ghosts of 75 million human beings, dead by the German lust for war and power, thought of his words—were there indeed ghosts. But I'm afraid that the dead, like the living, have no memories.

We are a nation without history. For us, there is no past, no memory, only today. We do not teach history, know history, or remember anything more important than baseball and football scores. We lie in a crazy miasma of the present, absorbed by television while our atmosphere is poisoned, our water polluted, our soil soaked with radiation and our future governed by airborne command posts, mini-general staffs directed by the Pentagon to be aloft in a plane if and when all organization and government and most of the population have been destroyed—so that those still alive in their airborne stations may continue their mission of depopulating the earth.

Ah well—three cheers, I suppose. The Berlin wall is down, and now the Germans can all get together and find a way to do it again. They may even beat the Pentagon to it.

February 19, 1990

Indecencies and Obscenities

A small note on the [1990] election, a matter that nobody appeared to have given much thought to—namely, Governor Mario M. Cuomo's commercials. I have always respected the governor as a man of principle and decency, and I have admired his stand on capital punishment. But when he boasts that he has built more prisons than any other man in America, I am ready to pull back and take another long, hard look. The very fact that he could put forward prison as a solution for crime means that he is either a sociological ninny or an unprincipled player to the crowd.

Does he realize, I wonder, that we have more men and women in our prisons that Adolf Hitler had in his concentration camps in 1939? Does he believe that a civilized society can prevail under these circumstances? If he had even indicated that he would fight to understand and change the social conditions that produce crime, I would feel differently. But when, according to a story in *The New York Times*, every other young person in the inner ghetto of his crown jewel, New York City, is armed with a gun, it's time for the governor to do some deeper thinking than prisons and cops.

* * *

And they've gone and elected Jesse again. What a strange lot we are! We put a kid who smokes a little pot in jail, and we put back into office Mr. Tobacco himself. Not only is Jesse Helms the voice of tobacco, the first fighter for the planters and their subsidies, the darling Philip Morris, but the tobacco interests have built him a museum and library. When you add up the tobacco deaths, our Jesse would be better called Mr. Scratch. It takes all kinds.

* * *

I have always been an easy mark for feminine beauty, and I shouted my own three cheers for the election of Ann Richards to the governorship of the State of Texas. I would give her points and buy her the best dinner in town if only for her performance during the Bush–Dukakis campaigns. The serious error there—and we may pay an awful price for it—was that Ann Richards was not the Presidential candidate. Anyway, the entrance of any woman into the government is cause for cheering and hope.

It must be noted that Ms. Richards's opponent, Clayton Williams, blew $8 million of his own money, as part of a $20 million election tab, namely $4.40 a vote.

So goeth democracy—with the happy exception of a single golden thread woven by Ms. Richards.

* * *

In another corner of the asylum, we find that sterling institution, the FBI, proving that idiocy is the first duty of government. According to Herbert Mitgang in *The New York Times*: "Although Pablo Picasso was born in Spain, lived most of his life in France and never visited the United States, the Federal Bureau of Investigation and the United States Department of State maintained a voluminous secret dossier on the titan of 20th-century art. . . . Even though the artist died 17 years ago at the age of 91, the Picasso file continues to be maintained in the FBI headquarters in Washington."

What is one to say? Some years ago, a minor theologian came up with the notion that God is dreaming us. Forget it! A third-rate television writer is writing us. If you have any other explanation, please write and tell me.

* * *

No one appears to have taken note of the fact that Jews are forbidden to set foot in Saudi Arabia under the threat of death. How about that! Has anyone culled the ranks to make sure that no Jews slipped through, and since thousands of Protestants have been circumcised, what if some poor kid is grabbed as he urinates? How does he prove he's not Jewish? If he just happens to have a crucifix hidden away, he can be whipped and stoned for being a Christian. It's somewhat better than being put to death for being Jewish—a practice we once deplored bitterly but which is now entirely acceptable in our new ally—but still it makes one wonder about the "good Arabs" we are ready to die for in a struggle against the "bad Arabs."

Also, it must be noted that a method of execution long since gone from civilized society, namely crucifixion, is still occasionally resorted to by those noble denizens of Saudi Arabia. One must add, in all fairness, that when the Saudis crucify a victim, he is mostly already dead.

* * *

While Golf-cart George and Stormin' Norman were occupied putting a nation to death, a city in the United States died quietly—not with bombs but with a small cry of agony. The city is called East St. Louis, and its 40,000 inhabitants eke out a hopeless and poverty-stricken existence amid the filth and ruins of what was once a vital and creative community. In East St. Louis, there has been no garbage collection in four years. The people, in desperation, burn their garbage, enveloping the city in a perpetual cloud of filthy smoke. The streets are broken, the roads impassable. No one repairs anything. The vanishing, often unpaid police force rides in ancient wrecks of cars. The electric power is an on and off proposition, and the sewer system has ceased to exist.

* * *

The other night, a physician friend of mine recalled an incident that occurred soon after he and his friend, Dr. Jonas Salk, were discharged from the Army. My friend then, in 1946, received a call from the Federal Bureau of Investigation. They wanted to know whether he had ever seen Dr. Salk at a radical meeting. Jonas Salk had apparently applied for a research grant, and if he was tainted with such an un-American act as attendance at a radical meeting, he would be marked a *commie* and the grant would be refused—and million-plus children who are alive and well today would have been either dead or crippled with polio.

November 26, 1990, and April 29, 1991

What Fate for Our Libraries?

Try this one on for size: We elect, as President of the most powerful country on earth, a silly old actor who has a reasonable amount of trouble writing his own name, and who has never gone much past that in literary efforts. And now, in his elegant Holmby Hills retirement, he is guest of honor in a fete to raise $40 million to buy him a library. Forty million dollars—you have to say it twice—as a repository for his papers. I'm a novelist, a teller of tales, but you can't invent such things, no way; you'd be laughed out of town. Only life itself can be impossible, ridiculous, laughable and inconceivable and get away with it.

According to *The New York Times*, 900 people paid $2,500 each to launch this library, said launching being a gala affair graced by the presence of James Stewart, among others, a fellow author whose book of poetry—recently on the best-seller lists—proved that even drivel will find a market if drooled by a movie star. As an item for those who can't find living space in these United States, it should be noted that this gigantic repository for the imperishable thoughts of a man who was semiliterate and hired every word he spoke out to speechwriters, will have 153,000 square feet of floor space.

What do we make of it? Will there be a Peggy Noonan hall, a Patrick Buchanan basement, stacks for the lesser speechwriters, bronze plates for researchers, gilded computers that were used by the busy little hands that composed the *State of the Union* addresses? Or will it be told to the innocents who enter this great hall of ignorance and deception that these works are from the hand of the master?

Small lies, big lies—none of it seems to matter anymore. Down in North Carolina the tobacco trusts, manufacturers and banks are building not only a library but a museum to the honor of one, Senator Jesse Helms, lord of the tobacco constituency, who fights the good fight to see to it that our Government continues to subsidize the farmers who grow what King James called the "sot weed." This business of building libraries to house forgeries and honor the unspeakable might simply be dismissed as another aspect of American lunacy and not too important when measured against our other lunacies, were it not for the crisis of the real libraries.

And there are real libraries, not mega-buildings that house the lies and infamies of regal Presidencies, but smaller spaces given to the writing of real writers and the thoughts and wisdom of the ages. These libraries—and happily, there are thousands of them in America—struggle desperately to find funds to buy books and to pay their librarians; but that is more and more frequently a losing fight, and perhaps nowhere more desperate than in New York City. Mayor Dinkins, besieged on every side in the drive for economy, turned on those least able to fight back, the public libraries, and slashed their budgets brutally. In all of his cutting, one might well say that "this was the unkindest cut of all."

I remember a lunch with that wonderful black writer Jimmy Baldwin, whose incredible talent is all too easily forgotten. We spoke to each other about our youth, about his black poverty and my white poverty, and we agreed that both of us, our lives and dreams and work, were made possible by the New York Public Library. I suppose the drinks and the being with each other made us a bit fanciful, for we saw the library as a place of magic and salvation, a shrine to all that is best in man's time on earth, a magic carpet that transcended race and poverty.

A few months ago, I was asked by a documentary film company whether I would be willing to participate in a film about the New York Public Library. They had read my book of memoirs of the time I had spent reading in the library, and would I go back to the same library and go through the motions of the child, now more than 60 years later? I said I would be delighted to, providing that the building still existed. It did, and we arranged to meet there one morning before the library opened.

The library in question is located on St. Nicholas Avenue and 160th Street. Unlike most city libraries, it is a three-story red brick corner building, designed by Stanford White, a fine old building that has been meticulously preserved. Time collapsed as I walked into the place after more than half a century. A few things had been changed, but not very much. The good hardwood banisters and mouldings pushed time aside, and the 15-foot ceilings and great windows retained their dignity.

But something else had changed; instead of Irish and Jewish and Italian kids, there was a new ethnic mix, black and Puerto Rican and Haitian and Central American—but the magic was no different. There were the same stacks, the same marvelous keys to all that man had done; but scrunched and stricken by poverty, making days when the library was closed and shortening the hours it was open, and making the replacement of books more difficult.

Yet that's all right, isn't it, so long as millions and millions of dollars can be raised to build the tombs of ignorance for Reagan and Helms and the rest of that scurvy lot.

February 25, 1991

Slogans

In the old days, when any dolt could make a nice living for himself in the rewarding profession of anti-Sovieteer, and at least a dozen prosperous funds gave chairs to anti-communists, Madam Jeane Kirkpatrick invented a neat twist to the language. Instead of the well-used and meaningful label of *dictatorship*, she divided the non-Western world into two categories, totalitarian and authoritarian. Totalitarian states were those in which the struggle for independence and freedom had more or less succeeded, as for example Nicaragua under the Sandinistas. Authoritarian states were committed anti-communist dictatorships, as for example El Salvador, where the Yankee-trained murder squads kept the peasants in line and power in the hands of a few families. Thus, authoritarian states could be our close allies, while totalitarian states were our sworn enemies. The former were the good guys, the latter the bad guys.

Language is indeed a marvelous thing. In the 1950s, when the Cold War was unleashed in its full fury—a war fought in America against free speech and free thought—a slogan was invented which became the battle cry of the cold warriors: "Better dead than red!" Like all slogans, it came without footnotes, so one was left without any explanation of why one was better dead than red, or of either the benefits of being dead or the threat of being red. Like all slogans, it substituted mindless imagery for rational thought.

Although Madison Avenue is keenly aware of this hole in the public head, they are by no means the originators of the use of the slogan to confuse and deceive. It has been around for a long time.

President Bush loves slogans. He doesn't invent them—he is not quite that witty—but he works them for all they are worth. What a delicious thing it was for him to spit out: the "L" word. Liberal is rather inoffensive; the schools are full of liberals, and often enough, you'll find one in your own home. But the "L" word, well, that's full of implications, sneaky suggestions, implied danger, a thing so foul that one does not speak it aloud, like the "F" word in the days when a kid's mouth could be washed out with soap and water. So when Mr. Bush or one of his minions speak of democracy, they line it up with "the two-party system" or "the free market," two slogans that are being worked to death the world over. Time was when we could be satisfied with pinning Mrs. Kirkpatrick's definition, authoritarian, on such bloody places as Iran, Iraq, Syria and a clutch of other client countries. But now, since the Gulf War slaughter ushered in a new concept of a gentle and kind policy, we have dropped the authoritarian approval and substituted the "two-party system," dividing the good guys from the bad guys with this sturdy political device.

Along with it, we push the "market economy," a related magic slogan. The trouble is that these two slogans, mouthed a thousand times a day, have not a scintilla of meaning in the real world—any more than the "L" word had meaning beyond invective.

Not that two-party systems do not exist. They do, all over the world, just as free market economies exist, but their existence is a litany, not a reality. Here in the United States, for example, the Republican Party controls the Federal Government—a party which is unabashedly the party of the great corporations, the munition makers, the suburban rich, the bankers and the trusts; and just as unabashedly the enemies of the cities and those who dwell in the cities, the working people and the poor. All this current agony about budget and the quality of life in New York City stems most basically from the disdain and hatred the Federal Government exercises toward the cities.

In a valid, working two-party system, the cities and the common people would have representation politically; and historically the Democratic Party has pretended toward that representation. But the Democratic Congress has become the brown-nosed follower of the Republicans. It apes the Republicans, whimpers over their packing of the courts, abdicates the struggle for civil rights, and joins in the massacre called the Gulf War in a manner so cowardly and degraded that it surrenders what shreds of populism still cling to it. So insofar as our Federal Government is concerned, there is no two-party system. The Republicans represent the establishment. No one represents the millions of ordinary folk who do the work and pay the taxes.

And the market economy which we demand the Russians install? When a nation drains the blood from its people to turn the major force of its industrial might into a gargantuan maker of armaments, literally becoming a killing machine, it's pure hokum to speak of a free market economy. Our factories manufacture death for profit; the people pay for this and receive nothing but yellow ribbon in return, and all the killing-machines, the tanks and the planes and the rest of it bring only death to the marketplace.

July 22–29, 1991

The U.S. Postal Service—At a Loss

I am still ambulatory and able to recall a name or two when the occasion demands it, yet I can remember when a first-class letter could be mailed with a 2-cent stamp. In fact, the first stories I wrote and submitted to unappreciative editors were mailed with 2-cent stamps. Certain perks went with the 2-cent stamp, as for instance two and sometimes three mail deliveries a day. And the letter that was posted arrived at the inscribed address, locally the following day and nationally in six days or less. Airmail was only beginning.

You may remember that in the stories of Raymond Chandler and Dashiell Hammett—both contemporaries of mine—the way to secure precious documents was to place them in envelopes and address them to oneself; such was the faith we had in our postal service.

Well, things change, but rarely for the better. Today, if one wishes to make sure that a letter goes to where it is addressed, one sends it by United Parcel Service or Federal Express, and pays a fat bonus for the privilege of doing so. Or one can put a 29-cent stamp on an envelope by going to the post office—any one of a number of branch offices in New York City. If one is part of a corporation, one can send a gofer, who can spend a fat chunk of the afternoon at the errand. But if you, like myself, run your own errands, you will recognize the experience.

I enter a room with 16 windows, service windows, but for reasons unknown only four of the windows are available for the patient expectations of ordinary mortals like myself. There is a line of people, enclosed in an imitation maze, that snakes back and forth, filling most of the interior of the large room, and here about 60 or 70 people await their turn at one of the four service windows available to the general public.

Not that the remaining 12 windows are closed, no indeed. Ten of the 12 are open, with post office employees dozing behind them. There are no lines at these windows. They are special windows for special services, and apparently no one in this curious institution has the audacity or inventiveness to shift one of those sleepy caverns to the use of ordinary folks who desire only to buy stamps or weigh a letter or mail a parcel or do any of the things that one goes to the post office to do.

Whereupon, I take my place at the end of the folded line. I stand on line, unhappily yet with a glimmer of hope that this line, like all lines of people or cars or trains, must eventually move. I comfort myself by telling myself that if I share the experience of people in Moscow and am privy to their boredom, I nevertheless do not have to undergo this punishment to buy a loaf of bread or a pair of socks—only in the United States Post Office. As with the other citizens on the line, my eyes begin to glaze over and I tell myself that the line has moved. Indeed, now there are a dozen men and women behind me, whereas before I was at the end of the line, yet the line in front of me has hardly moved. The afternoon wanes, and I begin to wonder at what time this office closes.

And then, miracle of miracles, I am at one of the four windows, and I offer $29 of cash money for a roll of stamps.

"No rolls. We're out."

"OK. Give me a sheet of twenty-nines."

"Out of twenty-nines. I can give you a sheet of twenties and a sheet of nines."

"I want twenty-nines. Maybe at one of the other windows?"

"Look, mister, I don't have the whole day to stand here arguing with you. Either take the twenties and nines, or move it."

Well, what does one expect? Like certain college professors, the man has tenure, and that gives him the right to grin at you and tell you to take your business elsewhere. Corporations can do that and, as I said, they have built United Parcel and Federal Express into two giant profitable enterprises. But for the little guy, the costs are too high.

Writing about the situation in the Postal Service, Charles Peters, editor of a remarkable magazine called the *Washington Monthly*, has this to say:

> Top postal executives were rewarded with nearly $20 million in bonuses between 1988 and 1990, when the post office not only was not making a profit, but was losing more than $1.4 billion. The rigorous standards used in evaluating the performance of these executives are suggested by the fact that, of all those who could have gotten bonuses, 97 percent received them. How did the executives justify the bonuses? Here's the defense offered to the *Pittsburgh Press*, by Frank Brennan, a postal service spokesman in Washington: "Hey, we saved $800 million off a projected $1.6 billion loss.

November 4, 1991

Where Insanity Prevails

A long time ago, when I was 11 or 12 years old, I was a rapacious fan of Edgar Rise Burroughs' Tarzan adventure books. In one of these, Tarzan discovers, hidden away in deepest Africa, a lost city of considerable structure and apparent culture, but with a population that is totally insane. As I was a small boy, just beginning to know the fact of mental illness—suggested mostly by special classes for retarded children in the public schools—and hardly capable of comprehending the nature of insanity, the proposition that Burroughs put forward was both fascinating and bewildering.

I remember asking myself whether such a community could exist. I knew something of the functioning of a community. Streets had to be cleaned, mail delivered, food distributed and sold—and, of course, law enforcement was necessary. Could a place where insanity prevails provide those elementary services and go on from generation to generation?

I still ask myself that question. Consider this recent *The New York Times* article: "Washington, Dec. 13—After billions of dollars in repairs and years of retraining operators and modernizing procedures, the Energy Department said today that it had begun the process of restarting a nuclear arsenal. The order to restart the K reactor at the Savannah River nuclear weapons plant near Aiken, South Carolina, was made this afternoon by Energy Secretary James D. Watkins. The reactor is expected to achieve a sustained nuclear chain reaction, from which the nuclear bomb fuel is produced, either on Saturday or Sunday, the Department said."

Edgar Rice Burroughs was not writing this one. After reading the above several times, to prove that one's eyes are not playing tricks, one might recall that the United States has at this moment a stockpile of some 30,000 nuclear bombs and assorted weapons, give or take a few thousand, enough to wipe out every particle of life on the planet Earth at least 20 times over. "Billions of dollars," for more and more and more atomic bombs.

On the very day the article appeared, three teenage kids were walking along a street in Brooklyn. Not doing anything, just walking. A car pulled up, and for no discernible reason except that one of the men in the car owned a rapid-fire assault weapon, said assault weapon owner poured 36 rounds into the three boys. Result: one dead, two others badly wounded. Random—no connection between the killer and the killed.

Two days later in *The Times*: "An anonymous gift of tainted Christmas candy given to seven teachers at the Ravena-Coeymans-Selkirk [New York] High School sent one instructor to the hospital this week, the state police said. . . . Tests on the candy revealed a chemical similar to insecticide was added to the candy. Other gift packages were shipped to the teachers' homes." These are the kind of items you can find in the back pages of any edition of *The Times*, and while the paper does its best there are certainly 100 unreported incidents for each noted and printed. Still, it does not indict an entire society.

What does indict an entire society? Half a century ago, Germans who called themselves Nazis exterminated, coldly and deliberately, over 10 million human beings. Six million of them were Jews; the rest were Poles and Gypsies and Ukrainians and Russians, other East Europeans and Germans who had opposed the Nazis. Here in our country, during the past two decades, a small movement came into being. They called themselves Nazis, shaved their heads and wore the same uniform as the original Nazis, hooked cross and all. One of their leaders, a man called David Duke, wore their uniform and preached their gospel of hatred, of death to the blacks and to the Jews. This was not a simple mental aberration, it was a reminder and a pledge to one day reprise the greatest mass murder in the history of the human race. This same man who was one of their leaders, proudly photographed in the uniform they wore, is today a candidate for President of the United States. Of course, one might say of Mr. Duke, "Crazy? Hardly, unless you say crazy like a fox."

But what of the media? By and large, he is treated with respect, his ideas are listened to, he is given endless photo opportunities and millions of words of copy: a state of things that gives one thought as to the possibility of an insane society functioning from generation to generation.

On that subject, it is well worth noting the arrival on the scene of Patrick Buchanan, another candidate for President. His war cry is "America First!" which he dug up out of the same past that yielded Mr. Duke's original images, the battle cry of those good folk who favored Hitler in World War II and worked day and night against American intervention. Mr. Buchanan rages against money for food and medicine to prevent chaos in what was once the Soviet Union—but about the billions spent to put our atomic bomb plant back into operation, neither Mr. Duke nor Mr. Buchanan has one word to say. And they have no words to say about the hundreds of billions of dollars we continue to pour into the Pentagon and the CIA.

And here I am, a lifetime later, still puzzled over Edgar Rice

Burroughs' suggestion that a totally insane society could function from generation to generation.

December 30, 1991

Chapter 16

War and Peace

Spies

I hate spies. I have always hated spies. The word itself has the smell of obscenity. The history books from which our children are taught the few bits of misinformation that constitutes history in American schoolrooms, have tried to give spying a good name by quoting Nathan Hale. This poor kid, sent from 125th Street in Manhattan downtown to count the British troops for General Washington, put it down on paper instead of keeping the numbers in his head. The Brits grabbed him and hanged him, and we are told that in the agony of his fear, he piped up with, "I only regret that I have but one life to lose for my country." Not content to be hanged once—what damned nonsense. But only a part of the nonsense we feed our kids, to prove that dying and killing are great fun games.

Spying is also very good for bad writers. James Fenimore Cooper, possibly the worst writer that America or any other country ever produced, set the stage with his worst book, if one can paste a superlative on a superlative, *The Spy*. Since then, he has been followed by a parade of sometimes skilled but rarely intelligent writers who deal with spies; and with the advent of film and television, an endless parade of TV shows and films that deal with spies. These films can be broken down into a set of categories, which makes it very easy for a producer to select the specific spy film he wishes to produce. But before I list these categories and give, free of charge, a valuable gift to every film and TV producer, let me dispose of any charge that I am prejudiced.

I hold in equal disgust and contempt the CIA, the KGB, and the Brits' MI-5. They share, quite equally, stupidity and other like virtues. And now to the categories:

1. Here a guy who looks like the uncle you hate most breaks into a CIA safe house and shoots everyone in sight. On from there.
2. A CIA guy goes over to the KGB. He's a good guy. Except that maybe he's a bad guy. Except that maybe he's both.
3. A KGB guy goes over to the CIA. He's a good guy, but really he's a bad guy, or maybe both.
4. A CIA guy who thought he was a good guy realizes, after a few years, that he was a bad guy, not a good guy, and he decides to leave the CIA, and they decide to kill him, but he outwits them, because every Hollywood director or producer knows that deep down in his heart every red-blooded American hates the CIA.

5. Same as above, but substitute KGB or MI-5 for CIA. It really makes no difference whatsoever. (Unless, of course, it's Sean Connery. If so, all bets are off.)
6. KGB and CIA team up because MI-5 is in the hands of a mole who is after the bomb, re terror.
7. Above, but we switch teams.
8. KGB guy goes bad. Good KGB teams up with CIA to get him and save the world. Or vice versa. Or vice versa with MI-5.
9. CIA super-guy saves: American ship; the world; USA, Moscow, New York, Washington. Or vice versa.

I could go on, but my space here is limited, and it is necessary to pinch ourselves and realize that these lunatics do not exist only in the movies, but that they have their counterparts in real life and that these real life counterparts not only spend billions of dollars of our hard-earned money, but augment their covert craziness by running a little dope and illegal arms here and there. It is also worth remembering that through their covert process of destabilization, they have brought about the deaths of countless thousands of people, as well as giving us such goodies as Vietnam, Chile, El Salvador, Panama, Nicaragua and Cambodia. But when it comes to the purpose for which they were established, namely the gathering of intelligence, it is almost impossible to discover one instance where they did what they were supposed to do. For example:

An atom bomb was tested off the South African coast. They never found out who did it. The Soviet Union had the atom bomb more than 12 months before the CIA knew it. Two hundred forty-one marines were killed in Beirut with no warning from the CIA. Fissionable material sufficient to make a dozen atom bombs disappeared from our facilities without either warning or knowledge from the CIA. Gigantic changes were taking place in the Soviet Union. The CIA either knew nothing about them or were unable to analyze them properly. A cruise ship was hijacked, five planes were hijacked and a 747 was blown out of the skies over Scotland, and the CIA anticipated nothing of this. And so forth and so on.

Intelligence? Get out of here!

April 17, 1989

From Star Wars to Canoes

D'emas, who is one of those foreign primitives with absolutely no concept of civilization, keeps harping on the poor and homeless in New York. He keeps asking why we don't do something for them, and I keep telling him that we simply don't have the money.

"But you're so rich," D'emas said the other day. "What do you do with your money?"

"We give it—or at least a great deal of it—to the Federal Government. It is called taxes."

"And what do they do with these taxes?" D'emas asked.

"Well, most of it goes for defense. Do you understand what defense means?"

"Oh, yes, of course. But on our island we don't spend a penny for defense."

"Because," I said with annoyance, "nobody wants your wretched little island."

Hurt, D'emas said that his island was larger than the Bronx and much more beautiful.

"I didn't mean to hurt your feelings, D'emas. On the other hand, you do know about Star Wars, which must cost us billions and billions of dollars."

"Yes, I read about it," D'emas said with unusual vehemence. "It is absolutely the silliest, craziest thing I ever heard of."

"Oh, no—wait a minute, wait just one cotton-picking minute. You are an uneducated primitive, and you dare to contradict a man like Ronald Reagan—"

"The other day you said Mr. Reagan was not bright, to put it kindly. I'm not criticizing Mr. Reagan, because he doesn't understand canoes. I come from canoe people. That's why I say Star Wars is nonsense."

"What on earth are you talking about, you silly savage?"

"Now I've upset you again," D'emas said. "But you see, on our island, everyone uses canoes. You are pouring billions of dollars into Star Wars to stop missiles that come through the air from Russia. But all the Russians have to do is rent some canoes from us, put the missiles on the canoes, and paddle them silently into New York Harbor. They can do this with one cheap submarine. They really don't have to use canoes; an outboard motorboat is much better. They could blow New York and Washington and San Francisco and every other seaport you have out of existence, while you wait for them to shoot the missiles through the air."

"That's the craziest idea I ever heard of!" I shouted.

"Can you pick a hole in it?" D'emas asked, grinning that foolish grin of his.

"We can sink their submarines."

"Yesterday," D'emas said smugly, "your *New York Times* said that the Russians' new submarines are so silent as to be undetectable."

I stared at D'emas for a long moment before I said, "If that is true, why has no one ever mentioned it?"

"You're asking me? I'm just a primitive savage. My goodness."

"You're trying to tell me we've been snookered? Had?"

"Well," said D'emas, uneasy because he had upset me so, "maybe there's an agreement between Washington and Moscow to shoot missiles only through the air and never to send a missile into a harbor by submarine and canoes and outboard motorboats?"

"That's just a dumb statement, D'emas, and you know it."

"Why? Would that be any stranger than all the other things your Government and their Government do? Look what your Government did in Vietnam. Look what their Government did in Afghanistan. You're always talking about people taking stupid pills. Maybe everyone who gets into government has to take stupid pills."

"For God's sake, D'emas, there's no such thing as stupid pills. It's just a turn of phrase."

"Oh? Well, I didn't know. I just don't know that much about civilization and government. I really thought you were explaining why civilized people do the things they do."

"Let me tell you something, D'emas," I said sternly. "No anchorman, no news writer, no commentator has ever mentioned what you say about how the Russians could blow our cities out of the world and never run into Star Wars. No one. Not once. Which proves absolutely that there's nothing in your whole idea."

"I suppose so," D'emas agreed. "No one could ever accuse an anchorman or a newspaper of deceiving the public."

April 24, 1989

War Stories

I am asked to talk at a book fair in the suburbs of Washington, D.C. I am picked up at the airport by a pleasant couple, who invite me, since we are early, to have lunch with them at their club. We eat and we talk, and I ask him what he does. I am always curious about what people do for a living.

"I sell armaments," the pleasant man tells me.

"Oh?"

He sees the expression on my face and says quickly, "Oh, no, not one of those. I work for the Pentagon."

"Oh? I thought the Pentagon buys armaments."

"Yes, quite so," the pleasant man agrees. "Americans look upon the Pentagon as an organization that orders arms for our defense. They do, you know. But at the same time, they are in the business and we are the largest armaments dealer in the world."

"You're kidding?"

"Not at all. It's no secret, you know."

"But where do you sell these arms?"

"Oh, not to the Communists or Marxists. Certainly not. But to the other side, wherever the other side is."

* * *

The little boy in Beirut stares at me out of my television screen. He is the same age as my small grandson. He has the same wide, wonderful eyes, and they look at me so uncomplainingly that tears come to my eyes. I don't know who made the shell that blew both his feet off, so that he begins life with two stumps where the feet God gave him should have been. I don't know whether the shell that did it was Russian, American, French, or German, and I can't do anything about it.

* * *

Count Leo Tolstoy, who was as wise as God ever permits a man to be, said, "Every story about war is a lie."

* * *

The kid in the crack army unit that we sent down to Panama also watches me from my television screen. He is strong and healthy, the way so many American kids are, proud and cocky, his carbine slung over his back, and he says, "I feel good. This is what they trained me to do. I'm glad I may have a chance to fight."

* * *

Mark Twain, who was also pretty smart, said, "No matter what they say about any war, it's got to be a lie."

* * *

The little Arab boy thinks it is a wonderful and exciting thing to throw stones at the bad people. If the older kids do it, there's no reason he shouldn't do it, and now he lies in his mother's arms with a hole in his forehead, filling my television screen, while the Jews and the Arabs and their masters in Moscow and Washington argue about land and God and history, and his mother weeps the way a hundred million mothers have since the lunatics took charge of our lives.

* * *

The poet Norman Rosten, in the army during World War Two, having a bowel movement, looked up and saw written on the wall of the latrine:

Soldiers who wish to be a hero
Are practically zero
But those who wish to be civilians,
Jesus, they run into the millions.

* * *

"The bombs we dropped opened like roses."

—Mussolini's son, a bomber pilot.

May 29, 1989

Explaining Civilization to the Uncivilized

My friend D'emas should not be faulted for his desire to understand Western civilization. Coming from one of those backward civilizations, he is something of a primitive, and very ordinary happenings are often beyond his understanding. For example, he said to me the other day, "I see that General Minoru Genda has finally died. Eighty-four years—he certainly took his time."

"That's not very gracious," I told D'emas. "He was a very important man."

"So I understand. He led the attack on Pearl Harbor, didn't he?"

"He certainly did. It was his idea, and he planned every step of it and led it as well. Absolutely brilliant. More than 2,400 Americans died in that attack, very fine young men, the very cream of our pre–World War II armed forces. At least that many more were gravely wounded. He destroyed 19 or 20 ships and 177 planes—a terrible blow. He also invented the idea of the suicide torpedo-bomber. We paid a terrible price to those torpedo-bombers—thousands of dead and wounded and many ships sunk."

"And as I understand it," D'emas said, struggling with the concept, as he always did when it came to matters of civilization, "a few years later Washington awarded him the highest honor that can be given to a foreigner, the Legion of Merit?"

"Oh, yes. Yes indeed. We had occupied Japan, and General Genda was given the task of rebuilding the Japanese Military Air Force. That was why we gave him the Legion of Merit."

"But as I understand it," D'emas said, "Japan was your enemy, and you had destroyed the Japanese air force. Why did you want it rebuilt?"

"To fight the Russians, of course."

"But the Russians were your allies. They had destroyed the Nazis and saved Western civilization."

"Oh, no. They were threatening all of Europe with Communism. Japan was anti-Communist."

"Yes, but this man, Minoru Genda, was a murderer—a mass murderer," D'emas said unhappily. "You said yourself that he engineered the death of thousands, perhaps tens of thousands of young men—your best and bravest young men. I don't understand why you would give him a medal for this."

"It was war," I explained patiently. "Coming from where you do, D'emas, you don't understand war. In war, you are given a uniform and a gun and the right to murder anyone who stands in your way. That is the essence of Western civilization."

"But you put people who murder in jail and in some states you even execute them."

"That is peace," I explained, still patient. "Those are people who don't have uniforms. People without uniforms are not allowed to commit murder. That is an act reserved entirely for people in uniform."

"Then if I buy a uniform—" D'emas began tentatively.

"Oh, no, no, no. It's not enough to buy a uniform. You must join an army—preferably one engaged in a war. You could join the Contras in Nicaragua or one of the armies in Lebanon or the police in South Africa—oh, any number of places as long as there is a war going on. Or you could join an army of one of the major powers. Of course, in that case you might have to wait months or years before you could do a reasonable amount of killing."

D'emas shook his head. There are times when I despair of teaching the man the simple basics of civilization.

"On my island," he said almost apologetically, "we would take a man like General Genda, give him what psychological treatment we could, and then keep him in our little hospital for the insane. But of course now I understand that such treatment would be improper."

"I'm afraid so."

"On my island, the missionaries work very hard to civilize us and to turn us into Christians. They keep talking about the Commandments of God. According to them, God says, *Thou shalt not kill.*"

"Absolutely—when you are not in uniform. That's the essence of civilization, D'emas. What kind of a world would it be if people went around killing each other because they had exchanged a few harsh words?"

"Pretty awful," D'emas agreed. "Then the whole world would be like New York City."

It's not easy, as you can see; to explain civilization to the uncivilized is difficult, but with patience and persistence, one can persevere.

September 11, 1989

Depraved Indifference

In Buddhist thinking, there is the dictum that one must always see things newly. This means that in the course of living, one should see everything as if one had never seen it before, a building, a tree, a lover, a mother—everything in life as if one looks at it for the first time. This is not easy, because it also applies to ideas—in the sense that no idea (or thing, or person) should be accepted without question. For one who tries to practice this, the world becomes a marvelous, living thing.

I mention this somewhat exotic notion because for the past weeks I have been absolutely intrigued by a section of the New York State Penal Code that was central to the two trials in Bensonhurst, Brooklyn [which concerned the beating and murder of a black youth by whites]. In the media it has been referred to simply as "depraved indifference"; in the Penal Code, it reads as follows:

> A person is guilty of murder in the 2nd degree when . . . under circumstances evincing a depraved indifference to human life, he recklessly engages in conduct which creates a grave risk of death to another person and thereby causes the death of the other person.

Now if one takes this part of the criminal code and examines it independently of what happened in Bensonhurst, but simply as a definition of a crime so repugnant to society that society specifies it as murder in the second degree, and if one looks at it newly, in terms I speak of above, the world shakes a bit on its foundations.

Let us for example look at what has been going on in El Salvador the past 10 years. We armed mercenary murder squads, trained them and then gave them a license to kill, and since then they have murdered some 70,000 men, women, children, nurses, nuns, a bishop of the Catholic faith and five Jesuit priests. The documentation on these charges is so enormous that it begs the point even to question it; but now I suggest that we think about it newly and within the framework of the criminal code of New York State. I understand quite well that this criminal code does not apply to persons not living in the state or to crimes not committed in the state; nevertheless, New York State is hardly insignificant, with its population of 18 million, with an area larger than England, and with its namesake city, possibly the most important city on earth, to crown its status.

So let us think of El Salvador in terms of the state's criminal code, and ask whether it does not apply to the murder squads of that sorry land and to others who "recklessly engaged in conduct which created a grave risk of death to other persons"? How do the actions of Joey Fama differ, not only in terms of a criminal code but in the moral sense upon which we attempt to structure criminal law, from the actions of a group of powerful Americans who created the situations in Panama and El Salvador and Nicaragua?

I am not trying to be judgmental or to condemn or to indict. I know the theories of the power of a sovereign state, and I know that history has not only chronicled and blessed and raised monuments to this practice, which in all truth can only be called "depraved indifference," but I also know that something must happen when one opens one's eyes and looks newly at clichés and maxims and absolutes that we were taught almost from the moment of our births.

There are no guiltless. No power structure on the face of this earth has not been guilty of depraved indifference, no state has not been guilty of it. I only ask that we at least try to make a giant step forward and open our eyes and look newly at these endless horrors that we have so glibly named civilization.

I think that there is a better measure of civilization, and the angry blacks who demonstrated in front of the courthouse in Brooklyn knew it and the people who framed the criminal code of New York State knew it.

The human race has somehow adapted itself to the proposition that there is legal murder and illegal murder. The Germans, a most law-abiding race, murdered millions, *most apparent*, but how *little apparent* is our own murder of uncounted thousands of blacks and American Indians (on our own soil), as well as those to whom we taught "democracy" in Central America. This so-called verity, this demented practice of the human race, is almost never questioned. In its utter nakedness, patriotism is not only the "last resort of scoundrels," as Samuel Johnson put it, but the ultimate accolade given to those who kill.

I suggest that we try to think newly, look newly and see newly, and that we question everything. Then, perhaps, a time will come when the people of this planet can call each and every bastard who holds the reins of power to an accounting and "depraved indifference" can top the criminal code of all mankind.

June 4, 1990

The Bottom Line

Readers will have already noted my views on the 1991 war in the Persian Gulf. Many more essays on this subject follow.

As a committed pacifist, and as someone who lived through World War II, the Korean War, the Vietnam War, I watched the approach and the nurturing of what became the Gulf War with horror and despair. The United States has designed and provoked wars in our past—wars where there was no real provocation on the part of our "enemies," as witness the Mexican War and the Spanish-American War, but these were in a past we sought to gloss over and forget; the Gulf War burst upon our supposedly enlightened present.

The New York Observer, *to its credit, was one of a handful of American publications that opposed it from the word go, and thereby I had the privilege of writing what I believed to be the truth about this horrible episode as it developed.*

Only a few days after the Oil War began, word out of Washington on August 12 had it that the Saudi incursion had already cost us $2 billion. The Pentagon was quick to deny this, claiming that the figure was too high by half a billion dollars, but other sources claimed that $2 billion was a reasonable figure, and *The New York Times* of August 13 confirmed it. It should be noted that the Pentagon, long separated from any reality, did not feel that a billion and a half was unreasonable.

But nobody in any part of the media, as far as I could discover, suggested that at wholesale prices $2 billion could buy better than 2 billion gallons of gasoline and that an additional few weeks of war cost would buy enough oil to last us the next 50 years. But any such notion or practice would have meant that common sense was functioning somewhere.

Instead, we took the easy path of lunacy:

We broke with the understanding at the United Nations and went into Saudi Arabia and the Gulf waters by ourselves.

We antagonized much of the Arab world.

We embraced the Emir of Kuwait, a somewhat less than democratic ruler. We embraced the Saudis, a gentle folk who treat their women as property and cut off the hands of thieves and stone to death women who have engaged in adultery.

We cried out to the world that what Saddam Hussein had done to

Kuwait was hardly comparable to what we did to Panama and Nicaragua, since Kuwait was bursting with oil and neither Panama nor Nicaragua had a dollop of oil.

And we declared, God help us, that we were righteous in our deeds.

Now, with that said, I will try to eschew questions of morality or right and wrong, and simply stick to that yardstick of our time, namely, the bottom line. The initial $2 billion is only a modest down payment. Every few days another billion dollars will be added to the bill which, like the savings and loan disgrace, must be borne by the American taxpayers.

Mayor Dinkins, chief executive of what is still the most important and wonderful city [New York] on the face of the earth, must crawl on bended knee to the "gentlemen" in Washington, pleading for a few million dollars to police this city properly. A single-day cost of the Oil War would not only give him the police he needs, but would rebuild most of the rotting bridges in the city, with enough left over for a desperately needed hospice for AIDS victims.

A single day of the Oil War's cost would finance the most expensive poison-waste cleanup in America, while a week of Oil War cost would probably rid us of the worst atomic waste spots.

Let's speculate about a month's cost of the Oil War. That would certainly provide enough funds to create a job for every unemployed person in America. Doing what? Cleaning streets for some, building and manning hospitals for others, repairing roads, fighting drugs, investigating solar energy and other novel sources of energy, such as tide and wind.

And let's go way out on a limb and talk about a six-month cost of the Oil War. With that kind of money, we could house every homeless man, woman and child in these United States.

And the net result would be a period of prosperity for us and for the world as had never been known.

As you see, I am talking the bottom-line language of the so-called minds in Government. I am talking dollars and cents (also sense), and carefully avoiding such extraneous matters as death and suffering and body bags and amputations and the guts of teen-agers spilled on the Arabian sands, and weeping mothers and heartbroken fathers, since none of that has the slightest meaning for the clowns in Washington.

But they do appear to have some understanding of the bottom line, and absolutely nothing I have listed is either difficult or unreasonable.

Of course, it would take a hell of a lot of pressure to force Congress to do something constructive instead of destructive. They love war. It makes them all feel so goddamned manly, and nobody ever got his ass kicked for spouting patriotism. As was well said, patriotism is the last resort of scoundrels.

And meanwhile, the real problems have been blown away, out of the media, out of sight, out of mind, and no one is snooping around, trying to discover whether the President's son is a crook or not, and the national debt blows up, larger and larger, like some crazy balloon, and who cares about the budget, and dope—well, dope is dope—all of the Establishment lives in the suburbs, and as long as we have golf carts and photo opportunities, all will be well, on earth as it is in heaven above. Amen.

September 3, 1990

The First Casualty of War

In the early days of television, *Gunsmoke*, starring James Arness as Matt Dillon, was one of the most popular programs. It touched something very deep in most people through the use of a simple formula. For the first 15 minutes of this half-hour, one watched an assortment of ugly "bad guys" inflict every sort of pain and humiliation on Dillon and the "good guys," to the point where the viewer's indignation boiled over. In the second 15 minutes, the tables were turned and Matt Dillon shot every one of the "bad guys" dead. Sometimes the small screen overflowed with the carnage that Dillon had wrought with his two six-guns, but we all watched with grim satisfaction. After all, the "bad guys" started it.

We are saturated with the "bad guy" philosophy. It eliminates a process that we dread above all else, namely mentation, and it allows us to rationalize almost any obscenity. I write of our own obscenities, not of theirs. Saddam Hussein is without question about as low and miserable a specimen of humanity as exists. He is a man without decency, compassion and honor, a murderer without conscience or soul—which does not justify the death of one American boy—yet the jingoistic outburst about this "beast of Baghdad" has been as loud and shrill and brainless as any justification of war in the past. Day in and day out we are confronted with the statements of citizens, men in uniform, politicos, women in uniform, Congressmen, Senators, and of course old "read my lips" himself, to the effect that we are defending our country and the American way of life; and day in and day out, this explosion of jingoism is underlined by some new loathsome act of Saddam Hussein.

But we are not defending our country. We are defending barbaric and cruel medieval monarchies called Kuwait and Saudi Arabia, ruled by oligarchs who are as deficient of compassion as Mr. Hussein, and of course we are defending the American oil companies who are their partners and the rigs and refineries that produce their oil. The thought of calling Saudi Arabia, a land where a woman accused of adultery is beheaded and where thieves have their hands chopped off, a democracy is laughable. So let it be said once and for all, we are not defending our country or democracy. We are fighting for oil.

As for the American way of life—unless we stop guzzling gasoline like lunatics, we will have only the American way of death to deal with.

Now with all this said, one must face the fact. The prince of lip-reading did not wait for the United Nations to vote an armed incursion of the Arabian desert, nor did he wait for Congress to convene. It is quite true that the Constitution of the United States holds that only Congress can declare war, but that's too slow for modern times, and before you could say Jack Robinson there we were in Arabia, with billions and billions of dollars' worth of high-class killing-junk and thousands of American soldiers all ready to die for Arabian oil if the heat didn't kill them first.

Truth is the first casualty in any war, and it usually requires at least 20 or 30 years before the truth underlying a war can emerge. But how can one evade the fact that Mr. Bush and the curious Mr. Sununu, who always lurks slightly behind him during the photo opportunities, have put their feet into one enormous trap? Unless Saddam Hussein pulls out of Kuwait and restores the Emir, what is Mr. Bush to do?

If he launches an attack against Iraq, he will be responsible for untold suffering, for a tragedy almost beyond computation either in human suffering or in dollars and cents.

If Mr. Bush does not attack Iraq and if the American press is alert enough to see to it that no incident is manufactured to provoke such an attack (like "Remember the Maine" or the "Tonkin Gulf") then we may be able, God willing, to avoid a terrible and senseless conflict.

But one thing that we cannot avoid or change, unfortunately, unless a new Government with some degree of sanity in its membership is voted into office, is our presence in Saudi Arabia. Going in gave us the opportunity to show the world what a brilliant response we could mount to a threat to our oil. No equivalent response has ever taken place in regard to crime, homelessness, drugs or the debt. Getting out is another matter entirely, and up to the date of this writing no one with a voice in the media has even considered the problem.

What then? Are we doomed to remain in that wretched desert for decades? Will it be like the 45 years of occupation in Europe? And will our troops be cautioned—also forever—not to wear crosses or the Star of David, since both appear to offend the sensibilities of the Saudis?

September 10, 1990

The Civil War

I watched *The Civil War*, all eleven hours of it, and as an amateur historian who has delved a bit into Civil War history, I doff my hat to it—certainly the finest and most original piece of television documentary history that I have ever seen. Making it must have been a monumental task of research and choice, eleven hours without, so far as I am concerned, a moment of boredom—and in some ways, a better picture and explanation of the Civil War than any book on the subject. This is due to the fact that it was visual—a superb accomplishment when one reflects on the fact that there was no motion picture film and that still photography depended on glass plates for negatives, thousands of which were lost or destroyed.

Perhaps my cheers for this work are to some extent based on a confirmation of beliefs that I have held for many years. These beliefs call for a massive but absolutely necessary revision of history. I list them below:

• The Civil War, in spite of the enthusiastic columns Karl Marx wrote for *The New York Herald Tribune*, hailing it and cheering it, was historically unnecessary. Enough sane discussion and intelligent give-and-take could have prevented it and thereby avoided the awful sacrifice of 650,000 human lives and the unmeasurable suffering of the wounded who survived.

• All the rationalizations to the effect that this had to be, that it was the beginning of the United States, that it was a glorious struggle against slavery, that it brought our nation to manhood—all of these are lies. The concept of good emerging from this awful, brainless slaughter is sheer manipulation of facts. Nothing good came from the Civil War. The emancipation of the black slaves, an afterthought when the Union had almost lost the struggle, was hardly a reality. It took another hundred years for the black man in America to take the meaningful steps toward freedom and civil rights. It gave the South justification for the repression of the blacks—and in this context, no one with any sense of history can doubt that manumission would have occurred in any case. With or without the war, slavery was intolerable. The Civil War destroyed the infrastructure of the Confederate States and burned their cities and savaged their people with brutality that almost matched Hitler's invasion of Russia. The lie, fostered for more than a hundred years, that Sherman's march to the sea ended or even helped materially to end the war, is still current. Like other inventions and rationalizations, it attempted to explain the unspeakable and justify a process of waste and barbarism rarely equaled in history.

The singular horror of the Civil War—no European war of the 19th century could even approach it in brutality and slaughter—had to be hidden from the American people, lest they should see it as it was and turn away from the lunacy of war as an answer to political problems.

The ennoblement of Robert E. Lee and Ulysses S. Grant as brilliant and compassionate military leaders is perhaps one of the greatest pieces of flackery in human history. The only accolade of intelligence Lee deserved was that awarded him by General Grant and the other Union leaders, since their ineptitude and sheer stupidity made some of Lee's actions appear to be intelligent. When Lee ordered General Pickett to lead his Virginia Division, 15,000 of the best men in the Confederate Army, in a frontal charge on an impregnable position on Cemetery Ridge, and slaughtered most of the 15,000 and perhaps struck the final blow that cost him the war, he honored with an apology the thousands of his own men whom he had brainlessly consigned to death. This incident is most often quoted as evidence of his compassion. God save us from such compassion.

The Civil War was fought without reason, without goal, without plan or purpose. In its entirety, it is a moment in human history so awful that for more than a hundred years, American scholars have been unable to face it. This is why it has become a pleasant fairy tale in our schools, taught without even an attempt to bare the truth; and until Public Television presented the history of that war in pictures and without apology, it has remained so far as the general public is concerned, a fuzzy happening guided by a superhuman being called Abraham Lincoln. It is not my purpose here to even attempt the truth of Abraham Lincoln. Others with scholarly credentials must face that task, sooner or later.

Tolstoy wrote, in *War and Peace*, that every account of battle is a lie, and at a moment like this, our country poised on the edge of a chasm, this must be remembered. It is not that only evil men lie; good men lie because the truth is so dangerous. But the lie is even more dangerous.

October 15, 1990

No Matter How the Killing Is Done

It needs only the smell of war in the air for all parties concerned to start working God. There never was a war when God was not on both sides, blessing the body count and all other aspects of slaughter; and I find it particularly difficult to find a religion, aside from the Quakers, that says forthrightly that killing one's fellow man is an insult to God and an unforgivable sin. Of course, a good many religions back up the "right to life" movement, but their zealousness in the defense of life extends only to the embryo still in the womb. Once the child is born, their interest wanes, and when it comes to the mass slaughter of young men, you don't get even a peep out of the lot.

In a marvelous story called "Captain Stormfield Visits Heaven," Mark Twain deals with the self-importance of religious leaders and their readiness to speak for God and God's will. Old Captain Stormfield dies, and on his way to Heaven, he is distracted by a comet and thrown off course. The result is that he reaches the wrong gate. As Stormfield tells it, no one at this gate ever heard of earth, and one of the heavenly clerks sets out with all good will to find it:

> He got a balloon and sailed up and up and up, in front of a map that was as big as Rhode Island. He went on up till he was out of sight, and by and by he came down and got something to eat and went up again. To cut a long story short, he kept on doing this for a day or two, and finally he came down and said he thought he had found that solar system, but it might be fly-specks. So he got a microscope and went back. It turned out better than he feared. He had rousted out our system, sure enough. He got me to describe our planet and its distance from the sun, and then he says to his chief—Oh, I know the one he means now, sir. It is on the map. It is called the Wart.

A very neat way of dealing with self-importance, and it's a pity we don't have a little bit of this kind of thinking around today.

Years ago, *Protestant Magazine* published an essay titled "The Bellhop God," which offered the image of a pitcher and a batter, both equally pious and both praying desperately, the pitcher for a strikeout and the batter for a hit—the essay noting that it put God in a very difficult position indeed. But the ambivalence of God must have resulted in a celestial headache for many centuries, watching His only son, a gentle Jew, not only crucified but used as a symbol for the murder and crucifixion of an untold number of Jews ever since—and in His name.

Well, I suppose that only God could work His way out of this kind of confusion. One hundred thirty years ago, a lady underwrote the mindless slaughter which we remember as our Civil War with the words that became the battlecry of the killing: "Mine eyes have seen the glory of the coming of the Lord . . . . " And only a few years ago, Saddam Hussein and the Ayatollah combined forces to send a million kids to their death in the name of God, whom both endorsed as the underwriter of the killing. But no matter how much killing Islam engaged in, it could not in a hundred years match the killing that Christianity indulged itself with—always in the name of the gentle Jesus, the Prince of Peace, and to the glory of God. And just to fill in any corner of the asylum left untenanted, let us remember again that a spokesman of God, an Hassidic leader in Brooklyn, who, on the eve of an election which would have been won by the Labor Party in Israel and which would have brought peace to Israel, informed two members of the

Israel Religious Party that God had instructed him to have them change their vote.

In many a church and in many a synagogue, on the wall behind the altar, are printed the words: "Eli, Eli, lamah azavtani," those in the Hebrew script, but translated thus: "My God, my God, why have you forsaken me?" Those were the words Jesus spoke as he hung from the cross, and given what we see in the world today, they might well be the desperate cry of all mankind. For two thousand years, the plain, common folk of this planet have been endlessly crucified in the wars their masters devised—and here we are again.

We stand at the edge, at the dangerous brink of an awful, murderous conflict that has been carefully crafted and promoted. It is a war to control the major oil reserves of this planet, and it is being put together by those who buy and sell and refine oil. That is all it is. It has nothing to do with God or freedom or anything else worth lifting a finger for, and those who say it has are lying as sincerely and blatantly as they have lied in the past. No war has ever been fought to the glory of God. Wars are fought to the greed and madness of men, and no matter how the killing is done, it is murder.

November 19, 1990

The Minds of Men Who Rule Nations

Saddam Hussein is a crazy, wild, cruel and terrible man, and therefore he must be destroyed. That's about it, isn't it? And why is he all these things? Well, obviously because he has absolutely no regard for human life, as witness his gassing of thousands of Kurds. People who do such things must be destroyed. General agreement.

Bear with me. Some 10 years ago, a much respected American newspaper man, Harrison E. Salisbury by name, wrote a book called *Without Fear or Favor*, a history of *The New York Times*. On page 478 of this book, he describes a discussion between Julius Ochs Adler and Winston Churchill, held in 1951. Adler handled business matters for *The Times* and was an important cog in the organization. Here is how Mr. Salisbury describes the discussion:

> . . . [I]n 1951 he (Adler) went to England to negotiate with Winston

> Churchill for *The Times*'s rights to publication of his memoirs and put down a meticulous account of Churchill's remarks, including the assertion that if he were Prime Minister he would bomb China and clamp a naval blockade on the China coast. Churchill declared that if he could get U.S. agreement he would send an ultimatum to Russia, telling the Kremlin that unless it yielded to our demands (specifics not stated) we would atom-bomb twenty or thirty Russian cities. Churchill was sure the Russians would reject the ultimatum but by the time the third city was wiped out would meet "our terms."

Remember that in 1951, we were just six years past World War II, a war that had to a large extent been brought to a victorious conclusion by the incredible courage of the Red Army of the Soviet Union. Without the Red Army, Hitler would have occupied Great Britain, and human history would have been very different. This is not my individual conclusion, but has been backed by statements of numerous military men.

So let's reflect for a moment on Churchill's statement. We know that he raised the matter with President Truman, since I have personal knowledge that Truman took up the possibility with the Joint Chiefs of Staff (see pp. 204, 205 of my recently published memoirs, *Being Red*). That was some 18 months before the conversations with Adler, and since no scientist consulted could guarantee that such an attack might not damage the earth beyond repair, the Joint Chiefs advised against the attack on Russia.

This matter, the discussion of an atomic attack on the Soviet Union, must be seen against the background of Harry Truman's decision during World War II to wipe out two Japanese cities, Hiroshima and Nagasaki, destroying their populations, man, woman and child—an action taken, incidentally, against the wishes of the Joint Chiefs, who preferred that the bomb be dropped on the Japanese fleet. Truman's wish was to save the Japanese fleet for an ultimate attack on the Soviet Union.

I mention these two bits of forgotten history because they represent a horror—one performed and one rejected—beyond the power of the mind to comprehend. Even the Nazi Holocaust pales in dimension when measured against Mr. Churchill's proposal, which if it had been carried out would have put at least 10 million and possibly 100 million people to death.

So what are we to make of Mr. Churchill's mind? We can say, of course, that he was our monster, our demented compassionless killer, but that he was all of these cannot be denied. Like Harry Truman, he wielded power without compassion, and since that appears to be a quality necessary to the leaders of this so-called civilized world, we might as well regard it forthrightly and clearly. We might also recall (see my memoirs) that during the Japanese drive toward India, the British, under Mr. Churchill's leadership, directed a corner on the rice supplies, bringing about a famine in which 6 million people died.

Such are the minds of men who rule nations. Saddam Hussein is a cruel and ruthless man, and his murder of the Kurds and so many others cannot be overlooked and put aside, but like both Churchill and Truman, he leads a nation at war and will justify any action, no matter how horrible or despicable, by his desire to win that war. But the bottom line is that he is Iraq's demented bastard, not our demented bastard.

Few Americans would hesitate to do whatever might be required of them in defense of our country; but this impending war in Saudi Arabia has as little to do with defending the United States as the small war that is fought day in and day out in Northern Ireland. It is a struggle for the oil of the Middle East, no more, no less, and all the trimmings around this simple, single purpose are lies, disgraceful lies.

If Mr. Bush is so blind, so ill-advised as to go ahead with this lunatic program for pain and slaughter, the whole world will pay an awful price. But our price here at home, where the price is measured in body bags, will be the highest. I don't know what mother in these United States is ready to give her son's life for oil. Perhaps Mr. Bush does know; if so, he has failed to inform us.

December 10, 1990

The Only Seat on the Aisle

I knew an Army pilot who flew his own small plane. He told me that when he flew, he sought always to have a landing spot in view, so that if his motor kicked out, he would have a place to come down, a road, a field, a lake. Other amateur pilots said much the same. My own variation at a lecture or a play where escape might be necessary, is last row on the aisle. Prudent and quiet, a small act of survival, and simply an exercise of common sense.

But common sense has never been very noticeable, either in the White House or in the halls of Congress. When President Bush made his foray into Saudi Arabia, the halls of Congress rang loud with praise and acclamation for his speedy action and for the manner in which he herded other members of the United Nations into line. Even the "liberals" rose and cheered—until the growing numbers of troops—American troops, mind you—in Saudi Arabia gave them pause; he was in. How does he get out?

Consider the situation. What are the choices of Mr. Bush and his advisors?

The first choice is to go to war, now that he has corralled the members of the Security Council, buying their votes with money, threats and promises. Forty-five days and you can begin to shoot.

But we have not won all of the optional wars. Panama was easy, almost as easy as Grenada, but in Korea and Vietnam, we devastated two countries, lost almost 200,000 dead, and inflicted almost 3 million civilian deaths on the countries where we fought. We were neither winner nor loser, and the agony of these adventures persists and the memory is very clear.

So it might be that Mr. Bush and James Baker and the curious John Sununu will decide that the price of war with Iraq is too great. In that case, what?

Let us say that Saddam Hussein does nothing. What then? We have half a million men in the Saudi Arabian desert; we have thousands of trucks, half-tracks, tanks and other engines of war. We'll try sanctions. But if we had a CIA bright enough to consult an almanac and read it, we would have known that between May and September, the heat in the Arabian desert frequently tops 150 degrees Fahrenheit. In that heat, few can live, much less fight. Depression is chronic. No Western nation troops can sit that out without disintegration setting in.

But let's consider another alternative. Suppose Mr. Hussein proves that he is brighter than your average member of Congress, and suppose he picks up and pulls out of Kuwait and allows us to return our dismal pack of emirs and sheiks and other apostles of oily democracy to their thrones. What then? We are sitting in Arabia with half a million men and piles of military junk. What do we do? Do we pull out and go home while the world, which doesn't love us to begin with, laughs itself silly?

And if we pull out, we leave Saddam sitting with his busy little fingers putting together atom bombs and gas bombs with the stuff we and the good Germans so generously supplied to him. But didn't Mr. Bush cry out that Saddam must not have atomic toys? Do we invade anyway? And what does the world say, when we attack an Iraq that had already pulled out of Kuwait? Oh, the Arabs will love us for that.

Or another alternative: We will build air-conditioned barracks for our troops and remain in Arabia for the next 40 years, just as we did in Europe after World War II. That way is costly, but on the other hand we will own Saudi Arabia and its oil body and soul, which was the intention in the first place.

But hold on now—it's not that simple either, because old Saddam Hussein is puttering away with his little pile of atom bombs, and by now every Arab in the Middle East hates us so much that they will be a dedicated cheering squad as the bombs begin to fall.

But, we have left out a very important fact. Saudi Arabia is not simply Saudi Arabia, a nasty desert sitting on large pools of oil. It is the holy place of Islam. And when I say it is the holy place of Islam, I am speaking not only of the Arabs, but of Iran and Pakistan and Indonesia and Afghanistan and Uzbekistan, hundreds of millions of Muslims, all of whom look upon Saudi Arabia as the holiest of the holy—and to have that place under the occupation and control of American troops will in time lead to an explosion that will make the current crisis look like child's play.

So there it is. Mr. Bush and Mr. Baker and Mr. Sununu have painted themselves into the most incredible corner that stupidity could devise. No landing field for them, no seat on the aisle, only a series of alternatives, each worse than the other—and we pay the price. He came to us with the loopy suggestion that we read his lips. We did, and here we are.

He could have closed the sea lanes and the air lanes, and his sanctions would survive and eventually take effect. No way. He had to have his war. How else are Presidents remembered? Well, there is still a way out. He can take the half-million American boys and the military junk and bring them home, and then he could talk, as civilized people do. Not a good way out, but the only seat on the aisle.

December 17, 1990

The Price Tag for the Pentagon's Lunacy

Since I work on a rather long deadline, this column will not appear until the 21st of January—at which time Baghdad might be pulverized, or, on the other hand, Mr. Bush might be having some second thoughts about the war process. And it might just be worthwhile to stick a few more pins into that hoary old legend of the good wars and the bad wars, a subject both Catholic and Jewish clerics are debating at this moment. As for the Protestant sects, they appear to be confused and divided by the fact that thousands of their constituents are beginning to ask uneasy questions about war in general, and whether Washington is not dishing out a fistful of lies.

Of course, ego and truth never sleep in the same bed, as so well portrayed by the Bush–Sununu–Baker trio, playing the last act of that overlong Republican tragicomedy, entitled: "We Are the Good Guys and No Matter What We Do We Are Still the Good Guys." That's a long title, but the show played for quite a long time. Recently, this trio, which bleeds for the proprietary rights of small nations, sent an armed helicopter over El Salvador's territory. It was shot down by rebels who have been fighting the dictatorship that the United States has supported for years. Bubbling with rage over the savagery of people who resist tyranny and who would dare to shoot down an enemy helicopter over their own territory, Mr. Bush and the curious Mr. Sununu urge Congress to vote another forty-million-plus for our long-sponsored *Death Squads*, who have already murdered more than 60,000 El Salvador citizens who dared speak up for their rights.

Yet they speak of truth and morality. "We fight and kill in the name of the Lord, the King, the Duke, the Leader, the President, the Nation, the gentle Jesus, the just Allah, the righteous Jehovah," and so forth and so on ad nauseam. The truth is that long, long ago, it was discovered that the quickest way to make a buck was to kill the other guy who had it.

And on that subject, let me quote from a piece from Scott Shuger, in the current issue of the *Washington Monthly*, one of the handful of courageous and honest magazines published in this country. Under the following title: "The Stealth Bomber Story You Haven't Heard," Mr. Shuger writes:

> In 1981, the Air Force estimated that a force of 133 B–2's (the Stealth)

> could be procured for $32.7 billion. By mid-1989, that cost had grown to $70.2 billion. [When in mid-1990 the Department of Defense (DOD) decided to acquire only 75 B–2's (10 have been funded thus far) the cost of that reduced purchase was estimated to be $62.8 billion.] Last September, the General Accounting Office (GAO) concluded that the total cost of buying and operating the 75 aircraft for their likely life span would be around $84 billion.

Let me spell it out: $84,000,000,000 for an idiot toy which, according to Mr. Shuger, " . . . doesn't work, and it will probably crash."

If you are, like me, a person who totals a checkbook laboriously and usually incorrectly, the above sum may be somewhat beyond your conception. It certainly is beyond mine, and I can only deal with it in symbolic terms. What might it accomplish in New York City, for example? Let's put down a list that still does not fill out the price tag for this Pentagon idiocy.

We could rebuild every bridge in the Metropolitan area.

We could double police and firemen.

We could make all repairs necessary to the subways.

We could give five percent pay raises to every city worker.

We could pay teachers adequately and get the very best.

We could care for all AIDS patients and build new hospitals as needed.

We could drop a cool billion into anti-drug measures.

And we would still have enough left over to take Mario Cuomo off the hot seat.

And whose money would we be spending if we had our hands on it instead of the turkeys in Washington? Our own, naturally. Where do you think those fancy hoodlums get it from? Sure as God, they create nothing. They only swill from the trough and dream of destruction.

But when you come down to it, the fault rests with New York's Mayor Dinkins and Governor Cuomo. If they had a little guts and if they would stop whining about their difficulties, they might speak up and point the finger properly. We pay the taxes. We are entitled to a proper return and *representation*, not deception by the cowardly crew we send to Washington. Our city crumbles and our civilization crumbles with it, and we are forced to watch a totally loony game in Washington spend our taxes on toys of stupidity and horror.

Address that, Mr. Dinkins and Mr. Cuomo, and stop the sniveling and whining. Prove to the world that your leadership means something and is not the same farce indulged in by every politician in this country.

January 21, 1991

The Not-So-Secret History of the Gulf War

"Truth is the first casualty of war."

Any war and every war, but more so when the war does not propose either defense or imminent danger, such as the Korean War and the Vietnam War. I remember well when I.F. Stone published his *Secret History of the Korean War*. There were all the lies, half-truths, dirty tricks and scams laid bare; but the war was fought and the dead were dead, and let the mothers weep. No one gave a good goddamn. Then the *Pentagon Papers*, and for a few weeks we squawked about being had—and then we forgot.

And how many were the civilian dead when we manufactured our recent war against Panama? Eight hundred? So some say, or perhaps four thousand, which is said by what we call in the trade, "reliable sources." Right now, it is anybody's guess, but sooner or later someone will come out with a book called, *The Secret History of the Panama War*.

In the January 7 issue of the *New Yorker* magazine, Milton Viorst writes a well-researched piece about the then perhaps impending explosion in Saudi Arabia. Speaking about the initial day of the Iraqi invasion of Kuwait, Mr. Viorst writes that

> Fahd (King of Saudi Arabia) did not at that time ask for a total Iraqi withdrawal. Instead, he proposed what seemed like a compromise: that the Iraqis withdraw to the disputed border area—a move that would have left them in possession of the Rumaila oil fields and the two islands. Whether that proposal represented to King Fahd the limit of possibilities, or was simply the limit of his aspirations, was not clear. What was clear was that he did not at any time express any fear that Saddam Hussein would order his troops into Saudi Arabia. Two days later, King Fahd sent a minister to Amman, who confirmed that Saudi Arabia saw no threat of Iraqi invasion. When President Bush an-

> nounced, on August 8th, that he was sending ground troops to defend Saudi Arabia, Iraq issued a statement that it had already notified the American Embassy in Baghdad that it never had any intention of entering Saudi territory. To this day, King Hussein of Jordan and his circle remain convinced that Saddam was telling the truth, and King Fahd knew it.

And why should we believe this? A good question, but then we should ask that very same question about any of the so-called facts and circumstances surrounding a rush toward war. Facts and information must be considered and appraised in terms of their origin and the trustworthiness of the reporter.

Our Congressmen had recourse to these facts and thousands of other facts. Each one of them has a staff of well-paid people. I do my own research, and the facts are not hidden from me. But a majority in both Houses saw fit to ignore them, to ignore the will of the people, to endorse the President's dismal desire for war. I heard no Representative or Senator address these simple matters, available to anyone who reads *The New York Times*:

1. If we fight to vanquish evil, then consider the evil of a Government which has spent billions, namely our government, to train and arm the *Death Squads* of El Salvador. Result: 60,000 civilian deaths in a population of three million.
2. If we fight against an evil dictator, then why did we make an ally out of Mr. Assad of Syria, perhaps the most repugnant functioning dictator, a mass-murderer who puts Mr. Hussein to shame.
3. If we fight for the sanctity of national territory, why is there still no apology for our raising, arming and paying a mercenary army—namely the Contras—to fight a war against Nicaragua on their own territory?
4. If we fight for democracy, then why are we willing to endure thousands of deaths in support of a feudal monarchy, whose billionaire owners will bask in luxury while Americans die to restore their ill-gotten gains?
5. And if this is in all truth a United Nations operation, why doesn't every nation involved send up the same number of troops, percentage-wise, that we are putting into the field; and why didn't one damned Congressman out of that whole stable that we coddle and feed and elect and re-elect speak up to the effect that we are the patsies of the whole world?

6. And finally, why didn't one Congressman say flatly that this is a war to control the oil of the Middle East and nothing more and nothing less?

Actually, there is no hidden history of the Gulf War. It all hangs out, brazenly and disgustingly; and even if it were honestly bespoken as a war for oil and for nothing else, then I would say that all the damned oil on the Arabian peninsula is not worth the life of one child.

On the other hand, maybe a friend of mine is right when he says that we brought it on ourselves when we called George Bush a wimp.

January 28, 1991

Blessed Are the Monsters

In 1941, an Iranian soldier who had made himself the Shah (or emperor) of Iran displeased the British and was forced to abdicate. He was succeeded by his son, Mohammed Reza Pahlavi. Mr. Pahlavi, being a second-generation emperor, succumbed to delusions of grandeur, decided that he was the proper descendent of such ancient luminaries as Cyrus the Great, built monuments to his progressive greatness and became as arrogant as most small men with great power. He also had very large reserves of oil.

Being suckers for the smell of oil and lands ruled by monsters, the United States adopted the Shah. We poured weapons into his country, sent advisors to show him how to operate the weapons of death we had given him and sent our experts into his country to train his police. In very short order, the Shah's police had won a worldwide reputation for torture and cruelty. In fact, the rule of the Shah became so unbearable that the whole nation began to simmer with rage. Having a Central Intelligence Agency that had cost us billions of dollars, we alone were unaware of this, and our Government continued to support the Shah until finally, in an outburst of rage, his people dumped him.

At this point, instead of supporting the revolution in Iran, we condemned it and supported the exiled Shah. A mob of enraged Iranians, 10 months after the Shah had fled, seized the U.S. Embassy and took hostage 62 Americans. A year later, Iraq attacked Iran.

We backed Iraq. We poured arms into Iraq. We poured ships into the Persian Gulf to help Iraq. We poured rage on Iran without end. We insulted their religion and their religious leaders. We made a hate-figure of the Ayatollah, and he became a target for every stand-up comic we had. When Saddam Hussein used his dreaded nerve gas, we sounded not a word of protest, even though he was killing not only Iranians but Kurds in his own country.

On May 17, 1987, Saddam Hussein launched an unprovoked attack on an American frigate on patrol in the Persian Gulf. Thirty-seven United States sailors died in that attack, not easy deaths, but burned by a fury out of hell—37 American seamen. I repeat the number because it is so much larger than losses in Saudi Arabia.

Sniggering, laughing at us, poor, stupid American fools that we were, Saddam Hussein apologized. And we humbly accepted his apology for murdering 37 Americans, and we went on feeding him arms. The Soviet Union, those other peace-lovers, had already given him a great supply of Scud missiles, but alas they had a range of only 150 to 200 miles, and that was not good enough to hit Teheran.

"Ah," we told him, "fear not, good Hussein, we have technical experts who can increase the range of those Scud missiles—so you will be able to hit Teheran and kill Iranian women and children and old people."

We are an energetic folk, and on July 3, 1988, an American warship shot down an Iranian commercial airliner, claiming to have mistaken it for an F–14 fighter jet. Two hundred ninety people aboard the Iranian plane died. It does no good now to recognize that fact that if we had helped the Iranian people to liberate themselves from the tyranny and cruelty of the Shah, there would never have been a hostage incident, and Mr. Reagan would not have been President, and this country might be economically sound instead of teetering on the edge of economic disaster. And our allies, the Iranians, would have made short shrift of Saddam Hussein.

But the saddest part of this whole dreadful business is that we are incapable of learning. With our bedsheets still warm from occupancy by an Iraqi murderer and pig, we have thrown back the coverlet to admit another, our new bedfellow, Hafez al-Assad, a fellow who puts Saddam Hussein to shame when it comes to the gentle arts of torture and murder. To Mr. Assad belongs the distinction of putting an entire city of his countrymen to death. He is second to none in torture, and his hatred of Israel is demonic. Out of his country, Syria, he runs a worldwide terrorist organization, and he is in part responsible for the kidnappings and hostage-taking in Lebanon. He is now our ally and the recipient of our largess.

Blessed are the monsters, for theirs is a partnership with the United States.

I have also heard, from reliable sources, that in Washington, in a corner of Georgetown, there is a small pharmacy that specializes in "stupid pills." I am also told that they sell thousands of these pills to Government people who would rather die than be mistaken for Northeastern intellectuals.

February 2, 1991

Report from Planet Earth

Report to the Galactic Council:

We have made a thorough study of the star and planets, listed on our charts as 51 degrees. Only a single planet of this system is fit for habitation by human beings. Its inhabitants call it "Earth." Our study was not interfered with; although there were many sightings of our ships, the inhabitants of this planet are so egocentric that they summarily reject the thought of any other sentient beings in the universe.

This planet Earth appears to be absolutely unique in the galaxy. While the human beings who inhabit it are similar to human beings elsewhere in the universe, they differ from all others in that their entire existence is dedicated to killing—that is, the murder of each other and of every other form of life upon the planet.

For the past two thousand years, they have pursued and refined this practice of mutual murder as well as the utterly merciless murder of other species.

The land mass of their planet is divided among groups of people usually speaking a common language, who call themselves *nations*. These nations have for centuries dedicated themselves to murder—mostly of the people of other nations, but not infrequently of their own people; and very often, the major part of their productive ability goes into the manufacture of weapons of death.

Their dedication to killing has created a sort of science, since in their development of the weapons of death, they have discovered various by-products, and since they must devise better means of killing than their neighbors, this scientific development proceeds apace; but so injurious is it to the ecostructure of their planet that even the non-weapons bring death in large numbers.

We have concluded that about tens of millions died in the practice of these mass killings—which they call wars—during the past 100 years. In the course of these great killings, some nations become more powerful and others less powerful. At this moment, one of these nations, the United States by name, is the strongest and most developed and in a position to unleash great killings at will. It is at present engaged in such a mass killing.

Through the centuries during which the people of Earth developed the art of killing, they have agreed on certain rules; for example, the right to kill is given to men and women dressed in a certain common manner, wearing what they call uniforms. If one does not have this uniform, one can be severely punished for killing. These measures enable the people to reproduce and generate the next generation of killers.

So highly regarded is the art of mass murder, that all over the planet statues and monuments are raised to men who led the great killings. All of these nations worship an entity which they call God, and very often they do their largest killings in the name of this God, and while they believe that there is only one such entity, they hold that He approves the killing of other nations' people. The record of their existence—which they call History—is largely an account of these killings.

Since they understand that the women and children must be preserved to raise the next generation of killers, they have agreed on certain rules concerning mass killing, and they have given these the name of "The Geneva Conventions." But the more generally destructive their weapons have become, the less they are able to distinguish among the various categories that they are permitted to kill or are barred from killing, and thus they tend more and more to ignore these "Geneva Conventions."

It must be noted that the desire to kill without mercy and without reason is so deeply implanted in these people that they have organized a worldwide game which they call "Hunting." Hunting differs from war in that it is directed against all living things but man, and to engage in it, one does not require a uniform. For example, the largest land animal, the elephant, has been hunted to near extinction. The area of the United States once had herds of over 2,000,000 bison. These were hunted and killed until only a handful survived. The same was the fate of the great sea mammals, the whales, and of numerous other species.

When the killing urge does away with an entire population of people—which is not unusual—they call it genocide, and many groups of people have disappeared in this manner. But curiously enough, they have no name for the process of destroying an entire species. Even though they do on occasion give lip service to the great universal love of charity and compassion, the moment they embark on another killing, all thoughts of compassion are immediately cast aside.

Our recommendation to the Galactic Council is that these people and this planet be avoided at all cost. Their lust for murder is so profound that it must be regarded as a disease, and left to themselves they will soon destroy their atmosphere and render their planet uninhabitable—after which children throughout the galaxy will sleep more soundly.

February 18, 1991

Saddam and the Bomb

Saddam Hussein does not have an atom bomb; if he had such a weapon, here is what he well might do: He could put it on a tanker or some other vessel, fly the colors of whatever nation he chose, and then, a few miles off our coast, transfer the weapon to a small sport boat, and head for whatever city he chose to destroy. He would have a wide choice, from Charleston and Savannah up the coast to Washington, Baltimore, Philadelphia, New York and Boston. He could come in at will and drop the bomb off wherever he chose, with a timing device to blow it up at his pleasure.

And then—poof. It would not be 500 women and children in a bunker, but all of Washington, D.C., if he chose that as his target. And all the Patriot missiles and all the Star Wars gimmickry in the world could not stop him. And do you know, sooner or later, he will have an atom bomb, and if not Saddam, then some other paranoid dictator, and some say that Pakistan—an Islamic country—already has the bomb, and we are not beloved of any Islamic people.

When the United Nations agreed on the exercise of sanctions against Iraq, there was a moment in the history of mankind that people of good will had dreamed about for centuries—a moment when an alternative to war was proposed and recognized and accepted by the world community. In due time, those sanctions would have worked, and this is not simply my own conclusion, but the conclusion of hundreds of notable and knowledgeable people. George Bush chose to substitute war for sanctions, and thus, the highest moment of mankind's hope was turned into that ancient horror of war and slaughter.

I place this in conjunction with the above speculation about the atomic bomb, because both occupy connecting slots in a file of gross stupidity. It is not merely the stupidity of Mr. Bush and the curious Mr. Sununu that must be condemned; as one watches the horrifying progress of this war, one must fall back on that famous phrase Leon Trotsky used, addressing a member of his group: "Sir, everyone has the right of stupidity, but you abuse the privilege."

What on earth could George Bush have been thinking when he unleashed his flood of technological slaughter? Did he imagine that he was preserving oil reserves? But already the world has lost tens of millions of gallons of oil reserves, and this is only the beginning. Did he imagine that we would endear ourselves to the hundreds of millions of men and women who practice Islam? Did he think that the Arab world would bless him? Did he think that he was helping Israel? Did he really think that all those promises of cash from other nations would be kept? Did he think that even if we took over Saudi Arabia the refineries and wells would be safe from terrorism? And did he think that in a world where atomic weapons are already beyond counting, our future would be safer?

Or does Mr. Bush operate without thinking? Whenever I turn on the "MacNeil/Lehrer Newshour" and listen to those cozy little clusters of Washington "experts" telling us the inner truths revealed only to them, I am renewed in my belief that stupidity is an absolute necessity for admission into any branch of government or for a sinecure in any one of the so-called "think tanks." As one watches and listens to the words and actions of government—a gift of this TV age—one becomes more and more convinced that behavior so mediocre, so witless cannot be described as evil, but only as gross stupidity. Long ago, in the lumber camps of the Northwest, a mythic character called Jesse Pyme arose. Lumbering is a dangerous business, and he who didn't have his wits about him could end up dead, whereby Jesse Pyme, the fool killer, appeared. I have mentioned Jesse Pyme in the past, for his mythic existence is deeply rooted in the truth. My little horror-tale of an atomic weapon in the Potomac or in the Hudson River is hardly a departure from reality. The more we picture our nation as a super-giant, armed with invincible gadgetry, the more we become dispensable to the human race. We could have halted the spread of atomic weapons 45 years ago—and even today this proliferation of destruction is not entirely beyond control; but such control is apart from the thinking of anyone in government, so enthralled and worshipful as they are of war in which only the enemy suffers.

But there is a school of opinion that holds that in the northern mountainous areas of Iraq, hidden deep in the earth, Mr. Hussein is well on his way to perfecting an atomic weapon. With this even as an outside possibility, one would imagine that someone in the government would begin to think in terms of the imminent reality.

March 4, 1991

They Know Not What They Do

There is an old and very wise saying, as follows: "He who saves a single life saves the universe, and he who destroys a single life, destroys the universe." It takes some thinking about, and it's worth copying out and looking at now and then. I quote it because in all the wild celebration of victory, the gleeful satisfaction of TV speakers and interviewers, the resonant pronouncements of anchormen, there is hardly a mention of compassion, pity or regret for anyone who did not wear the uniform of the United States. Even the dead and wounded of the French, British, Egyptians, Saudis and Kuwaitis were brushed aside and mentioned only in passing. And for the 80,000 Iraqis who met their deaths in the man-made hellfire that we created there in the desert, and for the 100,000 more who were injured, arms and legs blown off, testicles shattered, stomachs torn open—for them hardly more than a demographic snort of satisfaction.

We propose to believe in God. We say there is one God, and this is the creator of all things, and men and women are the children of God. In fact the act of going to war, the act of being a soldier in motion explodes the God thing in a million prayers, pleas, fears, and crying out to the same God, help me, save me, bring back my child, my son, bring back my son who is your son, who is on his way to kill as many of your other sons as possible, and let him kill as many of your sons as necessary to bring him back to me, safe and sound and whole.

Are we all crazy? Think about it.

The newest paladin is, of course, General Norman Schwarzkopf. "Stormin' Norman," as Barbara Bush told us on TV, grinning her delight in the great victory. Certain obscene things were done in Kuwait to Kuwaiti citizens captured by Iraqi soldiers, and as General Schwarzkopf put it: "Men who do such things are not human, they are not a part of the human race."

That's a very comforting thought, because when you take away a person's humanity, you remove him from the human race, and then, of course, killing him becomes an easy act indeed.

But hold on—the General was talking about Iraqi torture, and of course in the heat of things, he forgot about the men we sent to Argentina and to Bolivia and to El Salvador to teach the police of those nations the art of torture, and he certainly cannot be blamed for not mentioning, in the flush of his victory, that indulgence in torture is not a racial characteristic or a national characteristic or a religious characteristic.

I'm not putting down the General. War is his business and profession, and at that profession he is better than anyone else. At the same time, righteousness is the life-blood of slaughter, the rationalization of slaughter, and the satisfaction of slaughter. Every one of the 80,000 Iraqis we put to death—and don't even mention that it was a fair fight, the most technologically advanced nation on the earth, population 240,000,000 against a backward non-industrial desert nation of 17,000,000—every one of those Iraqis who died was a man of flesh and blood, each with dreams, with mother and father, with brother and sister, with son and daughter, with all the power to love that we possess and with all sense of pain that we possess.

And they brought it on themselves? What nonsense; and yet I hear it everywhere, they brought it on themselves. When all the voices for peace and sanctions raised here in the United States could not deter Mr. Bush from the course he had chosen for his own ego satisfaction, do you imagine for a moment that the protest of some poor Iraqi peasant could have deterred Saddam Hussein from the course he had chosen? These 80,000 human beings we have slain in the sands of a desert more than ten thousand miles from our shores bear no guilt; they are not the bad guys; they are people, plain people, simple people, poorly informed, deluded by their leaders as we in the West are also deluded by our leaders—indeed as plain people and poor people have been deluded by their leaders since history began.

Is anyone, in print or by voice on that electronic network which covers our nation, going to say that we have done a terrible thing, a thing that defies all reason and sensibility, that we have massacred a nation, that given the choice between peace and war, we chose war? Or are we going to celebrate the slaughter with victory parades and a thousand miles of yellow ribbon? If we have lost, not 80,000, but only a few hundred, it is not numbers but the useless death of boys hardly more than children—our own. Yet in a way, they are all our own.

A man who was nailed to a cross two thousand years ago, by Roman soldiers, said of his killers, "Forgive them, oh God, for they know not what they do."

That's all that's left to us, a plea for forgiveness.

March 11, 1991

Home Is Where the Oil Is

Some of you, who are longtime readers of this column, will remember my friend D'emas. He is a native of one of those obscure, far-off islands hardly touched by civilization, and during his visits to America, he is desperate and somewhat pathetic in his desire to learn and understand our civilization and the true meaning of democracy.

This time, however, he was disturbed by the victory parades, and I had a bit of a problem explaining that in the light of a great patriotic war and a great victory, such parades were an entirely proper response on the part of American patriots.

"But I always thought," D'emas said, "that patriotism was the defense of one's homeland."

"Quite true."

"But Kuwait, isn't that about ten thousand miles away?"

"Oh, yes. Yes, indeed."

"I don't understand."

"It's very simple. Where oil is, there is our homeland."

"Come on, you're joshing me," D'emas protested.

"Not at all. Let me say it again: Where oil is, there is our homeland."

"Now I may be an ignorant islander, but I do know that England has loads of oil offshore in the North Sea."

"Of course. But the Brits are white Christians."

"You mean where there's oil and white Christians, it's not your homeland?"

"Exactly. Kuwait is chock full of oil and dark-skinned Muslims."

"Which makes it part of your homeland?"

"Precisely."

"Do you know," D'emas said, "when I return from one of my trips, back to our little island, and I try to explain democracy and civilization, I find that I only confuse the people who listen to me. Now right here in *The New York Times*, it says that 80 percent of the American people supported Mr. Bush in the war. Do they all think that Kuwait is their homeland?"

"Oh, no. Only a select few, mostly in Washington, understand that Kuwait is our homeland."

"Then why did they support Mr. Bush and send their kids off to war?"

"D'emas, it's as plain as the nose on your face. They supported Mr. Bush because he told them that Saddam Hussein, the Iraqi dictator, was an evil man who had to be destroyed."

"Is he an evil man?"

"Oh, yes. Very evil."

"But if you're ready to go to war and kill 80,000 people because they live in the same country as an evil man, what about Syria?"

"What about Syria?"

"Well," D'emas said, "it says right here in *The New York Times* that the Syrian president, Hafez al-Assad, who you made an ally in the war against Iraq, is even more evil than Mr. Hussein."

"Yes," I explained, "but Mr. Assad did not invade our territory. It is very important for the United States to allow a man as evil as Assad to remain in power, because if we should ever decide that Lebanon is our homeland, we can very easily mount a crusade against Mr. Assad. You see, he did invade Lebanon and occupies it even now, but there is no oil in Lebanon."

"But I have heard," D'emas said pleadingly, since my simple answers to his questions appeared to confuse him, "that both Mr. Assad and Mr. Hussein became powerful dictators because of the arms and ammunition and poison gas that you and your European allies sold them."

"Of course. How else could they become so evil?"

"But isn't that terribly self-defeating?"

"Not at all, my dear D'emas, try to follow me. If we did not supply all these weapons of death, how would these evil men ever become evil enough for us to mount a crusade against them?"

"Oh? Well—perhaps. I'm beginning to understand. I mean that was also the case with Mr. Noriega, wasn't it?"

"With some slight variation, yes. You see, Panama is also our homeland, just like Kuwait and Saudi Arabia and the Oil Emirates, but not because there is oil in Panama. No, indeed. In Panama, it's the Panama Canal, and since the canal goes through Panama, Panama is unquestionably our homeland."

"And you created Mr. Noriega to be your evil man in Panama," D'emas said eagerly.

"Precisely. He allegedly ran a large drug business, which we cooperated with, with a lot of double-crossing of good people who had their fingers in the pot, and we had to mount a crusade against Mr. Noriega."

"I'm beginning to get it. Truly. I just never believed that democracy and peace could be so complex and so fascinating. But I hear that four thousand innocent civilians died in the war with Noriega."

"Quite so. You can't make an omelet without breaking eggs."

March 18, 1991

Half a Billion Dollars a Day

From *Fortune* magazine: "The U.S. has been dropping, launching, or firing about half a billion dollars a day in the Gulf."

Let's talk about numbers. The people downtown tell me that your run-of-the-mill New York City pothole, medium size, can be filled for $120. Since we blew half a billion a day for some 44 days, we could handle 166,000,000 potholes. Bridges are something else. At $4,000,000 each, give or take a bit, we could handle 6,000 bridges, 3,000 first-rate hospitals, 1,500 universities—or we could simply double the size of the police force in every major city.

But hold on, and don't go spinning off with crazy dreams—yet. I'm talking above only about disposables, what you might call the Kleenex, Pentagon-style. *Bombs*, that's all, just bombs. You want to talk about the other stuff—planes, tanks, trucks, military vehicles, soldiers' pay, clothing, food, blankets, tents, guns, rifles, carbines, shoes, socks—well, that puts it past my powers. I don't have a computer. All I can do is pick out a few numbers here and there.

Let's begin with the old thespian, who noodles away his well-earned retirement out there in Beverly Hills. In his time in office, Ronald Reagan spent $2,300,000,000,000 on the blessed Pentagon, and in case that's too many zeroes to read easily, it adds up to $2.3 trillion. There is no way in the world to estimate what that would buy in a sane country, because there is no precedent and an enormous institution would have to be created to spend it.

Also, that endless number we see above is by no means the end of the road. The road goes on, and through the months of the Bush Administration, the pace has increased. The only conclusion to be drawn from it is that the United States has become an industrial institution singularly devoted to the production of weapons of destruction.

It also creates a constituency motivated by survival, for the thousands of men and women who make these weapons do their jobs, not out of any hatred or malignancy, but simply to survive, to bring home a paycheck each week, to feed and house their families. Each of them must pay rent and buy food, and therefore what threatens their jobs threatens the existence of themselves and their families. But to fully understand this ghastly trap in which this nation is caught, and which will surely lead to terrible tragedy unless it is halted, one must include the other sections of this military-industrial complex, not as wanton killers, but simply as ordinary human beings, each treasuring his own nest. Let us look at each part of the whole:

First, the executive officers. According to *Fortune*, there are 25 great corporations that manufacture the bulk of the military arsenal.

The financial interest of each is enormous, and they are properly called the *Pentagon 25*. One of the top, General Electric, not only brings "good things to life," but almost $6,000,000,000 of not such good things to death, McDonnell Douglas $8,617,200,000, General Dynamics $6,899,200,000—and so forth and so on through all 25 companies. Like the blue-collar workers and the engineers and machinists, the executives fight for survival. They fight for the business and they fight for profits. If they lose business and profits, they can be out. Their stake is big, far bigger than the stake of the workers, but the fate of the losers is similar. They make the weapons of death, but trapped as they are, they have neither the wits nor the influence to change the pattern.

The next part of the complex is the Pentagon. Anyone who has ever touched base with our military machine can tell you that the perks are enormous and delicious. Except for the odd chance of war—where few senior officers die—the military executives live the good life to the full. They neither weave nor do they dig, and though they, like all humans, are subject to boredom, they manage to survive it very well indeed. Their only fear is that their institution might shrink, and with that in mind, they fight like tigers in defense of the great prime contractors who build their weapons—knowing full well that those military contractors will also fight to the death to preserve the only reason for their profits, namely, the Pentagon.

And with the third and final part of this military complex, we have the so-called *Congress of the United States*. They are key to everything, for they supply the military complex with our money; but unlike the officers or the executives, their jobs are not protected. They must be elected and re-elected, and the money for this process comes from the industrial part of the complex. Since the Congress is only interested in re-election, they have neither the courage nor the will to stop this process.

Now what we see here is not a conspiracy of villains, but rather a concordance of fools who blindly accept a situation that is self-sustaining and headed for doom.

He who prepares for war must go to war. This is both logical and inevitable. If the energies of the most productive country on earth are turned almost entirely to war production, then such production must be used. For years, we have tried to sustain the system by selling these terrible weapons to every nation that would buy. In the Gulf, we reaped the harvest of that, and we will go on reaping it. Kuwait lies in ruins, its air unbreathable. Iraq is destroyed. And this will go on and on. The more weapons we sell, the more need to destroy the buyers. And the house we live in, this wide and wonderful land, will die in the process.

April 1, 1991

How to Spend $95 Billion Without Really Trying

D'emas, whom you will remember as my friend from a small island far away, a very poor and backward island, is back here in New York, pursuing his desire to understand civilization and democracy. In this case he was upset by an announcement that the Feds had decided to rein in allocations of money for expensive medical health machinery.

"Well, there has to be an end to this kind of thing," I explained to D'emas. "Unless the Feds say, hold on, enough is enough, it can run into millions."

"But this is to save the lives of sick people," D'emas argued. "People will be healthier and live longer. Didn't your President Bush say he would bring you a kinder and gentler America? And here, in the same issue of *The New York Times*, I read that the Lockheed Company has won a contract for military planes that will amount to $95 billion."

"Of course."

"What do you mean, of course?" D'emas demanded. "Are you just sloughing this off? How can you say, of course?"

"Don't you see?" I asked the poor primitive. "Thousands of people in Long Island will have jobs, and they will eat well, and thereby we can dispense with the medical machines."

"But wouldn't it make more sense to spend some of that money for the medical machines?"

"Of course not. If you were a patriotic American, D'emas, instead of a primitive outlander, you would understand the need to defend the United States."

"From whom?" D'emas wondered.

"Oh, from any number of nations. Don't you ever read the newspapers?"

"I try," the poor savage pleaded. He always tends to collapse when I challenge his weird notions. "I have been reading everything I can get my hands on, and from what I read the Soviet Union is in a shambles and will not attack anyone in the foreseeable future."

"I'm not talking about the Soviet Union," I said sharply. "We don't fight wars with the Soviet Union. We just tell people what a terrible place it is and we sell them wheat, without which they would starve and our farmers would be bankrupt."

"Oh, I see," D'emas said weakly.

Obviously, he did not see, and I went on to explain: "I don't mean that we don't fight wars, D'emas. We just don't fight wars with the Soviet Union. We've fought wars with Germany, Austria, Italy, Turkey, Mexico, Nicaragua (with mercenaries), Korea, Vietnam, Grenada, and of course Iraq, and various and sundry small wars, but never with the Soviet Union."

"Then how on earth can you justify spending $95 billion on fighter planes, as well as the contract to General Dynamics that was just awarded, $2 billion for new atomic submarines, which is more money for fighter planes and attack submarines than all the nations of the world put together spend?"

"Precisely. The reason for that is the Soviet Union."

"But you just told me," D'emas pleaded, "that the Soviet Union is a shambles and cannot fight anyone."

"Of course," I agreed. "There never was any real threat of war with the Soviet Union. Not only was it logistically impossible, but if we went to war with them, who would buy our wheat? Believe me, Congressmen from Kansas, Nebraska and Iowa would have laid down their lives before they voted war with the Soviet Union. That's why we never went to war with the Soviet Union. Why should we drive our wonderful wheat farmers into bankruptcy? Do you understand now?"

He shook his head, poor savage. "No. I am absolutely more confused than ever."

"All right. Now listen carefully, $95 billion is a lot of money. If I say ninety-five thousand million dollars, it becomes more apparent what a very large sum of money we are talking about. It is enough to buy all the medical machines any hospital ever dreamed of owning. It is enough to rebuild the infrastructure of every large city in America. It is even enough to clear up the savings and loan mess with a tidy bit left over. It is enough to feed every hungry child on the planet earth for a full year. It is enough to train 10 million doctors to care for the people of the Third World. It is enough to build thousands of schools or hospitals. It is enough to pay a million researchers for a year to find the cure for AIDS or cancer.

"It is also enough to build 650 fighter planes."

"I should think," D'emas said, "that weighing the fighter planes against all the wonderful, heartwarming possibilities you list above, the American people would think that the government in Washington is totally insane."

"Now you're catching on," I said. "They certainly would, and don't think they would believe we need that stuff to fight Grenada or El Salvador. That's where the Soviet Union comes into the picture. No Soviet Union, no demented denizens of the Pentagon."

May 20, 1991

History True and False

Hannibal, born some 250 years before our era, was perhaps the only valid military genius in history. A thoughtful, gentle and well-loved man, he realized that sooner or later his country, Carthage, would be attacked and then incorporated into the Roman world, the fate of nation after nation at that time. Whereby, in Spain, partially held by Carthage, he put together a ragtag mercenary army together with a few dozen elephants, marched them across the seemingly impassable Alps, and in battle after battle defeated great Roman armies sent against him, took most of Italy and almost destroyed Rome. If reinforcements had come, he would have conquered Rome, but no reinforcements came, and in due time, Carthage, with its tiny population, was defeated by Rome.

It was upon this defeat that the Romans undertook measures that became a regular practice in the writing of history. They went about carefully and sedulously destroying every scrap of written material that described Hannibal's campaigns (the Punic Wars) or the history and being of Carthage from the Carthaginian point of view. They were determined that if history was to be written, they would write it and distort it themselves, a practice of those in power through all the centuries that followed.

The mendacity of the historian flows out of his conditions of servitude. He is rarely a creature of power, and most often he is taught, trained and paid by the establishment, and in order to keep his livelihood he dances to the tune the establishment specifies. Only in our years of naiveté could he be a Mason Locke Weems, who invented a George Washington and the war he fought out of whole cloth, with never even a small bow to the actual man. The historian today boasts of a judicious, refined and evenhanded approach to the distortion of events, but over the past few decades, at long last, he has been faced by a whole school of "revisionist" historians, mostly young scholars, back in school after the experience of World War II and thereby far more experienced than your average man of letters. While these "revisionist" historians are by no means free of the strictures of the universities, they are ready to look a little deeper into the facts of, at least, their own times, thereby setting an example for scholars that follow their path.

This is not to say that honest alternate histories were not written before our time. William Jay's *Review of the Mexican War*, published in 1849, challenges every official statement about the war and every book then written about the war; but such historical studies were rare indeed.

We have just been witness to the source, the development and undertaking of the Gulf War, and those of us who read the alternate press have been able to watch the historical lie take root and grow. There is a bitter and disgusting truth about this war, but such truth will not be taught in our schools, and the coming generations will be fed all the patriotic garbage that turns a massacre into a noble deed.

With Kitty Kelley's book about Nancy Reagan, another process is taking place. The book is so well researched that no one has yet challenged its facts in specific ways, which would be through the legalities of libel. Instead, the book is tossed off as worthless trash. In *The New York Times* of May 11, " . . . as 25,000 chanted her name at a Rose Bowl rally, Nancy Reagan heard herself described as 'a terrific mother, a devoted wife, and our guiding light.' " *The Times* goes on to say, "That public stance, and the choreographed appearances are the most obvious parts of a carefully planned campaign . . . . People close to Mrs. Reagan said that she plans more public appearances, including one in which she will be honored with General H. Norman Schwarzkopf."

Those who have not read Ms. Kelley's book have heard and read enough about it to be properly disgusted with the above. Nothing good has ever come out of living with lies, and would it really harm the children of coming generations to know that Nancy Reagan was a lousy mother—by the testimony of each and every one of her children, that she was a superstitious, greedy and malicious woman, that she moved into the Oval Office and took over the elective powers given to her witless husband?

Perhaps if this was taught as a part of history, children would learn that life or death can be determined by their vote, that the right to vote for government, such might armed with knowledge, is sacred to the existence of democracy, and that not to vote—almost half of the electorate does not vote—is to consign our future to men and women like Ronald and Nancy Reagan.

Nancy will stand beside H. Norman Schwarzkopf, both to go down in history as heroes, as people to look up to and honor, standing together, side by side, as thousands cheer. And why not, this woman who validated the "American way," that if you have no conscience and small compassion, if any, you can make it, and this smiling general who can say, honestly, "The CIA never told me that a bomb could set an oil well on fire," why not, indeed? It is our stamp of approval that defines them and will make them a part of righteous and false history.

June 3, 1991

A Money-Making Proposition

Back in the forgotten days of 1946, in speaking of World War II, people were wont to say, "He had a good war," or "He had a splendid war," or of those less fortunate, "He had a lousy war."

This is not to be interpreted as any sort of compassion for the 50 million dead, or joy over victory, or surviving without a wound—no, indeed. It was simply a statement of profit or loss. Wars can be very profitable, and if this were not the case, war would soon be a forgotten word.

Consider Kuwait. By now almost everyone in this country knows that Kuwait sprang practically full-grown out of the desert sand. It had no history, no childhood, no adolescence, no past as other cities and countries have a past, cowtracks turning into streets, streets turning into avenues, small buildings replaced by large buildings, music and art and literature joining to create opera houses, theaters, libraries—no, none of that. It was built, from scratch.

And who built it? Of course, many contractors had a piece of the pie, but the great refineries, the port, the heart and energy of Kuwait were created by a company called Bechtel. This is no secret. Even a casual reader of *Fortune* magazine knows that Bechtel is either the largest construction company on the planet Earth, or certainly the second largest, as some argue. And people reasonably well informed know that Caspar Weinberger was general counsel for Bechtel before becoming Secretary of Defense in the Reagan Administration, while George Shultz had been president of Bechtel before becoming Secretary of State in the Reagan Administration. Of course, this was a relationship of a company, and an Administration, with Kuwait never paraded before the American public. It is just amazing that with the largest news-gathering operation in the world, television and print, the American public knows so little of what goes on.

With all the hooting and shouting that accompanied our army's advance into Kuwait, no newspaper that I know of paused to inform us that our Government has signed a contract with the expatriate emirs of Kuwait, giving the U.S. Army Corps of Engineers full control of supervising and allocating contracts for the rebuilding of a city in the process of destruction. In other words, all those bucks we were spending blowing Kuwait and Iraq to pieces would come back to us in spades. Dirty? Well, war is dirty, as even General Stormin' Norman will admit.

As the war against Iraq continued, the family of Sheik Jaber al-Ahmed al-Sabah took residence in Taif, one of the more comfortable Saudi cities, and there, so as to speak, held court, letting it be known here and there about the world that the Kuwaitis would be offering better than $100 billion worth of business. Come and get it! The fact that Manhattan kids were sent to die to free the homeland of these utterly worthless rentiers who had fled their country in their Rolls-Royces and Mercedeses, meant absolutely nothing to them. There was business at hand.

And from all over the world they came, working together with the U.S. Army Corps of Engineers.

According to the Italian magazine, *Europeo*:

> Financiers, lobbyists, industrialists and bankers from all over the world

> had begun jockeying for a piece of the "big pie" of the 1990s, the reconstruction of Kuwait and Iraq. . . . The Army Corps has selected 36 companies for contracts. . . . The British Broadcasting Company has contracted to rebuild all of Kuwait's radio and television systems in a joint venture with the American firm Motorola. . . . The United States has 70 percent of the first 200 contracts . . . Bechtel, Brown and Root, Foster Wheeler, Caterpillar Inc., CBI Industries.

And so forth and so on.

But the biggest plum of this strange war is Iraq itself. Yes, our mortal enemy, an infrastructure which we smashed to smithereens, and the price of reconstruction is put at $500 billion, half a trillion dollars, and even today, before the war is properly finished and settled the deals are being made. Again from *Europeo*:

> The U.S. companies may be favorites in the race to reconstruct Kuwait, but the biggest deal concerns the reconstruction of Iraq. Almost everything needs to be rebuilt: factories, refineries, electric-power plants, roads, airports and houses. Before the contracts are given out, the political problems have to be resolved. The United States has proposed a Middle-East Development Bank . . .

to deal with this matter, a bank which, of course, we would control.

Did I hear someone whisper that those whom the gods would destroy, they first make mad? But if that's the case, then we're running a civilization that is absolutely loony from the word go. The mistake we made in Vietnam was not blowing the whole land to kingdom come, as we did in Iraq. If we had done that, Bechtel and the others could have gotten the contracts to rebuild from scratch, and thousands of people would have made millions in the proper American Way. No more Vietnams, as Mr. Bush is fond of saying. No more taking a loss. From now on, war must be a money-making proposition, as it always has been.

July 8–15, 1991

The Nuclear Threat

One day in 1981 my secretary turned up for work in what they call high dudgeon—indeed, very high dudgeon. After I managed to calm her and reduce her anger to rational speech, she told me the following story:

She was a divorced woman with a child of 7 years. Earlier that same day, her former husband, who had a government job in Washington and whom she loathed—not without reason—appeared at her home with a paper for her to sign. That was a year when the cold war had heated up to a boiling point. Her husband informed her that, deep under the national capital or vicinity, a great underground shelter had been built, packed with enough amenities to maintain life for a select number of people for years if necessary. A list of government people suitable for admission to the shelter was permanently in existence, but each week it was updated as some names were dropped and other listees perished. When the bombs began to fall and all life in the United States had either been extinguished or reduced to the Stone Age, these chosen worthies in their magnificent state-of-the-art bomb shelter would remain alive and vital, ready to carry on the human race and to govern, providing there was anything to govern.

My secretary's ex-husband had come to her that morning with the heart-warming news that he had been selected for survival and that, if she would sign a release, he could take her daughter—but not my secretary—into that wonderful ark, ready to sail into the irradiated future. Thus her very proper rage.

Now I do not know whether the above is true, and I do not present it as anything more than an explanation of a woman's anger. Myself, I believe it, but that is a reflection of a personal estimate of the intelligence of the men who govern the United States. If it is true, then it has been a well-kept secret and understandably so for, in all my life, in all my reading and study, I have never come across an idea more preposterous, heartless and egotistical than this—that the men who have the power to destroy the earth should plan for their own survival after they have executed the hundreds of millions of innocents.

I bring this tale out of the past because the media has gone into an explosion of joy at the news that George Bush and Mikhail Gorbachev have agreed to put away a few of their terrible toys—without pointing to the vast atomic armament that can destroy the world a hundred times over. Let me repeat a story I tell in my memoirs, *Being Red.* In 1949, one of the original atomic scientists had dinner with my wife and me and told us the following story: He and a number of other physicists had been called down to Washington to testify for the Joint Chiefs of Staff. The question asked again and again in various forms was this: "If 100 atomic bombs were to be exploded in a restricted geographical area, could the heat ignite the atmosphere and thus put an immediate end to all life on earth? Or create radiated winds that might do much of the same? Or what?"

To all aspects of these questions, my guest replied that he simply did not know. The possibility existed. Subsequently, he discovered that his colleagues answered in a similar manner, and perhaps through their testimony the world was saved—yet a hundred of the low-yield bombs that we had at the time could scarcely compare to the state-of-the-art weapons we and the Russians now possess. So I ask you—indeed I beg you—to consider the mentality of these powerful figures who could, by will or accident, put an end to this beautiful planet that might be the only place in the entire universe where life exists.

We were suckered by that cozy slogan, "Better dead than red," a piece of foolishness rarely equaled in a very foolish society. From the word go, it was arrant nonsense. There was never, never even the vaguest possibility of a Russian attack on the United States, and anyone who will give an hour to the historic Finnish-Russian relationship will understand that the menace of Russia was a swindle of the CIA–media–weapon makers combine, who together robbed our nation of a trillion dollars of wealth to put together this 45 years of demented gun making.

And today, in spite of the chortles of joy over the few steps toward sanity taken by Mr. Bush and Mr. Gorbachev, each remains in possession of enough atomic weapons to blow the earth into kingdom come, not once, but hundreds of times. It took the crazed Saddam Hussein to demonstrate that a small, backward nation could make a hydrogen bomb (he was working on it) that could blow half of Syria or Israel off the face of the earth.

Let's finally face the reality of the situation. We must understand that any incident of atomic warfare will change the world forever, and that the only hope for the future is to rid the world of these frightful weapons. For that, we need new men in government. We must not be deluded by the whine that Mr. Bush is unbeatable. He is absolutely beatable. He has had a career so lamentable that only a nation of fools would maintain him in power. Have we come to that?

Let me finish by quoting Peter Matthiessen, an important environmentalist, writing on Chernobyl in the October 14 *New York Times*:

> The official figure of 31 mortalities represents those who died in the original explosion. The actual toll of those who perished as a result of the "cleanup" is 5,000 to 7,000, and many thousands more throughout Southern Russia will die of radiation poisoning or related cancers . . . Dr. [Vladimir] Chernousenko [Soviet nuclear physicist] believes that at least 35 million people have been damaged.

Only a token. One reactor. Think of our 20,000 high-yield state-of-the-art bombs.

October 28, 1991

HOWARD FAST was born in New York City in 1914. An immensely popular novelist, he has written more than fifty books, including *Citizen Tom Paine*, *Spartacus*, *April Morning*, *The Hessian*, the five-volume Lavette saga, and, more recently, the best-selling *The Dinner Party* and *The Pledge*. Mr. Fast has also written plays, screenplays, history and biographies, and newspaper columns. His autobiographical memoir *Being Red* was published in 1990. Mr. Fast and his wife, Bette, live in Connecticut.